P9-DWK-006

TOKUGAWA RELIGION

Tokugawa Religion

The Values of Pre-Industrial Japan

By ROBERT N. BELLAH

THE FREE PRESS
GLENCOE, ILLINOIS
&

THE FALCON'S WING PRESS

COPYRIGHT 1957 BY THE FREE PRESS, A CORPORATION

PRINTED IN THE UNITED STATES OF AMERICA

DESIGNED BY SIDNEY SOLOMON

LIBRARY OF CONGRESS CATALOG CARD NO. 57-6748

To

My Mother

Lillian Neelly Bellah

whose respect for learning was early

communicated to her son

Preface

THIS BOOK grew out of the doctoral dissertation which I presented to the Departments of Far Eastern Languages and Sociology at Harvard University in 1955. The training which led up to the present study represents a somewhat unusual venture, in that this was the first time at Harvard that a joint degree was issued by these two departments. This training is reflected in the study in the combination of a theoretical approach derived from sociology with the methods of historical research developed by the humanistic discipline whose special concern is with Far Eastern civilization.

I am indebted to both the Social Science Research Council and the Harvard-Yenching Institute for financial support which allowed me to devote my full time to the research for and writing of this study. It was Serge Elisséeff who, in his lectures on Japanese literature, first interested me in Shingaku, and it was with him also that I first studied Shingaku texts. I am indebted both to Professor Elisséeff and to Edwin O. Reischauer for much in my understanding of Japanese history and culture.

My thesis advisors were John Pelzel and Talcott Parsons. Both were extremely helpful throughout; the former giving me the benefit of his extensive knowledge of Japanese culture and society and the latter providing the theoretical framework within which the thesis was largely carried out. Albert M. Craig read the manuscript throughout and made several suggestions which have been incorporated in the text. Tatsuo Arima was most helpful in checking my translations from Japanese and was kind enough to write the characters in the lists of terms and names at the end of the book.

Finally I want to express thanks for the many tangible and intangible services rendered by my wife. Besides editing the entire manuscript and doing some of the typing on it, she made several substantive suggestions. She was my best critic and at all times a source of encouragement.

ROBERT N. BELLAH

Contents

TOKUGAWA RELIGION

CHAPTER

I

Religion and Industrial Society in Japan

We have valuable studies of many aspects of Japanese religion in the Tokugawa Period (1600-1868) without which this book could not have been written. We do not have, however, any study in English of what the whole of Japanese religion in this period meant in the lives of the Japanese people. One of the purposes of this study is to fill this lack, even though cursorily, for a period of exceptional importance in Japanese history which immediately preceded and in many ways laid the ground for modern Japan.

In order to understand a people and their religion we need to know more than the formal creeds and doctrines to which they subscribe and the formal structure of the religious organizations in which they are enrolled. These are important facts but they tell us only about the husk of a religion. We must deal with the husk before we can come to the kernel, but it is the kernel, if such we can call the inner meaning of a religion in the personalities of individuals, which is really important for our understanding, though always difficult to grasp. Once we can grasp even imperfectly the place a religion has in the thoughts, feelings, and aspirations of individuals, then we can begin to see the way their religious commitment shapes and influences the whole of their lives, and how other parts of their lives in turn affect their religion. We will try to let Japanese of the period speak for themselves, through quotations, wherever possible.

A concern with living meaning will determine the way in which we handle the formal organizations of doctrine that go to make up the Japanese religious tradition. We will not be concerned, for example, with an exposition of the doctrines of Buddhism, Confucianism or Shintō for their own sake. It is only as active components of the religious life of the day that we will deal with them and we will indeed find that many of their most important doctrines still were exerting a powerful influence in the Tokugawa Period. We will find that Mencius, the great 3rd century B.C. Chinese Confucian, for example, was not just a name out of the dim past, but was a contemporary force in 18th century Japan, and as such, his doctrines must be dealt with here, even though he lived centuries before and in a different country. Similarly we will find that the method of enlightenment developed by Zen Buddhism in T'ang and Sung China was still widely practised, even by merchants and artisans, in our period, and so is relevant to our study. If we succeed in getting at the meaning of the Japanese religious tradition in the lives of ordinary people in the pre-modern period, we should not only deepen our understanding of Japanese history and society, but we should also get a more meaningful idea of the religious doctrines themselves, many of which in their abstract formulation seem so exotic to Western readers.

The study of any other religion and what it means to the people who hold it can be of great interest and can extend our understanding of religion and its place in human life. But the case of Japan is of especial interest. Japan alone of the non-Western nations was able to take over very rapidly what it needed of Western culture in order to transform itself into a modern industrial nation. Students of Japan have come increasingly to feel that this success is not to be attributed to some mythical faculty of imitation which the Japanese are supposed to possess, but to certain factors in the pre-modern period which prepared the ground for later developments. Among the factors frequently discussed are certain economic advances not shared by other non-Western societies. The sociologist influenced by Max Weber's great work[1] on the relation of religion to the development of modern Western society, especially the modern economy, naturally wonders whether religious factors might also be involved in the Japanese case. The problem stated baldly is, was there a functional analogue to the Protestant ethic in Japanese religion? This problem then will serve as a special focus of interest throughout the study. We shall attempt to understand as clearly as possible what Japanese religion actually meant to ordinary people, and we shall pay particular attention to any elements which might be connected with the rise of a modern industrial society.

In order to make clear the terms of the investigation it is necessary to define what the writer means by modern industrial society and by religion. By modern industrial society I mean a society characterized by the great importance of the economy in the social system and of economic values in the value system. It is important to be very clear about what is meant by economic values in this context. Above all I do not mean lust for profit, acquisitive instinct, or drive for hedonistic consumption. Many discussions of "capitalist" society have been plagued by the wholly unwarranted supposition that the "spirit of capitalism" is to be characterized by such terms.[2] Undoubtedly such motives exist in industrial (as in non-industrial) society. They in no sense characterize it.

By economic values I mean those values which above all characterize the process of the rationalization of means. In sociological theory these values are referred to as universalism and performance, two of the "pattern variables" of the theory of action.[3] In the process of rationalizing means, or what may equally well be called instrumental action, the ends of action are for the moment taken for granted. The only problem is how to achieve a given end with the greatest degree of efficiency and the least expenditure of energy. This involves above all adapting to the situational exigencies, for if there were no obstacles in the way of attaining a goal there would be no problem of means. In this process of instrumental or adaptive action there is no concern with particular objects as such. Every object in the situation is relevant only in so far as it has properties which bear on the problem of adaptation. Therefore we say that orientation to objects in the adaptive situation is universalistic rather than particularistic. Similarly the quality of objects in the adaptive situation has no relevance, it is only their performance which counts. In this situation it is not what an object is, but what it does which is important. Taking society as a whole as our frame of reference we can say that the economy is the system most concerned with the adaptive problem. For this reason we can refer to the values which define the adaptive process or dimension, namely universalism and performance, as "economic" values. Moving from the analytic level to the empirical we find economic values expressed in a high concern for productivity, a commitment to efficient production, which tends to become an overriding concern. In our own society, where these values are primary,[4] they are expressed in such phrases as "more and better things for more people" or "an economy of abundance." Actually the same values are expressed in non-economic spheres. There is a general concern with achievement, with "doing," which may be expressed as much in recreation as in business. Universalistic attitudes may be found in science and law as well as in industry. It is only because universalistic-performance values define the adaptive dimension of the social system and the adaptive dimension is coordinate with the economy that we are justified in speaking of "economic values."

Though the type case of a modern industrial society, the United States, is characterized by a primacy of economic values in the sense just defined, this is not a necessity. Nevertheless where an industrial society is characterized by the primacy of some other value complex, economic values as defined must have a very high secondary importance. Without such values it would be impossible to have a highly differentiated and rational economy, and thus to have an industrial society at all. They are necessary if there is to be a high level of formal rationality, in Weber's sense, a continuous process of the rationalization of means free from traditionalistic restrictions and governed only by formal rational norms. Of course no society could exist if economic rationality as here defined were absolutely unrestricted. Complete economic rationality is bounded by political, moral, religious, and other restrictions, even in societies where economic values may be said to have primacy. Nevertheless as against a traditionalistic society in which it is restricted to the narrowest of bounds, economic rationality must have a very broad area of free play in an industrial society. It is characteristic of a rational economy that, freed of those restrictions which keep a traditional economy static, it can not maintain the *status quo* but must continue its processes of rationalization into ever new spheres. This is the source both of the dynamism and of the instability of industrial societies. It is possible that the continuous rationalization of the economy may create such strains in the social system as a whole that the values legitimizing a rational economy may be threatened.

In considering the process of development from non-industrial to industrial societies, one of the most obvious facts is a shift in the basic value patterns. Thus medieval Europe was characterized by political and religious-cultural values[5] whereas the modern United States is characterized by economic values. It is possible, however, that an industrial society may develop without a shift in basic values, but rather through a process in which economic values become very important in certain spheres and the economy as a whole reaches a certain level of differentiation where it can develop freely and rationally with only minimal restrictions. Most European industrial societies seem to illustrate this latter development. So, in my belief, does Japan.

Japan is characterized by a primacy of political values, the polity takes precedence over the economy. Here as in the case of the term "economic values" the adjective "political" is to be taken in the very broadest sense. Formally, political values are characterized by the pattern variables of performance and particularism. The central concern is with collective goals (rather than with productivity) and loyalty is a primary virtue. Controlling and being controlled are more important than "doing" and power is more important than wealth. There is no need to spell out this value system in great detail here as many of the following pages will be devoted to this end. It is quite clear that political values in the generalized sense employed here are also of very great importance in the West, at times primarily, at other times secondarily.

Talcott Parsons has recently pointed out that there is a process of political rationality quite comparable to that of economic rationality.[6] Thus a society with high concern for political values may produce a situation in which power becomes generalized and extended relatively free of traditionalistic restrictions and governed only by rational norms. Of course political rationality can be no more completely unrestricted than can economic if the society as a whole is to continue to function, but here again the relative freedom which it has may have tremendous consequences. I am in no position to state how important such a process is for the rise of industrial society in the West. That its importance was considerable I think is beyond doubt.[7] The Renaissance state which broke through traditionalism in the political and other spheres and led to the development of the rational legal state of modern times, the phenomenon of nationalism, and related developments, all certainly had a major significance for the rise of industrial society. It is my belief that Japan gives a peculiarly vivid example of this process of political rationalization, and that it is only through understanding this that the specifically economic development in Japan can be understood. Economic values have come to have a high importance in Japan, but they have remained subordinate to political values, and linked to them in ways which it will be necessary for us to spell out in great detail in later chapters.

Having defined in a general way what I mean by industrial society and discussed some of those processes which lead to it, it is now necessary to discuss what I mean by religion, and the relevance of religion to the development of industrial society.

By religion I mean, following Paul Tillich, man's attitudes and actions with respect to his ultimate concern. This ultimate concern has to do with what is ultimately valuable and meaningful, what we might call ultimate value; and with the ultimate threats to value and meaning, what we might call ultimate frustration. It is one of the social functions of religion to provide a meaningful set of ultimate values on which the morality of a society can be based. Such values when institutionalized can be spoken of as the central values of a society.

The other aspect of ultimate concern is ultimate frustration. As long as frustrations are seen as caused by determinate factors such as manageable natural phenomena or appropriate social sanctions for moral breach, the normal person can deal with them as they arise and they have no character of ultimacy. However those frustrations which are inherent in the human situation, but which are not manageable or morally meaningful, of which death is the type case, may be called ultimate frustrations. The second major social function of religion is to provide an adequate explanation for these ultimate frustrations so that the individual or group which has undergone them can accept them without having core values rendered meaningless, and can carry on life in society in the face of these frustrations. This is done through some form of assertion that the ultimate values are greater than, can overcome, the ultimate frustrations and is symbolized in many ways—as the victory of God over death, of Eros over Thanatos, of Truth over illusion.

The "object" of ultimate concern, namely that which is the source of ultimate value and ultimate frustration, must be symbolized if it is to be thought about at all. We may speak of these symbols as denoting the "sacred" or the "divine." Religious action is any action directed toward the sacred or divine. In primitive or "magical" religions the conception of the divine tends to be extremely diffuse. It is symbolized in terms of a pervasive force or power which inheres in many objects or in terms of a complex conglomeration of gods, spirits and demons. The diffuse concept of the divine permeates daily life. The effect of this tendency is that a very high percentage of acts in social life are of a sacred or semi-sacred nature. Failing to perform them or performing them incorrectly would not only be morally wrong, involving social sanctions, but sacrilegious, involving divine sanction. In this way religion undoubtedly contributes to the stereotyping and rigidity of life in traditionalistic societies.

The new conceptions of the sacred and of religious action which mark the emergence of the great world religions out of primitive traditionalism are all characterized by a relatively high degree of rationalization. It was Weber's belief that the directions which these original rationalizations took had an enormous and in some sense determining effect on the subsequent development of those traditions. If we may characterize these more rationalized religions schematically, we may say that the concept of the divine which they hold is usually more abstract, in one sense more simple, and less diffuse than that of the primitive religions. The divine is seen in terms of a relatively few simple qualities which hold in all situations, it is seen as more radically "other" and its entanglements with the world are drastically reduced. Concommitantly religious action is simplified, is made less situational, and is concerned with a more direct relation with the divine, either in terms of carrying out divine commandments or in seeking some method for the direct apprehension of divinity. Frustration is seen as a general quality of human life, rather than primarily as an aspect of discrete situations. Man is felt to be in some radical sense "alienated" and in need of some radical salvation. The essence of these religions is to provide means to attain this salvation.

The great importance which these rationalizing tendencies have for students of society lies in the changes in attitudes and actions which may flow from them. Whereas traditionalistic religion may give a blanket sanction to myriads of discrete customs and thus help to slow or prevent any social change, salvation religions may, by depriving these discrete customs of any sacred character (in Weber's phrase, "freeing the world of magic") and substituting instead certain general non-situational maxims of ethical action, lead to a rationalization of behaviour which can have important effects far beyond the sphere of religion itself. Of course the two types we have been describing are seldom found in a pure form. Most primitive religions have elements of rationalization and most salvation religions have large elements of "magic." In Japan almost every religion and sect has both aspects. While remembering that they are interwoven with magical and traditionalistic elements, it is the rationalizing tendencies with which we will be most concerned.

From the above considerations about religion, some of its significance for the development of modern industrial societies may become evident. The processes both of economic rationalization and of political rationalization require a considerable degree of freedom from traditionalism before they can begin to have an effect in leading to the development of industrial society. Virtually the only way this freedom can be attained is through the re-definition of the sacred, so that values and motivation favorable to the rationalizing processes will be legitimized and traditionalistic restrictions overcome.[8] For Weber Protestantism is just such a redefinition of the sacred. A new conception of the relation of man to God makes rational mastery of the world a religious obligation and tends to lead to the institutionalization of the values of universalism and achievement. Weber has characterized this development with the phrase "this-worldly asceticism." In this case we may say that Protestantism contributed directly to economic rationalization. It will be one of the purposes of this study to show the ways in which the rationalizing tendencies in Japanese religion contributed to economic and political rationalization in Japan.

With respect to the pre-1868 Japanese development toward an

industrial society we shall concentrate on a single aspect, the religious, though we would insist that other aspects were also important. Since we have defined industrial society in terms primarily of economic values, we will have to show the relation of religion to these values and to economic rationalization. Because of the nature of Japanese society with its strong political emphasis it is impossible to show the connections between religion and economy without also discussing in some detail the connection of the polity and its structure with them both. In brief we are concerned with how the definition of the sacred and man's obligation to it influences values and motivations favorable to economic rationalization, and the possible importance of political rationalization as a mediating process.

After a chapter giving a brief sketch of Tokugawa society so that religious life may be seen in its proper setting, we shall go on to survey the principle manifestations of religion in the Tokugawa Period, relating them both to the strata in which they are most prominently found and to any possible trends toward political or economic rationalization. Following this general survey will come a more detailed consideration of the Shingaku movement, a merchant class religious and ethical movement of the 18th and 19th centuries. Finally in the concluding chapter we will return to some of the considerations raised in this introductory discussion.

Notes

1. See especially his *Gesammelte Aufsatze zur Religionssoziologie* (three volumes, Tubingen, 1920-1921) of which the following parts have been translated: *The Protestant Ethic and the Spirit of Capitalism, Ancient Judaism, The Religion of China,* and the three essays in the section on religion in *From Max Weber: Essays in Sociology.* See also *Wirtschaft und Gesellschaft* (two volumes, Tubingen, 1925) of which the following parts have been translated: *The Theory of Social and Economic Organization, Max Weber on Law in Economy and Society,* and chapters in the section on power in *From Max Weber: Essays in Sociology.* Complete citations may be found in the bibliography.

2. The following quotes illuminate the difference in point of view: ". . . we may say that a fruit of the capitalist spirit is that attitude adopted by a man towards the problems of wealth, its acquisition and use, when he holds that wealth is simply a means for the unlimited individualistic and utilitarian satisfaction of all possible human needs. A man governed by this spirit will, in acquiring wealth, choose the most effectual means among such as are lawful, and will use them without any anxiety to keep the result within certain limits. In the use of wealth he will seek indi-

vidualistic enjoyment; to the acquisition and enjoyment of goods he will recognize one limit only—hedonistic satiety." (Amintore Fanfani: *Catholicism, Protestantism, and Capitalism,* p. 29.) "It is the conception of an individual's 'business in life' as a calling in this sense, as a matter of moral obligation, which is to a comparable degree, distinctive of the modern world. It will be noted that acquisitiveness or a valuation of profit does not enter into this at all." (Talcott Parsons: Introduction to Max Weber: *The Theory of Social and Economic Organization,* p. 81.) For a general discussion of this problem see Talcott Parsons: "The Motivation of Economic Activities" in *Essays in Sociological Theory* (revised edition).

3. At this point it becomes necessary to introduce technical sociological terminology which may be unfamiliar to some. I will try whenever doing so to make clear the meanings of the terms in the given context. This is not, however, an adequate explanation of their significance, which can only be grasped through an understanding of the total conceptual scheme of which they are parts. It is clearly beyond the scope of this book to attempt an explanation of the total scheme. As I am using it, it is best expounded in Parsons and Smelser, *Economy and Society* (1956), and Parsons, Bales and Shils: *Working Papers in the Theory of Action* (1953), especially chapters three and five. Figure 1 is a paradigm showing the interrelations of most of the technical terms used in this study.

4. This statement is based on Parsons' analysis of the American social system, especially in his course on the subject.

5. In using the terms "political" and "religious-cultural" to describe values the same very broad level of generality is implied as in the case of the term "economic" above. Here we are merely trying to point to a more general level of those values clustering around "feudalism" and "Catholicism" in medieval Europe. The many problems of such an analysis lie outside the scope of this study.

6. In his seminar on the theory of social systems.

7. Weber repeatedly pointed this out, especially in his work on bureaucracy. It has also been stressed by a number of writers unsympathetic to Weber. For example Amintore Fanfani: *Catholicism, Protestantism, and Capitalism,* Chapt. IV, and H. M. Robertson: *Aspects of the Rise of Economic Individualism,* Chapt. III.

8. This is not an assertion of "one-way" causation, as non-religious factors, in combination with religious factors, will help to "cause" the re-definition of the sacred. All we are asserting is that, through whatever causal complex, a re-definition of the sacred is necessary.

FIGURE 1

Functional Sub-systems of the Social System

Pattern Variables	A — *Universalism*	*Particularism* — G
Performance (Achievement)	Economy "Economic Values"	Polity "Political Values"
Quality (Ascription)	Motivational or Cultural System "Cultural Values"	Integrative or Institutional System "Integrative Values"
	L	I

The Four Dimensions:

A Adaptation
G Goal attainment
I Integration
L Latency

CHAPTER

II

An Outline of Japanese Social Structure in the Tokugawa Period

THE BATTLE OF SEKIGAHARA (1600) in which Tokugawa Ieyasu decisively defeated his combined opposition and thus established himself as supreme in all Japan has been taken as a convenient point to mark the beginning of the Tokugawa Period, just as the fall of the last Tokugawa *shōgun* and the assumption of direct rule by the Emperor Meiji (1868) marks its end. Both of these events are, of course, mere moments in the continuous process of history, but there is no doubt that the period marked off between them is politically, socially and culturally a meaningful one. It is distinguished perhaps most strikingly from the periods which preceded and followed it by its peaceful character and its relative isolation from the outside world. These characteristics together with much that is apparently static in its political, social and cultural life tend to give one the feeling that for 268 years Japan floated in mid-air, existed in a state of suspended animation, until finally in 1868 the spell was broken and all the vibrant dynamism of the 16th century was unloosed again on an unsuspecting world. No student of the period, however, could agree with such a view. He sees the establishment of a national market, the victory of a money economy, increasing urbanization, an improved communications system, the impoverishment of the *samurai* class and enrichment of the merchants, the rise of a new artistic and literary culture appropriate to town dwellers rather than courtiers, monks or soldiers, increasing fervor of religious nationalism focusing on the person of the emperor, the propagation of a series of new religious sects, and so on, as indicative of the enormous social and cultural changes going on in the period, many of them directly leading to the Restoration of 1868 and the new Japan that rose thereafter. Nevertheless he would not deny that certain broad structural features of family, polity and social class, as well as many values and ideas, were relatively constant throughout the period. The constants are important enough, then, to distinguish this period from those which preceded and followed it. It will be necessary, however, in the present analysis, not to let a preoccupation with these constants obscure the enormously important changes continuously taking place.[1]

This outline of Tokugawa social structure will begin with a description of the value system as I see it. The analysis of the value system will be in terms of the categories already given above in figure 1. It is based on the assumption that the central value system of a society will tend to give primacy of emphasis to one dimension of social structure, though of course all four dimensions will have to be taken account of in any society. As has already been indicated, I believe that political values have primacy in Japan, which means, in terms of the scheme used here, that the goal-attainment dimension of the social structure is of special importance. Values governing the other three dimensions of social structure in this view are seen as derived from or strongly influenced by the values of the dominant dimension.[2]

After the description of the value system I will discuss the four functional sub-systems of the social system, the analysis again being based on the fundamental categories of figure 1. These functional sub-systems are thought of as analytical entities rather than as concrete structures. That is, a concrete structure such as the Tokugawa government, though primarily political in function, will also have economic, integrative and motivational functions. Concrete factual material in these sections is given then, not for the sake of its own particularity, but to illustrate the ways in which the basic functions are carried out. Finally, there will be a section devoted to concrete structural units which are oriented to situational givens, such as territory, biological relatedness and cultural tradition, as well as to functional exigencies. While I believe the discussion of the value system and of the functional sub-systems to be, though sketchy in content, essentially exhaustive in coverage, the structural units discussed represent only a small portion of the total, and even those chosen can be given but brief treatment.

The chapter will conclude with an attempt to point out those places within the social system where religion could have an important influence.

The Value System

We have already maintained that the Japanese value system is characterized by the primacy of "political" values. These may be defined by the combination of the pattern variables of particularism and performance, or as those values appropriate to the goal-attainment dimension of the social system; these being merely two ways of saying the same thing.[3] When we say that the primary concern is for the system goal, we imply the value of particularism. It is the particular system or collectivity of which one is a member which counts, whether it be family, *han*[4] or Japan as a whole. Commitment to these tends to take precedence over universalistic commitments, such as commitment to truth or justice. There was of course universalism and universalistic commitment in Tokugawa Japan. All we maintain is that particularism held primacy. The importance of the collectivity and of one's particularistic relation to it, is indicated by the enormous symbolic importance of the head of the collectivity, whether this be family head, feudal lord or emperor. This tended to be a representative role—the head stood for the collectivity—and very often not an executive role, actual executive functions being left to the chief clerk, or a leading retainer, etc. Thus one's particularistic tie to one's collectivity is symbolized as loyalty to its head. The enormous importance of loyalty in Japan is, then, a concrete expression of the values for which we are postulating primacy. It is important to note that this loyalty is loyalty to the head of one's collectivity, whoever that person may be. It is loyalty to a status rather than to a person, as such. There may be and often was a deep personal attachment to the head, but this was not a prerequisite for loyalty. This is important in connection with political rationalization. It implies the possibility of a deep loyalty to a person (e.g. the emperor or *shōgun*) with whom the individual has no personal relation at all, and thus of a powerful political influence far beyond the sphere of mere personal influence. This generalized particularism, then, may serve in certain ways as a functional equivalent for universalism in the process of the rationalization and extension of power.

Similarly, when we say that the primary concern is for the system goal, we imply the value of performance. The concern is primarily with system *goal* rather than system *maintenance,* and a goal must be attained. Thus performance or achievement becomes a primary value. The great importance of status in Japan had previously led me to postulate a primacy of quality or ascription in the value system. There is indeed no doubt of the very great importance which this value has. Perhaps, however, the primacy of performance will become clearer if one considers that status itself does not validate. Only performance in the service of the system goal is really validating. Even those in the very important representative roles, the heads of collectivities, are in a larger context subordinates engaged in laboring for the attainment of goals in the superordinate system. Even the emperor is responsible to his ancestors for his behaviour and must account to them. There tends not to be at any level in Japanese life a status style of life which, once attained, is its own validation (as against, say, the status style of life of the Chinese gentry). The importance of performance values is further illustrated in the family, where ascription normally holds primacy. Very intensive levels of performance were apparently demanded from children, with at least the threat of disinheritance for inadequacy or waywardness.[5] Conversely, masters in the arts and crafts not infrequently adopted especially gifted pupils as their heirs and successors. Loyalty in Japan implied not mere passive devotion but active service and performance. It should be noted that a high valuation of performance implies comparisons of relative achievement, and the standards by which such comparisons are made must be universalistic. This consideration together with the pseudo-universalism implied in the generalization of particularism discussed above, lead to the inference that universalism may be found to have a considerable if secondary importance.

It must be noted that though goal-attainment is of primary

concern in the value system, the content of the goals to be obtained is relatively variable. Naturally the goals chosen will, or it is thought that they will, increase the power and prestige of the collectivity. But the power and prestige of the collectivity may be increased through internal peace and prosperity, through victory in war, through imperialistic expansion, through becoming a model for other nations in peacefulness and a high level of culture, etc. The primacy of goal-attainment values, "political" values in the present sense, is not, then, dependent on the specific content of the goals chosen. Therefore even a radical and sudden shift in the content of the goal cannot be expected to have any seriously disruptive effect on the central value system.[6]

The central values, which, as has been shown above, give primacy to the goal-attainment dimension, naturally have important implications for values with respect to the other three dimensions.[7] With respect to the adaptive problem, those behaviours which are adaptive in the pursuit of the collective goals are most highly valued. The military is, in terms of the present conceptual scheme, exactly the adaptive arm of the polity. It is therefore not at all surprising that the military should have very high prestige in Japan. It displays the type case of adaptive action which is entirely subordinated to the system goal. Economic behaviour tends to be suspect because it may not be subordinated to the system goal but rather to some sub-system goal; it may be "selfish." But to the degree that economic behaviour can be seen as furthering the system goal, it is perfectly legitimate. In general, work itself is not a value, but rather work as an expression of selfless devotion to the collective goal is valued. The motivation to work, however, may be just as strong in such a society as in one in which work is valued for its own sake.

Integrative values are strong but tend to be subordinated to the goal-attainment values. Harmony must be maintained in the collectivity because conflicts between the members would not only be disloyal to the head but would disrupt the smooth attainment of collective goals. Thus harmony, willingness to compromise, unaggressiveness, etc. are highly valued, whereas disputatiousness, contentiousness, overweening ambition or other disruptive behaviour is strongly disvalued. In order to avoid friction a great deal of everyday life is formalized. Close conformity to a multiplicity of detailed prescriptions for behaviour tends to reduce all conflict to a minimum and ensure the smooth functioning of collective life. The emphasis on harmony, on the maintenance of the collectivity seemingly for its own sake is so great that it is likely that at some periods and for some groups the integrative values had primacy over the goal-attainment values.[8] It would seem, though, that the dominant pattern exhibited the primacy of goal values. Appeals to loyalty to the head of the collectivity and to pre-eminent system goals could override concern for harmony and motivate the breaking through of old social forms, the disruption of old collectivities, and the abandonment of old forms of prescribed behaviour. This potentiality contributed to the dynamism and ability for fairly rapid social change without disruption of the central values which differentiates Japan from societies in which system-maintenance-integrative values have primacy and are ends in themselves.

Finally, the sphere of "cultural" values seems to contain two distinct clusters of values. One of these is closely subordinated to the primary values already discussed, while the other seems to define an area sharply separated from that of the central values though in certain respects complementary to it.

The first group may be illustrated by the strong value on learning, study or scholarship (*gakumon*). This value which relates to the regard for the written word, for books, and for teachers and education in general, is not an end in itself. Rather it is valued because of its results in action. Learning for its own sake, as we shall see, tends to be despised. The merely erudite man is not worthy of respect. Rather learning should eventuate in practice. A truly learned man will be a truly loyal and filial man. The same considerations hold with respect to religion. It is, of course, impossible to deprive religion entirely of the character of being an end in itself, but there is a tendency in this direction. Or else there is a tendency to fuse the religious end and the secular end, religious values and the secular goal-attainment values. We shall have more to say on this in the sections on religion. An example of the tendency to value religion for its results in action rather than for its own sake would be the attachment of the warrior class to Zen

Buddhism in certain periods. It was seen almost as a system of training which aided in the self-abnegating performance of actions expressing loyalty to one's lord. The latter remains the central value and religion is subordinated to it (or subsumed in it). This general tendency to value cultural phenomena as means to action rather than as ends in themselves can probably be seen as inhibiting any very strong emphasis on theory as opposed to practice. The pursuit of theory whether in philosophy or in science does not seem strongly developed in traditional Japan. On the other hand, the strong regard for cultural phenomena which had visible results in action perhaps helps to explain the relatively strong attraction of the Japanese to Western science, even at periods when their access to it was difficult and even dangerous. It is interesting that the first subject to be studied was medicine. The 18th century Japanese physicians who studied Dutch medical textbooks were impressed by the accuracy of the information and its practical application more than by its theoretical sophistication.

The second cluster of "cultural" values which can be discriminated may be called the aesthetic-emotional values. As opposed to the values discussed above these tend to be ends in themselves rather than subordinate to the central values. They are, however, allowed expression only in certain rather sharply segregated contexts and under rather rigidly defined conditions.[9] It would be a mistake, however, to underestimate the importance of these values. For many individuals and even groups they have at some periods probably held primacy, and their existence probably always poses a certain threat to the central value system. These values center not on collective goals but on private experience. They define an area of individual expression and enjoyment. This may be in the aesthetic appreciation of nature or art, in the delicate ritual of the tea ceremony, in the vicarious thrills of the theater, in the refined eroticism of the gay quarters, or in sentimental and effusive human relationships of love or friendship. Such behaviour is legitimate and indeed very highly valued in Japanese culture. But there is always the possibility of its shading over into a sumptuous if sensitive hedonism, especially among those classes which can afford to gratify their tastes. In such a situation individual goal-gratification displaces collective goal-gratification as the central value and thus the strongest sentiments must be mobilized against it. Such a hedonism is the essence of "selfishness" which is the greatest vice, just as loyalty is the greatest virtue. In order to guard against such a consequence, aesthetic-emotional values are restricted to rather well defined areas and an almost ascetic austerity is highly valued in the area of consumption. The strength of the hedonistic tendency, however, is illustrated in the development of a refined, sensitive and often very expensive austerity, which serves rather to express than destroy its opposite, among certain circles.

So far we have had almost nothing to say about the family, which is so important in traditional Japanese life. This is because, in our view, the family is the polity writ small. Practically all that was said above about the value system of the total Japanese society can be applied to the family. Instead of loyalty the highest value is filial-piety (*kō*) but its function is the same. It implies the same attitude toward the head of the collectivity and the same central concern for the collective goal. In using the term family we mean to include lineage as well as nuclear family. The Japanese family is conceived as continuously handed down from the ancestors of old. Reverence for parents is subsumed in a larger concept of reverence for ancestors. The structural features of the Japanese family will be discussed briefly later on in this chapter, but we may point out here that lineages are related to each other in terms of main and branch houses, the main house being the line of direct inheritance and the branch being cadet houses. On the broadest level family and nation are one, the imperial family being the main house of which all Japanese families are branches. It is however the household, composed ideal typically of the parents, the eldest son, who will inherit the house, and his wife and children, which is the primary focus of the value of filial piety. It is very important to stress that in the dominant value system filial piety is subordinate to loyalty; polity overrides family; and in case of conflict of loyalty the first duty is to one's lord rather than to one's family. This is in clear contrast to China where the reverse holds true. These values are not seen, however, to be contradictory. Rather they are felt to be mutually re-inforcing. The filial son will make a loyal minister; the family is the training ground for social virtues. Further, the family tends to be the unit of society rather than the individual.

The status of family head is both internally central and externally the lowest "official" role in the polity. The family does not stand over against the polity but is integrated into it and to an extent penetrated by it. It does not serve as a locus for a different value system, but rather for a virtually identical one.

Above we have considered those values which are important at the social system level in that their institutionalization in a sense defines the social structure. We have not been concerned with the "metaphysical" underpinnings of these values nor with general orientations to time, nature and man. A discussion of these is reserved for the next chapter when their relation both to the social values discussed above and to the religious system can be analyzed.

The values discussed in this section were largely constant throughout the Tokugawa Period. If anything, they became more intense and more widely propagated as the period progressed, if we are to credit the influence of the many religious, ethical and educational movements which arose. The *samurai* class best typifies these values, at least in ideal, but they became quite general among all classes by the end of the Tokuwaga Period. On the other hand, there is no doubt that hedonistic values made considerable headway in the cities among both *samurai* and *chōnin*.[10] They were not, however, able to attain any semblance of legitimacy, and were constantly under attack from the moralists of all classes. There is a real sense in which the Meiji Period (1868-1911) was a culmination and intensification of the central values rather than a rejection of them, and they have remained strong throughout modern times. A discussion of the strains involved in the partial disintegration of these values in modern times and of the attempts to revive them lies outside the scope of this study.

The Polity

As was indicated by its central place in the value system there was a high input of loyalty into the polity, in Tokugawa Japan.[11] The Tokugawa rule represented a considerable step forward in the generalization and extension of power in Japan, but it did not succeed in creating a rationalized and unified power structure such as that of the Meiji Period. There were two main limitations on the generality of Tokugawa power. One was the extent of freedom left to the feudal lords, especially the *tozama,*[12] or outside lords. For many purposes the *han* or feudal domain was a more important political unit than the nation. It is true that all the major cities and many of the more important farming areas were under the direct control of the Tokugawa shogunate, and this gave a solid core to the nation, but the fact remains that large and important areas were unintegrated with this core. The other limitation was that on the legitimacy of the shogunate itself. In fact the shogunate was the actual central power in Japan. In theory the emperor held the central power and the *shōgun* was but an official. The charisma attaching to the emperor was always a potential threat to the shogunate, which was indeed overthrown by a polarization of all elements of opposition around this charismatic status. It remained then for the Meiji Period to dispose of these two limitations on the generalization of power by destroying the *han* and by making the imperial government the central government. The Meiji government then represented a logical fulfillment of a conception of the polity which already existed in the Tokugawa Period.

Loyalty, so central in the Tokugawa Period, remains somewhat ambiguous due to the limitations on the generalization of power stated above. The ambiguity derives from the question, loyalty to whom? Moral homilies on loyalty usually speak of loyalty to one's lord (*kun*), a term which is non-specific in its reference. There are also injunctions, especially to *samurai,* to be loyal to the lord of one's fief, to the people at large to be loyal to the shogunate, and to all Japanese to be loyal to the emperor. Though these ambiguities with respect to political authority are important and had significant consequences, they did not affect the way in which the relation of individuals and groups to political authority was phrased. The essential lines which we shall sketch below hold regardless of what authority is in question. There may have been practical limitations on how far the expected roles could be played, but the expectations remained.

First of all the compelling and overriding loyalty toward the political authority must be seen in the context of the idea of *on.* The political authority has the obligation of bestowing blessings (*on*) on the people subject to it. In the case of the *samurai* this takes the direct form of receiving a stipend, but the concept is much more general. For instance one of the great blessings which the shogunate bestowed on all the people was peace. This was frequently reiterated, especially in the early years of the period when, after a hundred and fifty years of almost constant warfare, it must certainly have been considered a great blessing. This fact was indeed one of the main ideological foundations of the legitimacy of the shogunate. Further, both *han* and shogunate governments carried out famine relief, flood control, land reclamation and similar projects which were "blessings" to the people under them. In general it was felt that favorable economic and political conditions were blessings bestowed by the political authority. In theory loyalty was not dependent on the actual carrying out of these blessings, but was an absolute obligation, but there can be little doubt that in fact the failure of "blessings" to materialize undermined loyalty, and the increasing misery, especially of the *samurai* class, weakened the power of the shogunate in its later years.

Coordinate with the concept of *on* is the concept of *hōon* or the return of *on*. This involves the general obligation to respect and comply with the orders of the political authority. The presence of the official notice board on which were posted the latest decrees of the *bakufu*[13] in every town and village, and the respect shown toward it, are evidences of the degree of compliance with political authority even at the lowest levels of the social structure. The relatively high degree of public order, as compared with China for example, is another instance of this compliance, as is the readiness of *samurai* to commit *seppuku*[14] or to go into exile when so ordered. These and other examples which could be given illustrate the rather considerable degree to which the political authority could exercise control through influence, that is through the manipulation of sentiments. The *bakufu* and *han* governments of course had force at their commands with which to compel compliance, but sociologically more interesting is the fact that in so many contexts compliance was voluntary. In the last analysis this depended on the fact that people identified with the polity. They felt themselves part of what became known as the *kokutai*,[15] the national polity, a symbol of great importance, especially in the Meiji and post-Meiji periods. They received gratifications through their identifications as members of the polity, they participated in the prestige and meaning of the polity, and thus they voluntarily submitted to the requirements of the political authority, feeling its interests to be identical with their own. Such a process of identification is apt to be most intense when there are definite system goals toward which the political authority is striving and which are clear and meaningful to all. Such identification is apt to be most endangered when the political authority has no goals but is purely conservative and concerned only with its own maintenance. It will then be difficult to maintain that high input of loyalty and high degree of control through the manipulation of sentiments which is, in a way, the essence of the sort of society with which we are dealing. Looked at in this context, we might say that the Tokugawa regime which had pushed political rationalization further than it had ever gone before, was "all dressed up with no place to go." The goal of restoring peace, order and prosperity may have been sufficient in the first decades of the period, but it tended to shade into a stagnant conservatism as the decades passed. It is no accident that the movement which finally overthrew the *bakufu* was characterized by two clear and dynamic goals: restore the emperor and expel the barbarians.

The relationship between the polity and the economy was one of the most vexed and troublesome of the Tokugawa Period. Taxation supplied the facilities with which the polity could operate. The major source of taxes was the peasantry, from which was exacted a land tax amounting to a considerable portion of the produce of the land. A singular weakness of the *bakufu* was that it received taxes only from its own land and not from the land of other feudal lords. It thus had to run a national government without a national system of taxation. Another weakness is that sources other than the land tax were not systematically tapped. The merchants paid heavily at times for monopolistic guild privileges and paid a land tax on their city lots but were, on the whole, very lightly taxed. They were subjected to forced loans and even confiscations, but these were not sources of income which could be regularly used without seriously damaging effects on the economy as a whole. Duties from foreign trade at Nagasaki supplied some income but the small volume of trade made this a relatively negligible source. The fact that the land tax was paid in grain but the nation had a money economy meant that low prices for rice and high prices for commodities would reduce the real income of the government.[16] All of these factors meant that the *bakufu* was chronically short of funds and had to resort to devices which in the long run weakened its position still further. Debasing the currency was tried on several occasions but was at best a temporary expedient. Reducing the salaries of the direct retainers of the *shōgun* was a still more dangerous expedient as it weakened the bonds of loyalty essential to the retention of power. The feudal lords were, with a few exceptions, in an even worse position. They had fewer expedients open to them and many were driven into the hands of the money-lenders. In spite of all these problems the fact remains that a large percentage of the wealth of Japan flowed through the hands of the political authorities and this undoubtedly did serve to sustain their power. Further, a few *han* which encouraged the growth of industry and trade and adopted policies favorable to agriculture had a healthy financial condition and were in a sense prototypes for the Meiji regime which was to rationalize the taxation system and put government finance on a sound basis.

The government attempted to maintain a rather tight control over the economic sphere but its efforts had mixed results. The most signal failure, perhaps, was the attempt to fix prices through edict. The government maintained some kind of supervision over guild organization, the operation of money and commodity exchanges, the licensing of formally free labor, shipping and highways, etc. Its sumptuary legislation attempted to regulate the minutest details of consumption. Though these and similar forms of control represent an attempt to regulate economic life in terms of over-all political concerns, it cannot be said that they were on the whole successful in their aim. By maintaining order and regularity of expectations the government probably aided economic advancement. By maintaining privilege and precedent and by arbitrary interference at times of fiscal difficulties it probably hindered it. The policy was aimed, however, not at the advancement or hindering of economic development, but at the maintenance of the political *status quo*.

The *bakufu* kept the major functions of lawmaking and law enforcement in its own hands.[17] It laid down a set of rules and precepts for even what was in theory the highest prestige group, the court nobles. Similar codes existed for the feudal lords, and for the retainers of the Tokugawa house. For the common people there were only the injunctions posted on the official notice boards. The laws governing them were kept secret from the public and were in the nature of guide books for magistrates, who were left with considerable discretion. Special ordinances were issued as needed by the *shōgun*. On the whole the legal system respected precedents and written documents. It was concerned that the ownership of property was based on legitimate claim and that contracts were fulfilled. It was especially concerned to see that the edicts of the *shōgun* were strictly enforced and further that the level of public morality was maintained. Since no rationalized system of jurisprudence existed, interpretation of the law was made in terms of the general morality as the particular magistrate saw it. Needless to say, his commitment was to the political authority, not to the law itself or to the "people." It was a tenet of the government, however, that its own stability rested on the maintenance of precedents and agreements and therefore it tended to support a relatively stable and consistent legal system.

The Tokugawa Period was characterized by a legal and hereditary class system. Its main outlines could be predicted from the value system: prestige correlates directly with power. It is power which determines status and not wealth, a situation which, as we shall see, led to some strains. At the apex of the system are the emperor, *shōgun* and feudal lords. Just below these is the *samurai* or *bushi* class, ranked high because it administers political authority either in military or official positions. A gulf separates the above mentioned classes from those below. Above are the rulers and below the ruled. The common people are prestige ranked in terms of traditional views as to their productivity. Farmers come first because they supply most of the income of the ruling groups. Artisans are next as they also produce for the rulers and merchants are at the bottom because they are considered to be unproductive. We shall see that this view of the merchants did not go unchallenged in Tokugawa times, but it was reflected in the official class system. Below the above mentioned classes there were several groups of outcasts, but they were relatively few in number and need not concern us.

There was some mobility between classes: a few merchants were given *samurai* status in return for extraordinary services to the government, some *samurai* gave up their rank in order to go into trade, many farmers moved to the towns and became artisans or merchants. Nevertheless, mobility was largely within classes rather than between them. It should be especially noted that the bureaucracy was recruited from the hereditary *samurai* class and not through an open examination system as in China. The son of a rich merchant, then, remained a merchant in Japan rather than entering the bureaucracy as so often happened in China.

It is worthy of note that the possession of wealth tended to have less and less relation to position in the class hierarchy as time went on. The merchants in particular became enriched as the *samurai* class became impoverished. This situation placed a considerable strain on both the groups concerned: one had wealth but not prestige and the other had prestige but not wealth. It is interesting that neither class attacked the central value system in seeking to right the imbalance. The merchants did not claim that prestige should be based on wealth or economic "success" but rather that merchants were faithful and hard-working subjects who performed indispensable functions for the collectivity and thus deserved prestige. There was no "bourgeois" ideology which directly attacked the "feudal" ideology in the Tokugawa Period and the 1868 Restoration can in no sense be seen as a "bourgeois revolution." If the merchants did not attack the central value system neither did the impoverished lower *samurai*. Rather they sought a reorganization of society in which that value system would really be expressed as it ought. Their attack on the shogunate was phrased in terms that it was not living up to the value system, and their devotion to the emperor represented an intensification rather than a weakening of their attachment to the central values. We may say that the increasing lack of correspondence between prestige and material rewards was another factor leading to the destruction of the Tokugawa regime.

The Economy

As Talcott Parsons has said, the generalization of exchange through the use of money "is a paramount condition of the high integration of the economy as a system and of its clear differentiation from other sub-systems of the society."[18] It is noteworthy then that the Tokugawa Period saw the establishment of money as a means of exchange for the first time on a national scale. It was indeed a period which saw a virtually continuous expansion and differentiation of the Japanese economy.

Agriculture remained the primary source of wealth throughout the period. The productive unit was the small peasant family farm, there being little if any development of "capitalistic" agriculture. Methods were traditionalistic and though the yield was relatively high it was obtained through the lavish use of hand labor so characteristic of Oriental rice agriculture. Most of the crop besides that needed to sustain the farm family was drained off by taxes and most needs were met by home production. Thus the farmers were on the whole fairly poor and relatively self-sufficient, being probably the group least integrated into the money economy. The *samurai* class was paid a rice stipend but this had in part at least to be converted to money in order to buy commodities other than rice. Most forms of productive work were denied the *samurai* on class grounds so they tended to be entirely dependent on their stipends. They were closely tied in with the money economy, then, and due to the constant fluctuations in the price of rice, they were in a very vulnerable position with respect to it. The city artisan and merchant classes were, of course, entirely integrated into the money economy. Finally there was an incipient group of "rural capitalists"—usually rich farmers who had begun *sake* brewing or textile industries.

As the vast majority of enterprises were small-scale family businesses, a great deal of the labor supply was obtained on a strictly kinship basis. Non-family labor both on the farm and in city businesses tended to take the form of fairly long-term indenture, on an apprenticeship or other basis, and the relation between employer and employee was largely assimilated to a kinship prototype. This of course is quite similar to conditions in medieval Europe. The cities did see the development of short-term indenture, for a year or half-year, and the beginnings of a formally free labor force, paid daily, weekly or monthly. The latter were largely unskilled workers but included some skilled workers as well. Relations determined entirely by the cash nexus rather than by "bonds of loyalty" run counter to the Japanese value system, as we have described it, so it is not surprising that there were serious checks to their development. In the first place the government kept a close eye on the formally free labor force and required all such laborers to register regularly with persons appointed for the purpose by the *bakufu.* In harmony with this scheme labor bosses developed with whom the worker had particularistic ties of a semi-permanent order. Regardless of restrictions, however, the development of some form of "free" labor force was probably required by an economy at the stage of complexity of the one in question.

As we might expect, relations between the purveyor of goods or services and the customer tended to be continuous and particularistic. Lafcadio Hearn remarks that even in the Meiji Period when one bought a house one also incurred obligations to retain the services of a particular gardener to do the gardening, a particular carpenter to do the repairing, etc., and that it would be difficult or impossible to obtain a man other than the one who "goes with the house" to do the work.[19] Settlement of terms under these conditions, and they were apparently very widespread, was personalistic and traditionalized. Here again, however, in an economy of such complexity all questions of the disposal and remuneration of goods and services could not be carried out in a particularistic framework. By 1800, the great Mitsui department store in Edo (modern Tōkyō) which employed over a thousand persons, had instituted a one-price cash-and-carry system. Even earlier we find injunctions to merchants to sell at the same price whether the customer was known or was a stranger. In general high standards of honesty (*shōjiki*) were considered essential in business life. As long as relations between purveyor and customer are particularistic and continuous the customer's confidence is supported by his diffuse relation to the seller and sanctions are relatively easy to apply, but when this relation becomes segmental, specific and transitory, confidence can only be maintained on the basis of belief that the seller is conforming to basic standards of honesty. That such standards did emerge is certainly related to the development of a highly differentiated economy, both as an effect and as a precondition. The same considerations which hold for specific and transitory relations between customer and purveyor hold also for relations between employer and formally free labor. In both situations universalistic norms were functionally necessary and did emerge.

The need for capital to meet current expenses was great in an economy such as that of Tokugawa Japan. Poor farmers who had exhausted supplies before the new harvest was in had to resort to usurers to tide themselves over. This was the basis for widespread relatively small-scale moneylending in the villages and towns. Further both *daimyō*[20] and *samurai* often found themselves in the same situation, they too had spent their income before the new harvest was in. They too turned to the moneylender. Some of the wealthiest merchants of the period specialized in loans to the *daimyō* which often ran into very large sums of money. Loans of the above types were often quite attractive to those with capital as rates of interest were high. Such loans can only be considered as a drain, however, if we look at them from the point of view of the economy as a whole. A great deal of money that could have been loaned for the expansion of productive capacity was turned into these essentially unproductive channels. Loans to the warrior class, nevertheless, had their drawbacks. The warriors still retained their control of the government, and more than once in the period the *bakufu* declared all outstanding loans to be null and void, largely as an aid to the hard-pressed *daimyō* and *samurai*. Further, the lenders to *daimyō* were vulnerable to direct government expropriation. More than a few of the richest of them fell like overripe plums at a word from the *bakufu*. Many merchants, therefore, came to the conclusion that loaning to *daimyō* was not a healthy thing to do. One of the early heads of the Mitsui family wrote a book in which he described the fall of some of the wealthiest of the lenders to *daimyō*, and warned the merchants against such loans. It became a cardinal principle of the Mitsui house not to make such loans, though on occasion they did so under political duress. Rather they preferred to loan to merchants who wished to use the money for expanding their operations. Thus in spite of the drain of capital in non-productive directions, the Mitsui and other merchants with similar policies did supply a source for productive capital.

Some of the large merchant houses and especially the money exchanges developed into institutions which fulfilled many of the functions of banks. They accepted money on deposit, issued drafts, etc. There was also the development of the bill of exchange which was especially useful for handling payments between Ōsaka and Edo, and thereby avoiding a long, costly and dangerous transportation of bullion. The legal system stood firmly behind these institutions. A charge of default on a bank draft took precedence over all other business in the Ōsaka courts and obligations were rigorously enforced. The high development of credit, by making for more flexible financing, certainly was a factor in the growth of the economy in the period.

Natural resources are not abundant in Japan but even those available were only spottily exploited in the Tokugawa Period. Land was intensively cultivated and a considerable amount of additional land was brought under cultivation during Tokugawa times, so much so that only a small amount has been able to be added to the arable land total in modern times. Water power was used a little for mills but its great exploitation had to await the introduction of electric power stations. Coal and a number of metals were mined but seldom on a large scale. Timber was used in building and in many other uses. A high percentage of mountain forest land had its advantages for the Japanese. Technology was for the most part relatively simple, traditionalistic and often ritualistic. The artisans in many instances exhibited a very high degree of craftsmanship, but rationalized techniques for large-scale production were virtually non-existent. It is interesting, however, that standardization was very widespread. Floor mats and other housing materials were made in standard sizes as was clothing. Such standardization undoubtedly helped to make possible the early introduction of the one-price system.

As has already been mentioned, most businesses were small-scale and organized along family lines, with non-family employees being assimilated to family roles. Above the level of individual businesses there was a widespread guild system. Of most interest are the large wholesaling guilds, comparable to the merchant companies of an earlier day in Europe, which were made up of large merchants combined for the exploitation of some particular market. A number of these wholesaling guilds combined to establish a shipping line between Ōsaka, the great supply center, and Edo, the great consumption center. A form of insurance was worked out so that losses of ships would be equally shared by the member guilds.

One would expect from the value system that "free competition" would not be highly regarded by the Japanese and that particularistic associations and combinations would be widespread in the economic sphere. As is indicated above this is the case. Though the guild system was abolished by the Meiji government, the existence of guild-like associations in the economic sphere by no means ended at that time. In fact, all through the modern period various forms of association among producers have been common; often they have received direct government encouragement. Though there were certainly abuses in such organizations and in many cases economic progress was hampered by them, it may be questioned if, given the Japanese value system, their effects were necessarily as pernicious as might appear from a purely Western point of view. Given the performance emphasis in Japanese values, these particularistic associations might serve to raise standards of efficient production and honesty in business dealings rather than inevitably to hinder these developments.

The Integrative System

The great extent to which social life was formalized in the Tokugawa Period, the extent to which it was determined by tradition and thus not open for innovation or hardly even for variation, certainly is an important fact for the integrative system because this formalization removed the possibility of conflict in a great many situations. Buttressing this adherence to prescribed forms was the principle of group responsibility. Serious failure to conform to the norms was considered not merely to be a matter of individual responsibility. Rather, family, five-family group[21] and even village or ward might be involved in the responsibility for the act of a single individual. Thus every person in his social actions was in a representative role with respect to his primary collectivities. A wrong step would jeopardize not only himself but could bring disaster upon his group or at best leave it open for contempt and ridicule. Further the group itself tended to place conformity with the social norms higher than group membership and thus, in addition to external social sanctions, a transgressor was more apt to receive rejection than support from his primary group in case of any very serious misdeed on his part. This situation leads to a close identification with the collectivity and a tendency for all sub-collectivities to support the morality of the total collectivity at whatever cost to themselves, which is perhaps close to what Durkheim was talking about when he used the term mechanical solidarity. This surely was very powerful and perhaps the chief integrative mechanism.

By contrast "organic solidarity" was relatively weak. The concept of mutually beneficial relations between persons belonging to different sorts of groups or between the different groups themselves, when related only by complementary function rather than particularistic ties, may have existed in theory but carried little weight.[22] Under these circumstances it is clear that when identification with sub-collectivities takes primacy over identification with the total society serious strains toward factionalism will appear. Factionalism was indeed rife in Tokugawa as well as in modern Japan. This whole situation seems to be closely related to the fact that particularism has primacy over universalism in the value system.

Solidarity based on common commitment to institutional religion is again relatively weak as a major integrating mechanism. This is because the great pluralism of sects meant that only relatively small numbers of people would be united in a single religious collectivity and that indeed religion formed one of the bases for the development of the factionalism noted above. On the other hand, to the degree that the major collectivites of the society, including the family and the nation, themselves were religious collectivites (this point will be discussed later), religion served specifically to reinforce "mechanical solidarity." Indeed it seems likely that this mechanism was as successful as it was only because it was able to combine with it the element of solidarity on the basis of common religious commitment.

The institution of property was rather well developed. Land was inalienable in theory but by means of universal legal subterfuges this provision was a dead letter and land was in fact often bought and sold. Freeholders predominated, but there was a considerable development of tenancy in the period though the landlords usually held relatively small amounts of land. That is, there was the development of a rather large class of small landlords rather than of a few great magnates. Not only was land alienable but many other kinds of property were as well. For example guild memberships were saleable, like seats in the stock exchange, and their value fluctuated with economic conditions. All sorts of rights and statuses became saleable on this same principle. It was even possible to sell one's status as a *hatamoto,* direct retainer to the *shōgun,* and there were men who had bought up a number of such statuses and so collected a number of stipends from the government. These were considered abuses at the time, but no government was able to stop them. Adoption into a *samurai* family was also a commodity on the open market and the price fluctuated at different periods. These examples show the penetration of the money economy into the feudal structure itself, and an introduction of a concept of alienability into an area where it could only have very disastrous effects on the status quo. It was indeed a mechanism whereby more mobility could take place in this economically expansive society than the ideal pattern would warrant. It was probably, then, a necessary safeguard against overrigidity. That it was at best an unhappy solution is perhaps one more fact behind the fall of the Tokugawa shogunate.

The Tokugawa Period saw the beginnings of a modern type of occupational system. There is considerable ambiguity about the concepts of status and occupation. The major status groups—warriors, farmers, artisans and merchants—were clearly in some sense occupational groups (*shokugyō*). Thus obligation to fulfill one's status in the sense of one's place in the "feudal" hierarchy merges almost imperceptibly into the obligation to perform one's "daily work." We shall have more to say about this later. In any case the period saw the emergence of an occupational system that was considerably more complex than that implied in the simple four-fold status classification. There was the development of a bureaucracy both by the *bakufu* and the *han* which, though drawn from the *samurai* class, was by no means coterminous with it. Many offices were filled on the basis of merit, that is by the application of universalistic criteria, though the group eligible to receive them was particularistically limited. The *bakufu* supported a "university" in Edo and a number of *han* had their own schools to which talented sons of *samurai* families could be sent. The education was indeed traditional and Confucian but officials were evidently often chosen from the products of these schools and they thus served in some sense as further "sieves" through which universalistic criteria could be applied.

There was the beginning of a professional class among certain groups in the major cities. The chief occupations involved were medicine, private teaching, and the several professions involved in a large-scale popular publishing industry. Probably most of these occupations were filled by members of the *samurai* class who were for one reason or another masterless. Not infrequently a *samurai* would ask to be relieved of his obligation to his lord in order to move to the city and pursue some private occupation. Nevertheless, most of these occupations were open to persons of any class. We shall see later, for instance, that Ishida Baigan (1685-1744), born a farmer and later working as a merchant, finally established himself as a private teacher. Some of the major writers of the period were of *samurai* birth and some were *chōnin*. The important thing in these rudimentary "professions" was that orientation was primarily to the occupation itself and the status of the person holding the occupation was irrelevant. Relations were entered into between professional and client on the basis of services required by the latter and not as the result of a pre-existing particularistic tie. It is to be expected, however, that relations between, say, teacher and pupil would be much more diffuse and particularistic once they have been inaugurated than would be true in the West. This remains true even in modern times when a Western educational system has been adopted *in toto*.

So far we have sketched a few of the "modern" tendencies in those occupations which are largely outside the sphere of the economy, that are primarily "political" or "cultural" roles. A relatively differentiated and complex occupational structure in the economy itself is, of course, implicit in the discussion of the economy which appears above.

The Motivational System

The motivational system as we are using the term is concerned with the regulation of motivation in personalities as it relates to the social system. This has a double aspect: on the one hand, the commitment to the values and functional needs of the social system, and on the other hand, the management of tensions arising in the personality in such a way that they are given adequate release without endangering the functioning of the social system.

Socialization, as we see it, is a very important function of the motivational system. This is the process through which individuals come to internalize moral norms and become committed to institutional patterns. As in all societies, the family was the primary focus of socialization. Though it is very hard to speak of socialization in the family in Tokugawa times, due to lack of primary data, we are perhaps not unjustified in inferring back from the evidence available on socialization among the more conservative elements in modern Japan. On the basis of such inference perhaps a few relevant remarks can be made, tentative though they may be. In early childhood children were treated on the whole with great indulgence and permissiveness. They were allowed to express aggression, assertiveness and greed to an extent far greater than adults. We can perhaps relate to this period of early permissiveness those tendencies to personal aggrandizement and hedonism which seem always latent in the Japanese character. On the other hand, certain disciplines, notably toilet training, were introduced early and rigorously enforced. Thus in some areas a child was expected to live up to rather meticulous standards from the start. As the child grew into the years of pre-adolescence the number of demands for conformity went up rather sharply. He was introduced into the world of rigid conformity with customary forms and high expectations of performance which would form the context of his adult life. There were, of course, wide differences in this respect between classes, the upper class expectations being considerably more demanding than the lower. The present description, then, is probably more accurate for the upper classes than the lower. The high expectations for conformity and performance were enforced more through psychological pressures than through physical punishment, though moxa cautery was apparently widely used by all classes for misbehaved children. The basic psychological pressure was the threat of rejection symbolized most pointedly, perhaps, by disinheritance. To be cast adrift without the support of relatives in a society such as the Japanese was indeed the worst of all possibilities.

The same basic attitudes expressed in the family were also to be found in the outside world. The schools spent a large amount of time on moral texts which repeated the same demands and injunctions learned at home. The five-family group, village, guild, etc., all had high standards of conformity and performance which members had to maintain. Further, breaches of these standards would not be condoned by the family but might bring on severe retaliation from it.

A second area of the regulation of motivation is the balancing of commitments to production and consumption. From what has been said before about the high level of performance expectations it is not surprising that in many instances this was reflected in the adaptive sphere, and that motivation to productive work was encouraged. In particular, skill and technical ability were highly regarded whether among artisans or artists. Though the main differences in prestige were blocked out by the hereditary class system, and within and between these divisions by the control of power, in narrower contexts prestige might correlate closely with differences in skill and productivity, which in turn might be reflected in a differential power position. For example, a clerk who showed himself extremely apt in handling his master's business might be set up on his own after twenty years or so of service. Though skill seems to have been a value in and for itself which in some contexts was seen as having an almost religious significance—the complete mastery of a skill involving a mastery over self akin to the state of enlightenment—productivity or work seems on the whole to have been valued as a contribution to the group goal or as a fulfillment of obligations rather than for its own sake. It would be hard to deny that work for the Japanese has any value in and for itself, but it is perhaps fair to say that this is a relatively secondary motivation. One indication of this is the relative ease with which Japanese men retired from positions of responsibility at a fairly early age to devote themselves to aesthetic or hedonistic pursuits and left the burden of work to younger men. This contrasts vividly with the great psychological difficulty which retirement has for many in our society for whom work for its own sake is a central value. It is also interesting to note that though the main burden of work may have been relinquished by these retired Japanese men, they often retained a fairly vigorous interest in and control over the manipulation of power. This indicates again the central position of the value of controlling others, of exercising power, compared to the value of productivity for its own sake.

With respect to consumption an almost ascetic attitude was pervasive in many spheres. Here as with productivity, however, one has the feeling that asceticism was not valued so much for its own sake as instrumentally, either as a means for furthering the collective goals or as a means of personal training and discipline. At times and in contexts where these considerations were not applicable a relatively unconflicted indulgence in sensual pleasures seems to have been rather common.

If this analysis is correct we may say that the actual amount of motivation committed to production or consumption was governed not by any rigid or relatively independent motivational mechanism but was closely and responsively dependent on collective and individual goals, variable both with respect to time and situation.

A third area of the regulation of motivation is the balancing of public and private interests. The central importance of the polity and of obligations to superiors which was characteristic of the period naturally led to a high valuation of public interest over private. Normally this was expressed through the maintenance of the appropriate behaviour of each status group. This was "knowing one's station." This implied a conformity to all the forms and customs as well as obligations of one's status and not trespassing on the rightful prerogatives of other statuses. Under these conditions, the pursuit of private interests was, of course, perfectly legitimate. In certain situations, however, such as threat to the security of the collectivity or the need of the collectivity head for assistance, the public interest took on an importance sufficient not only to override all private interests, including life itself, but the conformity to traditional customs or status obligations as well. It is evident that the balance between public and private interests was also quite sensitive to any shifts in the pattern of collective goals.

The problem of private interest, however, is not disposed of quite as easily as the above analysis might imply. The road to private aggrandizement was often the road of public service. Further, within solidary collectivities the struggle for power might often be acute. Factions as we have already noted were rife, but even beyond that an element of pure personal power seeking must be noted. This, after all, is to be expected in a society which places such a high valuation on political power. The aim of the ambitious man in this society was to gain control over the activities of others. Even the acquisition of wealth, as John Pelzel has pointed out, was often a means to this end. At the same time of course, this power seeking had to be cloaked in the guise of loyalty or service. The cloak may often have been threadbare but there were few indeed who could afford to discard it.

So far we have been discussing the regulation of motivation with respect to commitment to the values and functional needs of the social system. We must now turn to a brief discussion of the management of tensions arising in the personalities of members of the social system. It is not surprising that a society which requires such high commitment to system goals and is so intensely concerned with individual performance with respect to these goals, should generate a high degree of tension in the personality systems of its members. Management of such widespread tensions is of such importance to the functioning of the society that there must be socially patterned and institutionalized ways of handling them.

High degrees of demand for performance by the group, high penalties for failure to perform, e.g., rejection from the group, together with the fact that one's performance is always to some extent problematical, are apt to create considerable unbounded anxiety in the personality. The Japanese concern for "nicety," for having everything fit in a neat controlled pattern, can perhaps be interpreted as one way of handling unbounded anxiety. The creation of a neat and orderly world is the symbolic expression of an inner need to create neatness and order in the face of the threat from free-floating anxiety. A quite similar argument could probably be made for the concern for neatness and order in German society. But the contrast is highly illuminating. In Germany universalism is predominant over particularism and the order which is created is a universalistic order. It may be theoretical order, rational philosophical, or scientific, or it may be a concern for system and rationality in society itself, or it may find expression as "abstraction" in art or architecture. The Japanese concern for nicety and order, however, reflects the predominance of particularlism in the Japanese value system. It is more aesthetic than cognitive. With respect to nature its concern is not to find order through the most general abstract qualities of nature itself, through scientific laws, but rather to find it in that which unites man and nature, in the relation of outer form to inner feeling, in the creation of a harmonious communion between my soul and the "soul" of the universe. In society order is sought not through the systematic application of general prescriptions and principles, but through each person acting in accordance with what is "appropriate" in each particular relationship. Again in art, the Japanese are concerned with catching the particularity of an object, not in revealing its subjection to general categories. Japanese art is never abstract in the Western sense. Even in the philosophical art of the Zen painters the attempt is to show through a single swift glimpse that the nature of the world is its particularity, and that each particular is a total consummation. Zen art is not to be interpreted, as many Westerners have, as an attempt to point to a heavy Hegelian absolute standing behind all reality, a fact which D. T. Suzuki has repeatedly stressed.

Evidence of the free-floating anxiety of the Japanese is apparent in quite another area, health. The widespread almost hypochondriacal concern for health led to a very large medicine business. This is true of modern times as well when patent medicines have been very popular in Japan. Here the anxiety takes some somatic form and the attempt to gain order and control is made by means of the use of medicines.

It is important to remember that the family in Tokugawa society was in many ways a microcosm of the total society, it had largely the same value system and was penetrated with the same tensions as the total society. It was not, then, a refuge from society,[23] as it perhaps has become to some extent in modern America, where the family is an area for relaxation and emotional expression, set apart from the hard demands of the occupational world. And yet the Japanese with their high level of unbounded anxiety clearly needed such areas of refuge from the demands of society. It is in this context that the development of the gay quarters is to be understood. They offered areas of refuge in which tension could be released through sensual indulgence in wine and women or through vicarious participation in the theater. Certain types of effusive and emotional friendships between persons of the same sex played a similar role.

In concluding this discussion of the motivational system we turn to religion, which we hold to be concerned with the personality and its exigencies as they relate to society specifically in the area of commitment to ultimate values and the handling of ultimate frustration. The following chapters will treat Japanese religion in considerable detail so that here we need make only the most general comments. Religion supplied a context of ultimate meaning to the central value system through the fact that the primary collectivities in the society—the nation and the family—were conceived of as religious as well as secular bodies. Loyalty to these collectivities and their heads had not only a mundane significance, but also an ultimate meaning; fulfillment of obligations to them was in one sense a religious duty, in ways which will be discussed in some detail in following chapters. Acting in closest accord with the political values of the society, that is, giving one's full devotion to one's particularistic superiors, and expressing this devotion in vigorous and continuous performance with respect to the collective goal, was seen as the best means to acquire the approval and protection of divine beings or to attain some form of harmony with ultimate reality. It was precisely the attainment of such approval and protection of divinities or of a state of enlightenment which was the best way to handle the basic frustrations and anxieties of existence. Though the national and family religion was in many ways the most important aspect of Japanese religion in the Tokugawa Period, there were also a number of religious sects and movements which had independent institutional bases. Certain of these, which will be discussed in detail later, played an important role in intensifying commitment to the basic values by emphasizing the ultimate nature and importance of these commitments. They thus in turn affected the content and intensity of the national and family religion. By intensifying the commitment to ultimate values religion also had an effect on the other areas of the motivational system which we have discussed in this section. Namely, it reinforced the commitment to institutional patterns which is the primary concern of socialization, it intensified commitment to productivity over consumption, and it emphasized public responsibilities over private. By influencing the motivational balance with respect to these problems religion had an indirect affect on the other sub-systems of the society. The strength of commitment to institutional patterns has an important influence on the integrative or institutional sub-system. The balance of commitment to productivity or consumption has an important influence on the adaptive or economic sub-system. And finally the balance of commitment to public or private interests has an important influence on the goal-attainment or political sub-system. Not only were the relations of the motivational sub-system to the other sub-systems affected, but as a result of such influences the relations of the other sub-systems to each other were also affected. We will return to this problem in the concluding pages of this chapter. The book as a whole is indeed an attempt to trace and study these influences.

Concrete Structural Units

Above we have attempted to give a very sketchy picture of the four functional sub-systems of Japanese society. It is clearly impossible in this short chapter to go on and fill out the complete picture with respect to concrete structural units. A few strategic units will be discussed, however, to round out the picture of Tokugawa society. Only a very abbreviated treatment can be given even of those units selected here.

Territorial Units

The basic territorial unit of rural Japan was the village (*mura*). One of the village members was the headman (*shōya* or *nanushi*). This headman was appointed by the higher officials from among the more prominent families. The position was often hereditary. The headman was assisted by a group of elders (*toshiyori*) chosen by the villagers. These had largely moral authority. The headman was responsible to the higher officials for conduct in the village and for the payment of taxes. Within the village he was the highest judge and his approval had to be obtained for any legal action whether it were sale of land or disinheritance of a child.

Within the village the families were organized into companies of five families each (*gonin-gumi*). The head of this group was usually the head of the wealthiest and most prestigeful family in the group. The group was formed from contiguous families regardless of class differences. Legal actions had to have the approval of the *gonin-gumi* before going to the village head for approval. In addition all loans had to be sanctioned by the *gonin-gumi* and it was responsible for the defaults of its members.

The ultimate unit of the village as of the society as a whole was, of course, the family. It also had a formal head whose approval had to be obtained for any action of consequence by any member of the family and who was responsible to superiors for the conduct of all members of the family group.

There were a number of status distinctions in the village. In some areas there were the so-called *gōshi,* farmers who in pre-Tokugawa times had served as part of the local defense troops. After 1600 the *gōshi,* as opposed to the *samurai,* did not move to the lord's capital but stayed on their own land. Their income thus did not consist of stipends from the lord. In the areas where they existed they formed a sort of gentry class. Their status was recognized by the Tokugawa or *han* government, and it was possible for a *gōshi* to be made a *samurai*. In some areas *gōshi* were considered to be *samurai*. The 1868 Restoration abolished all feudal ranks and confiscated the "estates" of *daimyō* or *samurai,* which were in fact tax rights and rights to stipends. The *gōshi,* however, retained their land and survived as an important element in the rural gentry class of the modern period.[24]

There were further status distinctions in the village between landlords, those who owned their own land, renters, and hired farm labor. Only the first two groups participated in village affairs. There were distinctions between transient renters and those who had rented for twenty years or more, the latter having acquired certain rights of use by long possession and being hard to evict. There was another axis of status distinction depending on length of family residence in the village, the old "original" families having highest status. Such distinctions tended to run parallel to distinctions on the basis of land ownership, but this was not invariable.

The village owned grass lands, forest lands and mountain lands as well as some other types of land. Use of these village-owned lands went only to those who were sociologically members of the village community and not automatically to all residents.

It is interesting to note that the *gonin-gumi* had a set of written commands from the government to which its members formally subscribed. These were periodically read and explained by the village heads. This is an indication of the intensive penetration of governmental control down to the lowest level of the society. The village, *gonin-gumi* and family were all responsible to the government for the behaviour of individuals. Conversely an individual who was disinherited by his family was also excluded from the *gonin-gumi* and expelled from the village.[25]

We may take Ōsaka as an example of the city as a territorial unit. The commandant of Ōsaka castle, a Tokugawa appointee, was the over-all military officer. Two town magistrates appointed by the *bakufu* from among high-ranking *samurai* were the actual heads of the city. Under them was a numerous staff of *samurai* officials, judges, inspectors of commerce, inspectors of temples, inspectors of the family registers, etc.

There also existed a council of elders (at first 21, later 14 and finally 10 in number) composed of members of leading *chōnin* families on a hereditary basis. Its functions were to oversee trade, supervise the wards, manage assessment and payment of taxes, and appoint the heads of wards.

There were 620 wards (*chō*), but not every ward had its own head. Sometimes there was one head for two to five *chō*. When a vacancy occurred the people of the ward gathered to select a new head. From among three to five names suggested by the people of the ward, the council of elders chose the ward head. This office was not a full-time job, but rather an avocation, in this and other senses quite comparable to the office of village headman. The ward was a definite geographical unit with barriers at its boundaries so that it could be closed up at night. The ward head kept a register of all residents and was responsible for order and good conduct among them.[26]

As in the village, the *gonin-gumi* or five-family company existed as the next unit below the ward, and below this the family.

Though there were large urban concentrations of population in Tokugawa Japan, it will be seen from the above that they were not organized along modern Western lines. The main difference again seems to be related to the predominance of particularism in Japan. Even in the cities a strong particularistic nexus of relationships was maintained for purposes of social control. The city only to a limited extent represented a new form of social organization, that connected with the market and a differentiated economy. For many purposes it was merely a congeries of "villages" in close geographical contiguity. This, of course, is a common mode of organization of cities in many societies. Compare, for instance, the *bario* system in Latin America.

A fief (*han*) was a territorial unit of varying size. In a sense the Tokugawa domain was merely the largest and most complexly organized fief. Looking upward from the village, the smallest territorial unit of the fief, the first important official was the *daikan*. The *daikan* oversaw a certain area, usually one producing about 50,000 *koku* of rice. The duties of the *daikan* were to take censuses, forward taxes, supervise public works and public property and to judge disputes. Cases (especially land cases) could be appealed, however, to higher courts. The *daikan* had practically no military duties and was essentially a fiscal and judicial official. The selection of the *daikan* apparently differed in different areas. In some places the office was virtually hereditary in some local family. In the Tokugawa domain the *daikan* tended to be a paid official removable at will.

The central administration of a fief was carried on by the *samurai* living in the castle town of the lord of the fief. A close look at the *samurai* in one fief might give a useful indication of the general conditions of the *samurai* class in Tokugawa Japan. For this purpose we will rely on the summary given by Fukuzawa Yukichi of conditions in his own fief, that of Okudaira of Nakatsu.[27] In this fief there were 1500 *samurai*. They were divided in two main classes: the upper, about one third of the total, and the lower, about two thirds. Within these classes there were as many as one hundred distinctions in position and duties.

The upper *samurai* class contained the chief minister to the *daimyō* and the higher officials down to the Confucian scholars, physicians and *koshōgumi* or personal attendants to the *daimyō* (these were usually young boys). The top of the lower *samurai* group was composed of the calligraphers, followed by the *nakakoshō*. This latter category included a number of types of occupation such as groom or stablekeeper. Fukuzawa's father, who was a *nakakoshō,* was the keeper of the storehouse of the fief in Ōsaka. There were also the *tomokoshō,* attendants on the *daimyō,* and the *koyakunin,* who had light duties such as guarding the gate, patrolling the grounds, etc. The lowest group was the *ashigaru* or common foot soldier, who were sometimes felt to be not *samurai.* The lower *samurai* were organized in five-family companies as were the common people, but the upper *samurai* were not.

Mobility between upper and lower *samurai* was very small. In 250 years only four or five calligraphers got into the *koshōgumi.* On the other hand, the *koshōgumi* could rise very high in the officialdom and there was mobility in the ranks of the lower *samurai* as well. Peasants could by way of the status of *chūgen, samurai's* attendant, rise into the status of lower *samurai.* Clear status distinctions separated upper and lower *samurai.* A great deal of respect behavior was required from the lower toward the upper. The upper rode horseback, the lower went on foot. There was no intermarriage and even adultery was in the same class. Lower *samurai* were sometimes refused permission to go to other fiefs to study on the grounds that advanced learning was not proper to their stations.

The upper *samurai* received stipends sufficient to support themselves but the lower *samurai* did not. The latter had to supplement their income by means of spinning and handicrafts and not a few of them engaged in surreptitious trading enterprises. The upper *samurai* could afford luxuries but the lower could subsist only by the most careful economies. The upper *samurai* were educated in the polite accomplishments while the lower learned mainly writing and arithmetic (despised by the upper *samurai*) to prepare themselves for clerical work. As a result of these trends the lower *samurai* became very influential in actual administration. They could often hoodwink their superiors due to their greater practical knowledge.

We have dealt at such length with this matter because it was the lower *samurai* more than any other group which was responsible for the Restoration of 1868. Not only did they lead the central struggle which rallied forces around the emperor for the attack on the shogunate, but in the last years of the *bakufu* they seized power in many fiefs through *coups d'état,* replacing the upper *samurai* with lower *samurai* and taking the direction of affairs in their own hands. It was largely from their ranks that the new Meiji government was formed and they provided the leadership for many of the innovations, economic and cultural as well as governmental, of the new era. It is important then to realize what was their social position under the old regime. They were not a "nobility" in the Western sense of the term. They had a legitimized status as rulers vis-à-vis the common people but they had very little else which committed them in any rigid sense to the old system. They had no land and not even adequate stipends. On the other hand, their actual power and responsibility in the administration of government was considerable, so much so that their rewards were quite incommensurate with their performances. These social structural features of their situation together with ideological elements to be discussed later go far to explain the special role they played in bringing about the modernization of Japan.

The Family

The Japanese kinship system is a comparatively simple one. The kinship terminology is of Eskimo type, the main difference from our own being the discrimination of older and younger brothers and sisters. There were no clans or sibs, the lineage and nuclear family being the most important structural units. The definite legally recognized status of head of the family together with the bulk of the family property was inherited by one son usually on the principle of primogeniture. A younger son could establish himself as head of a branch family relative to a main family headed by his father or elder brother. This would be an independent unit but with close ties of loyalty and mutual helpfulness with the main family. Such ties of main and branch could extend over many generations but in most cases were fairly weak after two or three generations. If a branch family were particularly succesful it would very likely think of itself more as main family relative to its own branch families rather than as a branch relative to some remote main family.

The household might consist of several generations but was not usually of very great size since it did not include collaterals. That is, the family of only one son, normally the eldest, would usually live with the parents, the younger sons establishing separate households as they married. The obligation to support the aged parents naturally fell on the son who stayed at home, which in the poorer families, at least, probably served in part to balance out the inequality of inheritance. It should be pointed out that population was very nearly static throughout the Tokugawa Period. Younger sons could often find an inheritance by being adopted into a childless family or by marrying a daughter in a family without sons and being an "adopted husband." Thus the "problem of the younger sons," while it was undoubtedly acute in many individual cases, did not have great sociological implications until the great rise in the population after the Meiji Restoration.

The family was patrilocal with the exception of the so-called adopted husband who took his wife's family name and thus was assimilated to the patrilocal tendency in name at least. Marriage was arranged by families and usually served among the upper classes to cement strategic ties and among the lower to obtain a good strong additional worker for the patriarchial family. It was, then, a family affair and not a matter of individual attraction. Divorce was at the discretion of the husband's family; they could return the bride to her own family at any time. Adoption was common and the adopted child had the same rights as a natural born offspring would have had. This served both to preserve family lines that would otherwise have become extinct and to introduce an element of flexibility into a system in which heredity was of so great importance.

Within the household the central role was that of the head. He was treated with the greatest respect, and obedience to his word was considered absolutely binding on all family members. His was the power to divorce his wife or send away the wife of his son or disinherit any of his children, in other words the power of absolute rejection from the family. Having this latent sanction seemed to be enough to ensure his position in most cases and it was apparently rare for the head of the family to use physical punishment or other tyrannical means to enforce his commands. He was expected to take into consideration the feelings and opinions of other family members and he could afford to do so. The last resort was ultimately his.

The role of wife was ideally one of reticence and deference toward the husband. The wife was not, however, merely an ornament for her husband. She was expected even in upper class families to carry out intricate and very important responsibilities of household management and family obligations. She often worked hard and was capable of considerable planning and organization. It is not surprising then that women exercised more power in fact than their deferential behavior might indicate and that on occasion they were "the power behind the throne."

Among siblings boys in general had more prestige than girls and older siblings more than younger ones. The role of the son was somewhat differentiated with respect to whether he would inherit the family headship or not. The oldest son, whom it was expected would inherit, was trained to be more responsible, cautious —even solemn—than his younger brother. The weight of grave responsibility was on his shoulders from an early age. The younger brother, on the other hand, was encouraged to be independent, plucky, show initiative and cleverness that would not be countenanced in the future head. Such qualities would presumably be an asset in his struggle to make his way in the outside world.[28]

Girls were raised primarily with the expectation of marrying out. They were given the requisite training so that they could represent their family adequately in the household of their husband. The stresses and strains of this kind of family system on in-marrying daughters-in-law have often been discussed together with the phenomenon of "tandom aggression," the woman's making up for her own earlier discomforts by taking out her feelings on the wife of her son.

Commercial Houses

The emphasis on the relation between lord and follower, on loyalty, and on self-abnegating service for the collective goal which we have found characteristic of the Japanese polity and which had even penetrated the family to a considerable extent, was also markedly characteristic of the commercial firm. Of course the ideal expression of these values was in the political sphere proper and the *samurai* were supposed to embody them most fully. It would seem, however, that such values were just as strictly institutionalized in the *chōnin* class. Of course the *chōnin* were often attacked for luxury and immorality, but they had no monopoly on these qualities. They had their share of the luxurious and immoral as did the *samurai* class. There is no reason to believe that the conspicuously immoral in either class should be taken as typical. The ambivalence with respect to the merchants was not, I submit, primarily because their values were different or their morals more lax than the *samurai*. On the whole they had the same values and strict morals. The ambivalence was over what collectivity was to take precedence. The *samurai* were oriented to "public" service and, increasingly as the period came to an end, to "national" service. The suspicion with regard to the merchants, one which, as we shall see, some of their apologists went to great lengths to allay, was that they were oriented to service only with respect to ends of their own firms.

Employment in a merchant house began normally with apprenticeship. The apprentice (*detchi*) entered service around the age of ten. Usually the merchant house would seek its apprentices from its branch families, then from related or friendly families and if there were none available from these two categories it would take an apprentice from an unknown family. If the apprentice was from a branch family no documents would be signed, but otherwise the family of origin and other relatives of the apprentice signified in writing that he was to be apprenticed to such and such a merchant house. The apprentice was taught to read, write and calculate and was given food and clothing by his master. His consumption was restricted in various ways—for example he could not wear a tobacco pouch or clothing of certain of the finer qualities of material. At first the apprentice had lowly tasks to do such as sweeping out the shop, cleaning the tobacco tray, helping in the kitchen, attending the master and the like. When he became a little older he was sent on tasks in the neighborhood. At 15 or 16 the apprentice "entered half-way into manhood" and assumed the status of a *hannin-mae*. He now began to assume some of the functions of a full clerk (*tedai*), such as ordering, selling, paying and taking in money. He was still an apprentice and received no pay. It was common even in well-to-do families to have children serve apprenticeships with another house to ensure that the proper commercial education would be received and that the child would do well in his own family's business.

At 18 or 19 the apprenticeship ended and the status of full clerk (*tedai*) began. On this occasion a new contract was made out again calling for the signature of members of the clerk's family. For a while his duties were about the same as those of the *hannin-mae* but gradually he was given more responsibility. He might be assigned to do bookkeeping or to lay in goods or to wait on customers. He was allowed some discretion in the transactions which he handled, and was not severely scolded for mistakes of judgment. It was felt that only through error could one learn and that too severe scolding would make the clerk overly dependent on others and destroy his business spontaneity. Positive misconduct, however, was not treated leniently and would incur discipline or dismissal. The latter action would keep the dismissed from any further employment in that line of business as other houses would be informed through the guild organization.

One step above the *tedai* were the *bantō* or chief clerks, who were either especially responsible clerks, or clerks in charge of a group of other clerks for some special function. Highest on the scale was the *shihainin* or general manager. In a large firm with several shops one *shihainin* would be in charge of each shop. In general the *shihainin* was second only to the master. He was given the greatest responsibility not only for the business but for the household economy. He often advised on family matters such as the marriage of the son. If the master were dissolute it was the *shihainin's* duty to restrict him and maintain the standing of the business. Here we see clearly the predominance of performance values over status values. The collective goal was the highest aim and if the *shihainin* was more active in performance with respect to that goal he could, for practical purposes, supersede the master, the holder of legitimate status, in the decision-making process. The *shihainin* might ultimately marry a daughter of the house and be set up as head of an official branch family.

An employee who had served well for twenty years or so could ask the master to set him up in a branch business. The master house supplied the capital, house and fittings, and the name of the new house. Indeed, even some of the customers might be turned over. Business and ceremonial connections remained strong for at least the first few generations between main and branch house. They might gradually die out but in some instances they remained strong and served as means for the building up of great commercial networks.

If some one of the branch houses performed some especially important service on the occasion of a crisis in the main house, it would thenceforth stand in a special relation to the main house. Its members would always be treated as guests in the home of the master family and would share its fate with it. This custom was clearly derived from similar usages among the feudal families.

Finally we must mention the status of *chūnen*. The *chūnen* was a clerk who did not serve a normal apprenticeship but was hired after his coming of age (*gembuku*). The chūnen was considered less reliable than those who had served a normal apprenticeship and he had low prestige in the house. He would usually never be entrusted with major responsibility and the status of *shihainin* was usually closed to him. This is a striking example of particularistic considerations taking precedence over universalistic ones.[29]

Religious Organization

The last of the very selective group of concrete structures to be briefly discussed are the religious sects. Here we are concerned only with the social structural aspects; other aspects will be discussed in detail in later chapters.

As a measure to combat Christianity the Tokugawa government required all Japanese to be registered members of some recognized Buddhist sect. This implicated a large part of the Buddhist clergy in the social control structure of the Tokugawa state, and made membership in a sect a matter of political obligation rather than religious conviction. This fact has been cited to explain the general lethargy and uncreativeness of Buddhism in the Tokugawa Period, though actually Buddhism had been at low ebb even before 1600. In any case, it is a fact that the vital religious movements of the age did not emerge from the Buddhists. For most people, apparently, the temple to which they belonged was only visited but rarely on special ceremonial occasions and the major function of the priests was to act as undertakers. Priests were recruited for monasteries and temples on the basis of a period of novitiate, not too dissimilar from an apprenticeship system. Except for the Shin sect, which allowed a married clergy, the monks and priests were supposed to be celibate but this was not rigidly enforced in Tokugawa times, at least in many sects. The sects were organized relative to a definite religious tradition, often singling out one or a few of the numerous books of the Buddhist canon for special veneration. Within these large religious traditions there were many sub-sects deriving from minor doctrinal differences, disputes between temples, rival founders, etc. Each sub-sect had a chief temple or monastery which kept certain controls over the clerical organization of the sect.

The social structural aspects of Shintō are rather more complex than those described above for Buddhism. Shintō is a name which is used to cover a multiplicity of phenomena. In the first place the annual agricultural ceremonial cycle of the rural peasantry has been called Shintō, though many Buddhist and Chinese elements are to be found in this "folk" religion. From the social structural point of view this phenomenon represents a low level of differentiation because the religious ceremonial is a function of the entire village community and in a sense inseparable from it.

Secondly we can distinguish the widespread veneration of certain deities like Jizō or Inari. These we may speak of as cults; there is no special clergy or organized group of followers. Specially important shrines to these deities might indeed have attendant priests, but the cults had no over-all organization. Rather they existed in the daily behaviour of many thousands of Japanese. In this respect they merged with and became part of the "folk" religion.

Thirdly we may consider the cults which had a definite shrine center, such as those of Ise and Izumo, and which at the same time were dedicated to deities central to the main Shintō myth cycle, often being on the spot of important mythological happenings. These shrines had hereditary priesthoods which were responsible for their maintenance and the performance of ceremonies. These cult centers had important relations both to national Shintō and to sect Shintō which will be discussed below. Mythically, of course, the relation between the Shintō deities and the imperial family was continuous, and the imperial family retained certain responsibilities for the worship of its ancestral and related deities. This was especially true with respect to the great shrine of Ise which was dedicated to the Sun-Goddess, the original ancestress of the imperial family. On the other hand, these great shrines became the centers for the development of sect organizations. This was so of Ise and of Izumo. The hereditary priesthoods of these shrines developed fairly elaborate theological systems with, of course, a considerable admixture of Buddhist and Confucian elements, beginning at least as early as the 13th century in the case of Ise. The Tokugawa Period saw both the continuation of this theological tradition and the beginnings of a sect organization. The priests of the Ise shrine took long trips throughout Japan and established confraternities (*kō*) in the various towns and villages for the purpose of the Ise pilgrimage. This may be considered an intermediate stage between cult and sect.

National Shintō centered around the court and the person of the emperor. Its canon was composed of "historical" works which fused the national mythology and the early history of the ruling house. As we have noted above, the great cult-centers are at least partially integrated into the structure of national Shintō, representing a differentiation of sacred specialists within it. This differentiation, however, was far from radical, the emperor and the functioning of the imperial government retaining a strongly sacred character. In a structural sense national Shintō was rather weak in the Tokugawa Period. Formal organs and mechanisms for its propagation were few outside the immediate court circles. All of this was to be drastically changed in the Meiji Period when every device of the central government in the way of education and propaganda was turned toward the strengthening of national Shintō. But the structural weakness of national Shintō in the earlier period should not lead one to Chamberlain's conclusion that modern state Shintō was an invention of a few clever leaders of the Meiji Restoration. Almost every expression of Japanese nationalism in both the Tokugawa and Meiji Periods (and, indeed, earlier) can be seen as an expression of national Shintō. In fact national Shintō can perhaps best be understood as a sacred form of nationalism. National Shintō in this sense then was steadily on the increase throughout the Tokugawa Period, and certainly by the end of it there would have been general consensus on its primary tenets concerning the special divine ancestry and nature of the emperor, and Japan as "the land of the gods" among those of almost all religious commitments. In this sense of Japanese nationalism, national Shintō was not incompatible with other religions and this is the basis of the assertion by the Meiji government that state Shintō is "not a religion."

Sect Shintō, our fifth category of Shintō, is a term which describes a group of religious movements with little in common theologically, often borrowing as much from Buddhism and Confucianism as from Shintō, which for historical reasons have been classed as Shintō. They all have organized and centralized clergies and relatively definite bodies of adherents. They are all fairly new, though those growing out of the Ise and Izumo cults have, of course, very old roots. Not all of them even have their origin in the Tokugawa Period and those that do originate in its latest phase.

It has been argued at length whether Confucianism can be considered a religion at all. Some have maintained that it is only an ethical system and not a religion. Though this could be seriously argued for early Confucianism it can hardly be seriously maintained with respect to the Confucianism of the Sung Period, the so-called neo-Confucianism. We have defined religion above as man's attitudes toward his ultimate concern and his actions with respect to it. Neo-Confucianism has a well developed metaphysical position with explicit conceptions of and attitudes toward man's ultimate concerns. Further, it has well worked out and elaborated methods for the attainment of enlightenment which is seen not as mere cognitive understanding but, in a sense parallel to the Buddhists, as an ultimate religious reconciliation.

Japanese Confucianism was largely neo-Confucian though several schools of neo-Confucianism were represented. It had no ecclesiastical structure, but rather structurally was comparable to the philosophical schools of the ancient world, being handed down from teacher to pupil and occasionally being represented by a more or less continuous educational institution. Its greatest influence was on the most literate elements among the city-dwelling *samurai*. The importance of Confucianism, however, far exceeds that of a separate differentiated religious movement. It had for many centuries seeped into the consciousness and customs of the Japanese people. Such central concepts as loyalty (*chū*) and filial piety (*kō*), though they may have been thoroughly Japanized, never lost, as at least part of their significance, the full meanings of these terms in the Confucian tradition. The practical ethics of both Buddhist and Shintō sects were largely of Confucian origin, and at least the latter were strongly influenced by neo-Confucian metaphysics (which in turn, of course, had been the product in part of strong Buddhist and Taoist influences). Especially for our purposes it is important to note that almost every important new religious movement of the Tokugawa Period showed a strong Confucian influence.

Finally we must note Japanese family religion, which focused on "ancestor worship" and was more or less integrated with Buddhist, Shintō or Confucian religious traditions. Each home had its small shrine before which simple ceremonial acts were performed daily. Here, as in the case of national Shintō, we have an important example of the lack of differentiation, or perhaps better, of the only partial differentiation of religious and secular functions in Japanese social life.

The above sketch of Tokugawa society is intended to serve as a general background for the material on religion which is to follow, and specifically as a rough working model of the society by means of which the relations between religion and other aspects of the society can be made clear. We have already discussed the place of religion in the motivational system and some of the effects a pietistic intensification of religion would have had on that system. An increase of motivational commitment to the institutional patterns would strengthen the ability of the integrative or institutional system to control and channel social action, in a word, it would lead to an increase in social discipline. The particular characteristic of the Japanese institutional system was its strong emphasis on the vertical axis and relatively small reliance on horizontal ties. That is, the institutional structure was held together largely through ties of loyalty between superior and inferior. A strengthening of this system then meant a strengthening of the intensity of loyalty and thus affected the relation between the political and institutional systems. Being able to count on a high level of loyalty, the powers of coordination which the political system could exercise vis-à-vis the institutional system were also strengthened. With respect to the problems of modernization and industrialization it is clear that such intensive controlling powers of the political system and the disciplined response of the people to them were a major advantage.

An increase in the motivation committed to production and inhibition of consumption through emphasis on austerity and frugality had an obvious significance for the economic system. Devotion to work and thrift are important motivational prerequisites for economic rationalization. Further, the powerful controlling position of the polity had its effects on the economy. We have noted above that the polity took considerable responsibility for the functioning of the economy. More on this will be included in Chapter V below. The important point here is that if from the point of view of power advantage it seemed useful to develop the economy, the polity was in a position to support strongly such a development.

Finally, the intensification of public commitments over private supplied the motivational basis for the rationalization of political power, and especially for the 1868 Restoration which carried that rationalization to new levels. The political innovations of the Meiji government, which were radical in some ways, required such a motivational commitment if they were to be carried through. A lack of just such a commitment was a major stumbling block to all efforts to reform from above in China. The importance of political rationalization for modernization and the development of economic rationalization has been pointed out above and will be discussed further below.

In all these relationships between the sub-systems of the society the influence of religion is clearly only one element. It would be possible to start from any segment of the model and trace out the interrelationships with all other segments. We are not arguing for either one-way or one-factor causation. It does seem useful, however, to attempt to isolate the single factor of religion and follow through systematically all its influences and ramifications. Though we are not yet able to estimate in quantitative terms how important any single factor is in such a complex process as the rise of a modern industrial nation, it is only through such a process of isolation that the nature and effects of a single factor can begin to be gauged.

The following chapter will be devoted to a more extensive treatment of Japanese religion, pointing out its relations with the central value system and the ways in which it regulated motivation. Chapter IV will then treat the relation between religion and the polity and Chapter V that between religion and the economy. After a case study of a single religious movement and its various social ramifications we should be in a position to estimate, even if very roughly, the role of religion in the rise of modern Japan.

Notes

1. In a survey chapter such as this one, drawing as it does on my entire reading on the Tokugawa Period, it is impossible to document every statement of fact or even acknowledge indebtedness for every interpretation. The general treatment of the period in Sansom's *The Western World and Japan* and his *Japan: A Short Cultural History,* and the relevant volumes of Murdoch and Takekoshi (see bibliography for all citations of books mentioned in these notes) have probably provided the main factual basis, though numerous articles and books dealing partly or wholly with the period have also been consulted. With respect to interpretation the influence of Benedict and Pelzel has been pervasive. I have tried to give specific citation when points were derived from these authors, but feel sure that a number of such points have slipped past unacknowledged. An article of John Pelzel, "The Small Industrialist in Japan," must particularly be mentioned. I did not have occasion to read it until after this chapter was written but was gratified to discover a close correspondence between the analysis of the overall pattern of Japanese society contained there and that which is set forth in this chapter, particularly with respect to the key importance of the political aspect in Japan. This is of particular interest as the two analyses started from largely different empirical materials and entirely different theoretical premises. In the sociological interpretation of Japan and especially of the contrasts between Japan and China I am indebted to the published and unpublished work of Marion J. Levy.

2. An example of such an analysis for the American value system is contained in a paper by Talcott Parsons, "A Revised Analytical Approach to the Theory of Social Stratification" contained in his *Essays in Sociological Theory* (revised edition).

3. The reader is advised to refer to figure 1 as an aid to clarifying the relations between these terms.

4. *Han* is the Japanese word for "fief." This term is often translated "clan" but as it is a territorial unit under a feudal lord and in no way a kinship unit this term seems unadvisable.

5. This point may be illustrated by a story told about one of Ninomiya Sontoku's most prominent pupils, Tomita Kokei. When starting off from his home village early one morning to attend the Confucian school in Edo, he heard footsteps and turned around to see his mother running after him. He asked what was the matter and she replied, "If you do not succeed, you need not return home." (Armstrong: *Just Before the Dawn,* p. 153.)

6. This point has been made by Ruth Benedict in *The Chrysanthemum and the Sword.*

7. The approach to the analysis of values used here is configurational. The values we are discussing are not primarily a matter of presence or absence. All societies have, in the broad sense in which we use the term, political values. But not all societies give pri-

macy to these values as the Japanese seem to have done. Values which other societies hold primary are not necessarily absent in Japan, but are of secondary importance and usually strongly influenced by the primary political value cluster.

8. Professor Parsons has suggested that this may be a matter of phase alternation. The four dimensions of figure 1 when viewed temporally may be considered as four phases. There may be inherent strains in a basic commitment to goal-attainment values which require a periodic shift of emphasis to integrative values. The same kind of shift can, I think, be seen in China, but there the primary emphasis is on integrative values and the shift to goal-attainment values seems to be the more temporary.

9. This point is made by Ruth Benedict in *The Chrysanthemum and the Sword.*

10. *Chōnin* means "townsman." This term was used to cover the merchant and artisan classes and was often used as a synonym for *shōnin,* or merchant.

11. The four functional subsystems are considered to be related through a series of input-output balances. That is, each subsystem makes contributions to each of the three others and in turn receives certain contributions from them. Loyalty is considered to be an input into the polity from the integrative or institutional system. The corresponding output is the power of coordination.

12. The *tozama* were those lords who submitted to Tokugawa rule only after Ieyasu's final victory. They were excluded from the inner circles of the shogunate and placed under various restrictions but at the same time were not taxed and were very nearly independent within their own fiefs.

13. *Bakufu* means literally "tent government" and is used interchangeably with "shogunate."

14. *Seppuku* is the more common Japanese reading for what is known generally in the West as *hara kiri.*

15. A further discussion of *kokutai* may be found in Chapter IV.

16. For a discussion of taxation in the Tokugawa Period see Honjō, "Views in the Taxation on Commerce in the Closing Days of the Tokugawa Age." He estimates that the sources of tax revenue of the *bakufu* in 1842 were as follows: farmers, 84%; *samurai,* 12%; and merchants, 4%.

17. For an interesting discussion of Tokugawa law see Henderson, "Some Aspects of Tokugawa Law."

18. *The Integration of Economic and Sociological Theory,* p. 32.

19. *Japan: An Attempt at Interpretation,* pp. 441-443.

20. *Daimyō* is the term for the feudal lord of a *han.*

21. The functions of the five-family group (*gonin-gumi*) will be described later in this chapter.

22. John Pelzel notes the difficulties involved in establishing mutually beneficial credit or other business relationships between concerns of essentially equal status. Almost all important business relationships were between firms of inferior and superior power and status. The relations were essentially patron-client relations. Partnerships, for example, were extremely rare. See "The Small Industrialist in Japan."

23. Here again we must note considerable differences between classes. What is said here applies most typically to the upper classes, but this includes upper *chōnin* as well as *samurai.*

24. For a discussion of *gōshi* in Tosa see Grinnan, "Feudal Land Tenure in Tosa."

25. For local institutions in the Tokugawa Period see Asakawa, "Notes on Village Government in Japan after 1600," and Simmons and Wigmore, "Notes on Land Tenure and Local Institutions in Old Japan."

26. For government of Ōsaka see Simmons and Wigmore, *ibid.,* p. 52, ff.

27. See Fukuzawa Yukichi, "Kyuhanjō."

28. This point has been made by John Pelzel.

29. For merchant organization see Kachibe, "Sekimon Shingaku Shiron" and Simmons and Wigmore, *op. cit.*

CHAPTER

III

Japanese Religion: A General View

AS THE TITLE to this chapter indicates, there is some validity in speaking of Japanese religion as an entity in spite of the variety of its manifestations. Especially by Tokugawa times so much borrowing had occurred between the various major religions that one can abstract out certain elements which are nearly universal and label these "Japanese religion." In the national and family religions all the great religious traditions were represented and almost inseparably fused. Confucianism and Shintō had borrowed Buddhist metaphysics and psychology; Buddhism and Shintō had borrowed much of Confucian ethics; and Confucianism and Buddhism had been rather thoroughly Japanized. In spite of considerable homogeneity, however, some sects stressed certain of the common tenets more than others, and in each the common tenets were formed into slightly different configurations. Consequently there will be frequent occasions to discuss the different religious strands separately.

Some further remarks concerning the theory of religion which underlies this work must perhaps be made before turning to the descriptive material. The chief social functions of religion as we see them are to supply a context of meaning for the central values of the society and to meet the threats to these values posed by the ultimate frustrations of the human situation. Both of its primary functions require orientation to a superordinate system characterized by the attribute of ultimacy. The superordinate system supplies a metaphysical context for the central values and thus some ultimate basis of meaning for them. It also supplies a source of ultimate power and meaning which can support and fulfill human motivation in the face of the ultimate frustrations. Within certain limits threats to the social system which cannot be met on the reality level, and thus generate an unreleased reservoir of tension, can be met by the religious mechanisms of ritual, rationalization, expiation, etc. Beyond these limits, however, such threats may undermine the institutionalization of the religious system itself. The old metaphysic may be felt to be inadequate to give meaning to new conditions and the old source of power inadequate to handle new threats. Under these conditions the old conceptions of the superordinate system may be altered and new religious institutions develop which channel the flow of religious motivation in new directions. Changes may also occur in such situations which do not involve the development of new religious institutions. The old religious system may lose some of its power to maintain the value pattern and manage tension without any compensating tendency. This would result in greater *anomie* and higher levels of tension in the society with consequent impairment of the nonreligious functions as well. Beyond certain limits such tendencies would lead to the destruction of the society but societies can continue to function even with rather high rates of *anomie* and tension and there is probably a considerable variation in these respects from society to society. Conversely to what we have just discussed, change without the development of new religious institutions in a situation of strain may occur as a strengthening of the old religious system. Religious efforts to maintain the pattern and manage tension may become more intense and systematic, and more motivation may be channeled into some of the nonreligious subsystems, rather than less.

This last situation would seem to be that of Japan in the Tokugawa Period. No really new religious orientation developed, but in response to strains in part due to the growing differentiation and complexity of the society itself, the existing religious system was strengthened and its effects ramified. It is the purpose of this chapter to discuss the old religious system as it existed at the beginning of the Tokugawa Period. The following two chapters will then discuss some of the intensifications and ramifications of that system which occurred during Tokugawa times.

Underlying Conceptions

There seem to be two basic conceptions of the divine in Japanese religion. The first of these is that of a superordinate entity who dispenses nurturance, care and love. Examples include the Confucian Heaven and Earth, Amida and other Buddhas, the Shintō deities, as well as local tutelary deities and ancestors. This category shades off imperceptibly into political superiors and parents, both of whom are treated as in part, at least, sacred. Religious action toward these entities is characterized by respect, gratitude for blessings received, and attempts to make return for those blessings.[1]

The second basic conception of the divine is more difficult to explain. It might be described as the ground of being or the inner essence of reality. Examples are the Chinese *tao;* the neo-Confucian *li,* often translated as reason, and *hsin,* heart or mind, when identified with *li;* the Buddhist concept of the Buddha-nature; and the Shintō term *kami* in its most philosophical interpretation. Religious action toward these entities is the attempt on the part of the communicant to attain some form of union or identity with this ground of being or essence of reality. These types of religious action will be discussed in detail in a later section.

The two conceptions of the divine should not be thought of as competing. They are both to be found in almost every sect and they were not felt to be in any way mutually exclusive. Any potential conflict was resolved by a theory of levels of truth, the second conception of the divine being considered perhaps more profound. Only some of the more extreme forms of Zen, however, radically rejected deities of the first type. The Pure Land sects, on the other hand, stressed devotion to Amida, a deity of the first type, in rather exclusive terms, but always left the door open for metaphysical interpretations which could approach the second type of conception of the divine. Between these extremes most of the various sects and movements stressed some combination of these conceptions.

The conception of nature shares both aspects of the attitude toward the divine. Nature is both a benevolent and nurturing force toward whom man should express gratitude, and a manifestation of the ground of being. Man may attain insight into the essence of reality and union with it through the apprehension of some natural form. Nature is not alien to the divine or to man but is united with both.

Man is the humble recipient of endless blessings from divinity, nature, his superiors, and quite helpless without these blessings. At the same time he is both "natural" and "divine." He is a microcosm of which divinity and nature are the macrocosms. He is a "small heaven and earth," he contains within himself the Buddha-nature, or the *tao,* or *li,* or his true heart (*honshin, ryōshin*) is the same as *li.* Clearly from what has been said here human nature is conceived as good. Mencius' solution of the problem of human nature, then, can be considered typical of most Tokugawa religion. It should be pointed out, however, that it is only man's basic or true nature that is good. In actual life this nature may be obscured by the dirt of selfishness and personal desire.

Radical evil tends to be denied in man, nature, or divinity. Evil is explained either as relative, only seeming evil but in a larger context not really so, or as a sort of "friction" attendant on daily living or "weight" due to our having bodily substance. This friction or weight diverts us from our true natural orbit. Freeing ourselves from selfish desires will allow our natural selves to take their appropriate places without hindrance. The Buddhist conception of evil as due to the moral working out of causes in a former existence was also widespread in the Tokugawa Period.

What has been said about the unity of man, nature and divinity should not be interpreted as a static identity. Rather it is a harmony in tension.[2] The gratitude one owes to superordinate benevolent entities is not an easy obligation but may involve the instant sacrifice of one's deepest interests or even of one's life. Union with the ground of being is not attained in a state of coma but very often as the result of some sudden shock in daily living. Something unexpected, some seeming disharmony, is more apt to reveal the Truth than any formal orderly teaching. Japanese art and aesthetic attitudes toward nature are also concerned with the unexpected, with moments of tension which reveal the inner life of the object in all its particularity. Symmetry is abhorred. There is harmony, but it is a tense harmony.

All three of the main religious traditions were oriented to a historical past when things were felt to be better than in the present. For the Confucians it was the age of the sages; for the Buddhists the present age, the *mappō,* was a corrupt age during which it was hard to understand the Buddha's teachings. The revival Shintoists harked back to the days when the emperors ruled in pristine Japanese simplicity. The Buddhist and Confucian theories of historical change were essentially cyclical. Better times are followed by worse in endless succession and the contemporary period was seen as merely a temporary trough. The Shintō belief was not cyclical, however, but one-way. It alone of the major religious traditions had the concept of a creation, even if in the form of a rather primitive myth. To Shintō Japanese history could be seen as the unfolding of the will of the gods, and religious ends might be fulfilled in time and history as the destiny of the Japanese people. Nichiren adapted some such view in his own unique form of Buddhism and in the Tokugawa Period various Shintō movements made use of it.[3]

The above very condensed exposition of the underlying conceptions of the divine, nature, man and time may serve as an introduction for the discussions which follow.

From Magic to Metaphysics

In this section we must review briefly certain lines of development of Japanese religion which precede the Tokugawa Period. These developments reveal a tendency toward rationalization on both philosophical and ethical levels which went far in freeing the world of primitive magic. Such a development was a precondition for the use of religious motivation in rationalizing the world in nonreligious spheres and so is of the first importance for the present study.

Early Shintō was concerned perhaps more than anything else with fertility. Ceremonies for praying for harvest and thanksgiving for harvest had a prominent place in the ritual calendar. In the villages phallic rites were employed to ensure fertility through a sympathetic magic, and even in the formal state cult the reliance was primarily on offerings and the promise of praises to the deities if good harvests were forthcoming. The *Engishiki,* a document dating from the early 10th century, gives the text of a prayer for harvest given annually on the 4th day of the second month by a member of the priestly Nakatomi family at a large ceremonial gathering in the capital. An excerpt from it will perhaps give some of the flavor of this early Shintō:

> I declare in the presence of the sovran gods of the Harvest. If the sovran gods will bestow in many-bundled ears and in luxuriant ears the late-ripening harvest which they will bestow, the late-ripening harvest which will be produced by the dripping of foam from the arms and by drawing the mud together between the opposing thighs, then I will fulfill their praises by setting-up the first fruits in a thousand ears and many hundred ears, raising high the beer-jars, filling and ranging in rows the bellies of the beer-jars . . .[4]

We have a number of texts of early ceremonies for the warding off of calamity from fire, storm or pestilence, and for settling spirits in their sanctuaries. Purification held a central place in early Shintō ritual. Offenses, deliberate as well as inadvertent, were felt to bring contamination or pollution and required various acts of purification such as lustration, fasting, abstention. Leprosy, tumors and "calamity from creeping things" were given in the same list as wounding and killing, incest, and bestiality as causes of pollution requiring purification.

Fertility, purification, and similar forms of ritual continued down to recent times in more or less the same "primitive" forms as have been sketched above, but beginning at least as early as the 13th century there developed, especially around the cult center at Ise, a marked trend to philosophical and ethical rationalization. There is no doubt that this occurred under the stimulus of Buddhist influence, but it is a genuine reworking of the Shintō tradition and not merely a Buddhist overlay.

One of the earliest documents which reveals this trend is the *Shintō Gobusho* compiled by the Gekū priests of Ise probably in the 13th century, some of its materials undoubtedly being of even earlier date. With respect to offerings it says, "The gods desire not material gifts, but offerings of uprightness and sincerity,"[5] and with respect to purity, "To do good is to be pure; to commit evil is to be impure. The deities dislike evil deeds, because they are impure."[6] The monk Musō-Kokushi (1271-1340) recounts a visit to the Ise shrine not long after the period of the presumed compilation of the *Shintō Gobusho*. His account is as follows:

> At the Ise Daijingū offerings are not allowed, neither is the reading of any Buddhist sutra or incantation. When I went to Ise I stopped for a while near the Gekū and questioned a Shintō ritualist styled Negi whom I met there on this point and he said, "When anyone comes here to worship there is both an outer and an inner purity. The former consists in eating clean food and observing the ritual purification and keeping oneself from defilement, but the latter means ridding the mind of all ambitious desire." The usual thing is to make offerings at shrines and have *Kagura* performances held in order to petition the deities for some benefits that are desired, which is very far from inward purity and so is declined here.[7]

Here we can see how the old ideas of offerings and purification are given ethical and symbolic significance. The implication of this idea of inner purity for the relation of man to the divine is brought out in the following quote from a 14th century visitor to the Ise shrine:

> And particularly is it the deep-rooted custom of this shrine that we should bring no Buddhist rosary or offering or any special petition in our hearts and this is called "Inner Purity." Washing in sea water and keeping the body free from all defilements is called "Outer Purity." And when both these purities are attained there is then no barrier between our mind and that of the deity. And if we feel to become thus one with the divine, what more do we need to pray for? When I heard that this was the true way of worshipping at the shrine, I could not refrain from shedding tears of gratitude.[8]

The earlier notion of deity, one that continues to be held down to modern times, is in the above passage tending to be replaced by the second concept of the divine which was discussed above in the section on underlying conceptions. This is clearly brought out in a statement by the 14th century Shintō theologian Imbe-no-Masamichi in his *Shindai Kuketsu* (1367):

> *Kami* [the native Japanese word for deity] is from *kagami* [mirror]. This is abbreviated and read *Kami.* The Divine Mind, like a clear mirror, reflects all things in nature. It operates with impartial justice and tolerates not a single spot of uncleanness. That which in Heaven is *Kami,* in nature is Spirit and in man is Sincerity. If the spirit of nature and the heart of man are pure and clear, then they are *Kami.*[9]

To round out the discussion we may turn to a very popular Shintō work of the Tokugawa Period, the *Warongo* or *Japanese Analects.* In the following quote we can detect both of the basic conceptions of deity and the final assertion of the pre-eminence of inner over outer purity:

> That the God dislikes what is unclean, is equivalent to saying that a person who is impure in heart displeases God.
>
> He that is honest and upright in heart is not unclean, even though he be not ceremoniously so in body.
>
> To God, inward purity is all important; mere external cleanliness avails not. This is because God is the Essential Uprightness and Honesty, and therefore, it is His Heavenly Ordinance that we should lead an honest and happy life in harmony with the Divine Will.
>
> If a man is pure in heart, rest assured that he will ever feel the Divine Presence with him, and possess the immediate sense of the Divine within him.[10]

Buddhism in Japan underwent a course of development very similar to that sketched above for Shintō. Though there were undoubtedly from the first a certain number of sincere Buddhist monks who understood something of the more philosophical forms of their religion, it would be hard to deny that the importance of Buddhism in the early centuries of its development in Japan was largely magical. Sutras were read often not for their intrinsic content but for the magical results such reading was thought to bring. For example, in the 7th century we have records of sutras read to bring rain, the *Maha-megha-sutra* being thought especially suitable for this purpose. Other sutras were read to stop rain when floods were feared. Ritual vegetarian feasts were given for large numbers of monks to gain various ends such as restoring the health or lengthening the life of some noble patron or for the benefit of some departed soul. Large convocations were held to read certain sutras in various special ways, that is, facing certain directions or speaking with a certain degree of loudness or softness, etc., to obtain various magical results. The *Ninnōkyō* or *Sutra of the Benevolent Kings* was often read in such convocations. Its principal aim was to ensure peace and prosperity to the empire, but it was also read to bring rain, to stop pestilences of smallpox, leprosy or other epidemics and to avert the evil consequences of bad omens such as eclipses, comets, etc. Virtuous acts, such as the granting of a general amnesty, or issuing a prohibition against the killing of animals, or having some pure person retire from the world, were also employed to obtain results like the ending of a drouth or the recovery of a sick emperor.[11]

At the personal level, Buddhism in these early years was largely a matter of spells and charms and devotions to especially favored Bodhisattvas. Certainly a considerable amount of this sort of thing continued in general practice right down to modern times, but nevertheless the 12th and 13th centuries marked a great turning point in Japanese Buddhism during which a strong trend to free the religion from magic took hold. This is most markedly shown in the three great sects or congeries of sects which arose in those centuries, the Zen, Nichiren and Jōdo or Pure Land sects.

Eisai (1141-1215), founder of the Rinzai school of Zen in Japan, taught that knowledge of the Buddha-mind could only be gained intuitively through meditation (*dhyana*), and not by worshipping Buddhas, reciting sutras or other such religious practices. He held that no physical media could express or symbolize the Buddha-mind. It could only be found within one's own mind through meditation. "Find Buddha in your own heart, whose essential nature is the Buddha himself," he said.[12]

Zen did not consider the older religious practices as "abominations" but merely as inefficacious, and so did not lead a drive to eliminate them. Among its own adherents, however, and these numbered among the more important intellectual and military figures of the upper classes, it did serve as a definite force in breaking the hold of the old magical religious attitudes.

Nichiren (1222-1282), founder of the sect which bears his

name, taught worship to only one Buddha, the Buddha of the *Lotus Sutra*. Worship of any other Buddha he felt was not merely inefficacious but wicked and disloyal to the true Buddha. He urged the repression of all other sects on these grounds. His message was primarily ethical and he did not stress performing rituals or engaging in mystical contemplation as proper means for worshipping the Buddha. Rather he taught that faith should be reposed in the Buddha, to be signified by the repetition of a brief phrase in praise of the *Lotus Sutra,* sacred above all other sutras and in some way identical with the Buddha himself. Faith ought to be actualized in life through ethical actions, chief of which are, he held, reverence for sovereign, teacher and parent.[13]

The Pure Land sects went in some ways the farthest of any of the new currents in Buddhism in the direction of freeing religion from magic, superstition and ritual. The Jōdo Shinshū, founded by Shinran Shōnin (1173-1262), went farther than any other of the Pure Land sects in this direction and, since it is much the largest not only of the Pure Land sects but of all the sects of Japanese Buddhism, the following remarks will be confined to it.

The core of the Shinshū belief was that only faith in Amida could bring salvation. Shinran wrote:

> Two things are essential to Faith. The first is to be convinced of our own sinfulness; from the bondage of evil deeds we possess no means of emancipating ourselves. The second is, therefore, to throw our helpless souls wholly upon the Divine Power of Amida Nyorai in the firm belief that His Forty-eight Vows were for the express purpose of saving all beings who should put their trust in Him without the least doubt or fear. Such souls will be born surely into His Pure Land.[14]

Since faith in Amida alone is efficacious it follows that all ceremonies, charms, worship of other Buddhas, etc., is in vain. Shinran said:

> An evidence of the increasing degeneracy of the world is visible in the religious life of both priests and laymen of the present time. They are Buddhists in outward appearance, but in reality followers of a false religion.
>
> How sorrowful it is that they look for "lucky days," worship other gods on earth and in heaven, indulge in fortune-telling and practise "charms."[15]

The stress on "faith alone" made many of the older Buddhist practices seem to be outmoded superstitions. The prohibition on clerical marriage was dropped, as was the prohibition on eating meat. Consequently occupations which were formerly held in disrepute were now exonerated. Shinran said:

> There is no difference among those who are living upon fishing with a line or net from ocean or river, those who are dragging out an existence with hunting game or fouling on field and mountain, and those who are getting along in trade or tilling the soil. Man may do anything (whatever), if moved by his karma.[16]

Rennyo Shōnin (1415-1499), often called the second founder of the Shinshū because of his great influence on its development, extended the work of Shinran. He opposed the practice of austerities and meditation as merely giving the mind an opportunity for evil thoughts. He insisted on the practice of the Confucian virtues in daily life and on obedience to state authorities, while at the same time one's inner life was to be wholly given up to Amida. Rennyo opposed any worship of Shintō deities and it is due to him that there are no *kamidana* (household Shintō shrines found in most Japanese homes) in Shinshū homes to this day.

Confucianism needs only a mention at this point. It had gone through a process of rationalization comparable to that discussed above for Shintō and Buddhism many centuries earlier in China. Arthur Waley sees this as a transition from an "auguristic-sacrificial" stage to a "moralistic" stage, a transition which began about 400 B.C. or perhaps earlier and was essentially completed by the time of Hsün Tzu (c. 298-c. 238 B.C.).[17] Thus Confucianism in Japan was from the first a rationalizing influence in the sphere of ethics. Later when the neo-Confucian philosophy of Chu Hsi (1130-1200) and others began to be imported (beginning in the 13th century) largely by Zen priests, Confucianism had some rationalizing influence in philosophy and psychology as well. This reached its greatest extent during the Tokugawa Period when philosophical Confucianism had its most prosperous days. Needless to say the importations of popular Taoism and other folk belief from China had an effect in the opposite direction.

The importance of the rationalizing processes we have been

describing is that they create the possibility of religious action based on a rather small number of premises and applied systematically in a wide number of contexts. The earlier magical stage tended to have few ethical or metaphysical generalizations with relation to which behavior could be ordered but rather contained a vast number of discrete and often contradictory prescriptions and prohibitions almost all of which had compulsive moral legitimacy in their own right rather than with reference to some more general obligation. It is our next task to examine this relatively highly rationalized religious action in some detail. Having done that we will be in a position to determine the relation between this religious action and action in other spheres.

Main Types of Religious Action

As we have indicated above, traditionalistic religious action of a generally magical type has remained important throughout Japanese history. No religious movement has been able to break through it as decisively as Protestantism has done in some Western countries, though Jōdo Shinshū went fairly far in this direction. Though never utterly broken, this type of religious action was often overridden by religious action of a more rationalized type. For our purposes the magical variety needs no further discussion, though its prevalence should not be forgotten in the following discussions. Attention will be focused here on the types of religious action with respect to the two main categories of the divine as previously analyzed.

Action with respect to deity as a benevolent superordinate gets us at once into the theory of *on*. Deity in some form dispenses blessings (*on*) and it is the obligation of the recipient to make return for these blessings (*hōon*). Religious action, then, is the various forms this *hōon* may take.

The term *hōon* is probably of Buddhist origin. It does not appear, apparently, in Chinese literature earlier than the Six Dynasties Period, when Buddhism had already become popular. The term *on* does appear in the *Mencius* and in the *Li Chi* several times, and a term somewhat similar to *hōon*—*hōtoku*—appears in the *Analects* and the *Li Chi,* etc. But *hōon* seems to be of Buddhist origin and reflects an important aspect of early Buddhist ethics, the stress on indebtedness or return for kindness. The *Anguttara Nikaya,* an early Buddhist work, quotes the Buddha as saying, "The wicked person is one who is not grateful and who does not bear in mind any good rendered to him."[18] Another quote from the *Anguttara* is interesting because it shows the early connection of the theory of *on* with filial piety and because it maintains that *on* can never be fully requited:

> We may carry our mothers on one shoulder, and our fathers on the other, and attend on them even for a hundred years, doing them bodily services in every possible way, and establishing them in the position of universal sovereignty: still the favour we have received from our parents will be far from requited.[19]

In the *Mahayana-mulajata-hridayabhumi-dhyana-sutra* (Nanjo 955) the Buddha is described as having preached on four sorts of debt which the Buddhists owe: to parents, fellow-beings, sovereign, and the three holy treasures of Buddhism (the law, the church and the Buddha).

The theory of *on* and *hōon* is found prominently in Japanese Buddhism, especially in the great "reform" sects of the 12th and 13th centuries. To start with Zen, the 13th century founder of the Sōtō branch of that sect wrote, in a manual for his students:

> That we can now see Wisdom and hear the law, is a mercy that comes to us from laying hold of the actions of former founders of religion. If the founders of our religion had not handed it down, how would it have reached to our day? We must be thankful for the kindness that gives us one maxim or one law. Much more therefore must we return thanks for the great mercy of the unsurpassed Great Law. The sick sparrow never forgets a kindness: the rings of the three Great Ministers are no surer token. The distressed tortoise forgets not a kindness: the seal of Yofu is no surer token. Beasts even show their gratitude. How shall men not feel it?[20]

Nichiren in his work "Recompense of Indebtedness" held that "the most significant aspect of ethics, namely, the signification of life, consists in the recompense of indebtedness or grace, and he firmly believed that the true orders of human society will be born from it."[21] In his great work *Kaimokushō* Nichiren quotes with great approval the following passage from the *Saddharmapundarika-sutra*:

> We are greatly indebted to Sakyamuni. He loved us and taught us and bestowed on us grace. We cannot repay his great benefits to us even if we endeavored to do so for countless aeons. Even if we offer to him with hand and foot and worship him with bowed heads, we cannot repay his favors toward us. Even if we take his feet on our upturned palms and carry him on our shoulders through aeons countless as the sands of the Ganges, or honour him with all our hearts, or offer ambrosia or innumerable robes or richly worked cloth of gold, or costly bedding, or offer precious medicines or build for him great monasteries with wood of sandal and adorned with precious jewels, or if we spread the floors of the monasteries with rich carpets, yet shall our debt remain unpaid.[22]

This sentiment is echoed in a common exhortation of the Jōdo Shin sect, "One returns thanks to the source of the Buddha's benevolence by pulverizing one's body and breaking one's bones for countless kalpas."[23] The Pure Land sects, indeed, are among the most fervent in insisting that men owe everything to a single deity, Amida, and that ". . . our whole life must be one long expression of gratitude: we must regard life as a service which Amida demands of us."[24]

Many Confucians stress the importance of *hōon* often in connection with the duty of filial piety but also often with a more general metaphysical underpinning. For example, Kaibara Ekiken (1630-1714) says,

> Man is greater than all other beings, and owes the universe an extremely great debt of gratitude; for this reason, what men should do is, needless to say, to serve their parents with all their power and at the same time to revere the universe all their life, in order that they may repay their great debt.[25]

And in a similar vein Nakae Tōju (1600-1648) wrote,

> All men acknowledge the duty of gratitude, and filial obedience is merely showing the edge of gratitude. Even crows feed their parents, and lambs show their respect by stooping as they eat. It is the beginning of all the virtues, and when we forget it we cloud the soul with lust, dim the illustrious virtue, and are astray in the night.[26]

It would be possible to continue to marshal evidence from various periods and various religious sects and movements as to the great importance of *on* and *hōon* in Japanese religious thinking, but in order to avoid needless repetition we may close this discussion with a rather long quote from Ninomiya Sontoku (1787-1856), founder of the Hōtoku movement which will be discussed later, as this quote admirably sums up the very broad application of this theory.

> My teaching is that we should reward grace and virtue. If asked for an explanation I would say this means that we make return to heaven, man and earth for gracious benefits we have received from them. Heaven's blessing is given in the light of the sun and moon. The sun rises and sets. The four seasons come and go. In every living creature there is both development and decay. In these and other ways heaven's blessing is manifested toward us. Earth manifests her favor in the growth of grasses, trees, and grain; in the fact that birds, animals and fish live. Man's grace is manifested in the fact that sages teach the truth; emperors govern their subjects; high officials protect the country and people; farmers distribute commodities. We all live by the grace of heaven, earth and man, and so we must make it our first principle of conduct to make return to them for their gracious contributions to our welfare. From the Emperor on down to the humblest peasant, this spirit must prevail.[27]

Religious action conceived as a return for blessings from a benevolent superordinate, then, is based on a view of man as weak and helpless by himself. Only with the help of benevolent beings can he live, and the blessings he receives are so much greater than his ability to return them that actually he can only return an infinitesimal amount. By devoting himself utterly to returning these blessings he assures to himself the continuation of them, and in some sense he is thereby saved from his weakness. But he can never repay; he always stands in debt. This theory, it would seem, has some of the dynamic potentialities of the idea of original sin. It presents a fundamental "flaw" in human nature which cannot be overcome by man alone but only by some intervention from above. It is only in this sense that they are similar; in other respects they are quite different. It is interesting to note that the theory of *on* holds for superordinates within the social system, such as parents or political superiors, in exactly the same terms as it holds for entities above the social system, gods or Buddhas, etc. The significance of this will be commented on at a later point.

The second major type of religious action is that which seeks to attain unity with the divine conceived as the "Great Ultimate," or the *Tao,* or whatever the term may be. We can distinguish within this second major type two main divisions. The first attempts to attain this unity through private religious exercises or experiences, through withdrawal from the world. Elaborate techniques of breath control or meditation may be devised to attain this end or it may be considered that only giving oneself up to a life of "pure experience" and waiting for enlightenment to burst forth at some unexpected moment can attain it. Stated theoretically, this approach seems to be an attempt to destroy the self as an ontological entity, to destroy the dichotomy between subject and object. The second main division attempts to attain unity with the divine through the accumulation of ethical acts or "works of love," through participation in the world rather than withdrawal from it. The ethical acts may be relatively specific "acts of charity" or they may merely be those acts which make up a "good life." Stated theoretically this approach seems to be an attempt to attain unity through the destruction of the self as an ethical entity, by destroying the division between self and other, mine and thine, in a word by destroying self*ishness.*

Fung Yu-lan makes this distinction with respect to early Chinese philosophy. He gives the Taoism of Chuang Tzu as an example of the first type and the Confucianism of Mencius as an example of the second.[28] Sir Charles Eliot seems to be making the same distinction between the two main branches of the Zen sect in the following quote. He says the Sōtō sect

> ". . . lays greater stress on the need of good conduct and morality in spiritual life, whereas the Rinzai, without being in the least open to the charge of immorality, emphasizes the importance of a sudden spiritual enlightenment without insisting so strongly that a good life is the best training for such an enlightenment and a sure result of it."[29]

Both of the divisions of the second type of religious action are to be found in Japan. The first, unity through cognitive experience, we are probably safe in saying, had only a limited influence among the upper classes, whereas the second, unity through moral action, has had a fairly broad and general influence and is, in fact, closely linked with the first type of religious action, that based on the theory of *on.*

Mencius is undoubtedly the major source of the idea that mystical unity can be attained through moral action or acts of love. It would be difficult to overemphasize the influence of Mencius on the thought of the Far East, at least since the Sung Period. He was, of course, extremely familiar to all educated Japanese of the Tokugawa Period, so that he must be considered not only as the beginning of a long line of influences but as a continuing contemporary influence throughout the Tokugawa Period, and indeed even up to the present.

Following Fung's tentative interpretation that Mencius' famous "moving force" (*huo jan chih ch'i*) is the spiritual quality of those persons who have attained the state of mystical unity, let us note what Mencius has to say about this force:

> Such is the force (*ch'i*): it is most great and most strong. Being nourished by uprightness (*chih*), and sustaining no injury, it fills up all between heaven and earth.[30]

And on how to develop it, he says:

> Such is the force: it is the correlate of righteousness (*i*) and morality (*tao*). Without it, [man] is in a state of starvation. It is produced by the accumulation of righteous deeds, and not to be obtained by incidental acts of righteousness.[31]

The whole Confucian practice of moral self-cultivation, then, is to be seen as religious action of this second subtype, the attempt to attain unity with the universe through moral action. Already with Mencius we get the idea that the mind (*hsin*) within man is in its true form identical with essential nature, and needs but to be cultivated in order for this identity to be fully attained:

> He who has exercised his mind to the utmost, knows his nature (*hsing*). Knowing his nature, he knows Heaven. To keep one's mind preserved and nourish one's nature is the way to serve Heaven. To be without doubleness of mind whether one is to have untimely death or long life; and having cultivated one's personal character, to wait with this for whatever there may be: this is to stand in accord with Fate (*ming*).[32]

It was the neo-Confucians of the Sung Period that developed this idea, incorporated aspects of Buddhism and Taoism in it, and made it one of the most important religious influences in the Far

East ever since. Fung Yu-lan summarizes the views of one of the greatest of the neo-Confucians, Ch'eng Hao (1032-85), as follows:

> According to Ch'eng Hao, man's original state is that of union with the universe which, however, becomes lost through the assertion of the individual ego. Hence the aim of spiritual cultivation is to destroy the barriers created by the ego, and return to the state of universal oneness.[33]

Spiritual cultivation consists precisely in the cultivation of the classic Confucian virtues. Oneness with the universe can be achieved by the following means, says Ch'eng Hao:

> The student must first comprehend love (or humanity, *jen*). The man of love is undifferentiably one with other things. Righteousness (*yi*) propriety (*li*), wisdom (*chih*), and good faith (*hsin*): all these are love. Get to comprehend this truth and cultivate it with sincerity (*ch'eng*) and earnestness (*ching*); that is all.[34]

Japanese Confucians of the Chu Hsi and the Wang Yang Ming (1472-1529) schools both held views of spiritual self-cultivation which were variations on what has already been said. The differences between them are considerable and the controversies not uninteresting, but for our purposes these can safely be ignored. Here what we wish to stress is that which they had in common, the notion of a process of moral self-cultivation with the religious aim of some sort of identification with the universe.

This basic type of religious action was not confined to the Confucians. Rather it permeated a great deal of Japanese religious thinking. Many of the quotes above, especially of the Shintō rationalizers, show a similar notion. The following is from a popular Shintō work of the 17th century:

> The heart of man is the abode of God (*kami*); think not that God is something distant. He that is honest, is himself a God (*kami*), and if merciful, he is himself a Buddha (*hotoke*). Know that man in his essential nature is one and the same with God and Buddha.[35]

An even more vulgarized version of the same basic idea is to be found in the *kakun* or family instructions of a Tokugawa *samurai*, Ise Teijo (1714-1784):

> If the heart is honest and in the right way, even though you pay

them no worship the gods will vouchsafe their protection. Hence the saying that a god makes its abode in an honest man's head. If a man's heart be not honest, and he loses his grip of the five moral constants and the rules of the five social relationships, then, even though he pays them worship, the gods will not grant him their protection. On the contrary, retribution will overtake him.[36]

It is selfishness which obscures the true self and keeps us from attaining the state of oneness. Consequently moral self-cultivation is a constant effort to combat selfish desires. Only the sage is finally successful in this effort. For others, the eradication of selfish desire is approached but not absolutely attained. The obligation to make the effort, however, like the obligation to return *on,* is unrelenting, and not dependent on the feasibility of the task. Here is another dynamic factor in Japanese religious action.

It is interesting, I think, to view the two main types of religious action to which we have given considerable attention not merely as two parallel types but as reciprocals, as two sides of the same coin. The first type, that concerned with the return of *on,* focusses primarily on the relation of the individual to objects outside himself. The second, that concerned with self-cultivation, focusses more on the integration of the individual's personality within itself. For both, selfishness is the great sin. It disrupts the proper repayment of obligations without, and it disrupts the true harmony of one's nature within. Selfless devotion, on the other hand, establishes a "perfect" relation with the benevolent superordinate and at the same time allows the individual to identify with him, lose himself in the divine. Through this identification he finds his own inner nature fulfilled, because his own inner nature in its essence is identical with the divine.

We must remember that both the main types of religious action call for vigorous activity in this world. If the Chinese neo-Confucians at times leaned in the direction of contemplation and quietism and a rather static sort of harmony, this is not true of the Japanese —Confucian or otherwise. Japanese Confucians were vigorous in praising activism and attacking quietism in all its forms. The next stage in the argument, then, is to discuss exactly what sort of activity in the world was implied in the Japanese theories of religious action.

Religion and the World

It might be well to begin this section with a few concrete examples of *hōon*. What follows is a continuation of the remarks of the Japanese founder of the Sōtō branch of the Zen sect which were quoted above on page 71:

> In showing this gratitude, men need not go to extraneous or superabundant laws; the performance of daily duty is the path of justifying (proving) one's gratitude. That which is called reason is the not neglecting of one's daily life, nor wasting it in selfishness.

As an amplification of this we may quote a Shinshū tract:

> The will of the Buddha is manifest everywhere and in everything, it is present in the person of our teacher, parents, brother, wife, children, friends and also in the state or community to which we may belong; the Buddha is protecting, nourishing, consoling, and instructing us in every possible way. What we owe to the Buddha is not only when we are carried into his Pure Land, but even when we are living our daily life on earth, for which latter fact we must also be deeply grateful. Let us not forget how much we are owing to our present surroundings, and to regard them with reverence and love. We must endeavor as much as we can to execute our duties faithfully, to work for the growth of Buddhism, for the good of family, state, and society, and thus to requite a thousandth part of what we owe to Amida. To work thus for the world with a sense of gratitude is the true life of the Buddhist.[37]

The method of attaining "true knowledge," the aim of the second type of religious action, turns out to be not far from what is enjoined above. Muro Kyūsō (1658-1734), one of the more famous Tokugawa Confucians, says,

> Read, learn the "laws" and then search them out in conduct and affairs; this is the true knowledge, the knowledge that is the beginning of right conduct. The "Way" of the Sages is not apart from the things of every day. Loyalty, obedience, friendship, all the relations are in this "learning" and not a movement, not even our resting, is without its duty.[38]

The above quotes may serve to give an indication of a view which had become quite common in the Tokugawa Period. Religious action, whether it be *hōon* or the quest for personal enlightenment, took primarily the form of fulfilling one's obligations in the world. Ritual, prayer or meditation all took second place to the primary ethical obligations. What concretely tended to be most stressed was obligation to political superiors and obligation to family. In the above quotes such obligation might be considered as the temporal fulfillment of more ultimate obligations. A further example of this would be Nichiren's injunction to a *samurai* disciple: "Consider your daily works in your Lord's service as being the practice of the *Hokkekyō* (*Lotus Sutra*)."[39] But there was also a tendency to make these moral obligations ends in themselves, that is to endow them with ultimacy and make them "religious" in their own right. Such a tendency is strikingly illustrated in a quotation from the *Warongo*:

> All ye, my people, high and low, rich and poor! Before you pray to Heaven and Earth as well as to the myriad other deities, it is essential that you should first show filial piety by being obedient to your parents, for in them you can find all the gods of "Within" and "Without." It is useless to pray to the gods who are "Without," if you do not serve your parents Within (at home) with filial piey.[40]

We may cite one interesting and rather extreme example of the tendency to fuse what we would separate into the categories of religious and ethical. This is Nakae Tōju's cosmic interpretation of *kō* (filial piety):

> Before the heavens and the earth were conceived *kō* was the divine way of heaven. The Heavens, earth and man, yea, all creation were conceived by *kō*. Spring and summer, autumn and winter, thunder and rain and dew had not been except for *kō*. Benevolence, righteousness, propriety and understanding are the principles of *kō*.[41]
>
> *Kō* dwells in the universe as the spirit dwells in man. It has neither beginning nor end: without it is not time or any being; there is nothing in all the universe unendowed with *kō*. As man is the head of the universe, its image in miniature, *kō* endows his body and soul, and obedience to the way is the very pivot of existence.[42]

The true understanding of *kō* leads to a perception of man's identity with the universe:

> If we seek for the origin of things we find that, as our bodies are divided from our parents but still are one with them, so are their bodies divided from the spirit of heaven and earth, and the spirit of heaven and earth is the offspring of the spirit of the universe; thus my

body is one with the universe and the gods. Clearly perceiving this truth and acting in accordance with it is obedience to the way.[43]

As for the destruction of self, *kō* is the best means:

> Let us take counsel from our original nature, for it is still pure though we be ignorant and wicked. It will teach us that unfilial conduct is the pain of hell and the source of all evil. All we have, body and soul, are derived from our parents. If we injure ourselves we harm what is not our own but theirs.[44]
>
> All the errors of mankind arise from "self" as we think "this is my body," "this is mine," but *kō* slays self.[45]

The above material is interesting because it presents a rather complete "theology" for a "religion of filial piety." Moreover this theology is derived entirely from elements of the general religious system which we have been discussing above. It is, however, a religion with no necessary connection with sect, shrine or temple. It is indeed a family religion, and it is to the family that we must look for one of the most vigorous foci of religious life in Tokugawa Japan.

The "family religion" of Nakae Tōju cannot, of course, be considered as typical. It represents an extreme of philosophical sophistication and explicitness. Nevertheless it is an expression of the underlying spirit of that religion, only more refined and abstract than most of his contemporaries would have understood. This family religion which was virtually universal in Tokugawa Japan is what is generally called ancestor worship. Every family had a household shrine, usually two, one Shintō and the other Buddhist, in the latter of which tablets or other memorials of the ancestors of the family were kept, as well as statues or symbols of deities. A brief ritual was performed before the shrine each morning and evening, a lamp was lighted and some small offering of food was given. This ancestral cult was a constant reminder of the sacredness of the lineage and of the obligation of all family members to it. Motoori Norinaga (1730-1801) wrote:

> Forget not the shielding love shown for ages by your ancestors. My parents for generations are my family Gods, they are the Gods of my house.[46]

From ancestors to parents is but a step, and the step was easily taken. Motoori also wrote:

> Father and mother are our family Gods, they are our Gods, child of man take greatest care and worship them.[47]

As we have seen above a "theology" of filial piety showing it as a means of attaining union with the universe, so similarly a theory of filial piety based on the concept of *on* was very widespread. It was often said that one's obligation to one's parents was "higher than heaven and deeper than the sea." Such an obligation could never be repayed. Hirata Atsutane (1776-1843) said:

> Should a child support his parents there is no reason for him to talk about his affection. Through whom was it that he was given birth and grew up and who made it possible for him to keep his parent? Was it not through the parent? If this is well considered then no returns of love can repay the parent for rearing the child. The parent never thought of any return in the way of support when rearing the child, out of a truly loving heart he gave his body to nourish the child and his love is ten times more strong than that which expects a return of love or keep.[48]

The family was not only the locus of the ancestral cult. It was the most frequent place of worship for the deities as well. We have noted that most homes had Shintō and Buddhist shrines. Various Shintō and Buddhist deities would be worshipped along with the ancestors. Almost every home had a piece of the shrine of the Sun Goddess at Ise and thus participated to some small extent in the worship of the divine ancestress of the emperor. Visits to shrine or temple were infrequent and when they were made it was usually the family head who went as a representative of the whole, except on festival occasions when the whole family went. Popular preaching was widespread and the reading of sermons and tracts extensive in the Tokugawa Period. Still we must assume that a considerable amount of the religious indoctrination took place within the family.

Just as we can speak of a "religion of filial piety" so also we can speak of a "religion of loyalty." Actually this term has been used to denote *Bushidō,* the status ethic of the *samurai* class, on which we shall have more to say in the next chapter. That loyalty had a religious compulsion that could override other religious commitments is indicated by the following incident:

> When the priests rebelled against Ieyasu at Mikawa many hesitated to fight against the holy brotherhood, but Nagayoshi Doi, taking up

his spear, rushed into the enemy's line crying aloud, "The benefaction of our lord is apparent and at hand, while the punishment of Buddha is in the dark and far away. If we were to be burnt in the lurid flames of hell, how could we help saving our lord from the hands of the rebels? If we fail to serve our lord in this emergency, we break the duty of man and become brutes.—If ye understand me, ye rebels, surrender and sue for our lord's pardon."[49]

Loyalty was one of the prime tenets of the family religion. Filial piety did not compete with loyalty, it reinforced it. Nakae Tōju, when questioned as to whether the obligation to preserve one's body as a gift of one's parents would prohibit one from going into battle, replied that the obligation to preserve one's virtue was higher than to preserve one's body, and that if need be one should willingly die for one's lord. This is true filial piety. We may see in the following quote from Nichiren that filial piety in the last analysis for the Japanese meant loyalty:

. . . when a father opposes the sovereign, dutiful children desert their parents and follow the sovereign. This is filial piety at its highest.[50]

Conclusion

Especially in the last section the close relation between Japanese religion and the Japanese value system as outlined in Chapter II has become apparent. We have seen how the two types of religious action, one derived primarily from Buddhism and the other primarily from Confucianism have come to reinforce the central values of achievement and particularism. They establish the particularistic relations to superiors as sacred and insist on a high level of performance of obligations to them as necessary for religious justification or salvation. They provide a metaphysical basis, a view of the nature of man and deity, which makes these central values meaningful in some ultimate sense. They promise some ultimate salvation or enlightenment, the victory of meaning over ultimate frustration if the values are adhered to, and misery in the abyss of selfishness if they are not. It is quite possible that it was on the level of religious action that these values first received their clearest and simplest formulation. This involves a period before that with which we are dealing. All we can assert here is that in the Tokugawa Period religious action reinforced the central values.

In the view of deity which sees it as a benevolent superordinate we may say that the values of performance and particularism are seen as defining the religious object. The deity performs benevolent acts with respect to those who stand in a particularistic relation to him. This involves the reciprocal obligations of loyalty and the return of gratitude. The view of the divine as "the ground of being" defines the religious object by the values of particularism and quality. The religious object does not "act." In fact it is not really an object because it is beyond subject and object, it is an identity of self and other which can be attained by the religious actor. Performance norms are built into this process of attainment, but are perhaps so greatly stressed due in part to the great influence of the concept of deity of the first type. At any rate the importance of this second concept of the divine may indicate that integrative values are very important in the Japanese value system and that the need for some form of personal resolution beyond any demand for performance may be a compelling result of the strains inherent in the particularistic-performance pattern.

There can be little question that a religion of the type described in this chapter would have the effect of reinforcing a strong motivational commitment to the institutional values of Japanese society. This is another way of saying that it reinforced the values of performance and particularism. What we have seen of the relation of religion to loyalty and filial piety is a concrete example of this. Put in the most formal terms we may say that religion reinforced the input of pattern conformity from the motivational system into the institutional system.

In Chapter II we saw that the various segments of society were subjected to somewhat diverse forms of strain. The problems of the *samurai,* merchants and farmers were all somewhat different. It is therefore not surprising that the reactions to strain of these groups which took on a religious aspect were also different. Broadly stated, each main class had a status ethic, a form of the central value system especially adapted to its situation. The religious and ethical movements of the Tokugawa Period both codified and formalized these status ethics, and introduced new and dynamic elements into them. Of course certain of the more important new trends cut across class lines. As we have indicated before, the main direction of these new movements was not to introduce new values or weaken the old but to propagate stronger and more intense forms of the old values. Two main areas affected by this intensification of the old values were the political and the economic. The next two chapters will, therefore, be devoted to an analysis of the relation between religion and the political and economic systems in Tokugawa Japan. In carrying out this analysis the main lines of the different status ethics will be sketched in and most of the major new ethical and religious movements will be summarized.

Notes

1. Certain of the examples of the divine mentioned in this paragraph, especially the Confucian Heaven and the Shintō deities, may not originally have been viewed as nurturant in character, but by the beginning of the Tokugawa Period they were generally viewed in this way in Japan.
2. The concept of harmony in tension was suggested by John Pelzel in order to dispel any implication of rigidity in the notion of harmony. The idea is that for the Japanese harmony always implied potential movement, was an active and not a static idea. Albert Craig has objected to the noun tension or the adjective tense as having psychological implications which the Japanese idea of harmony does not have, and in fact is strongly opposed to. In lieu of a better term we have decided to retain the present one, but warn the reader to disregard any implication of psychological tension or anxiety which the word may carry.
3. This concept of history was undoubtedly not characteristic of the earliest Shintō but arose in medieval times and was further developed in the Edo Period.
4. Satow, "Ancient Japanese Rituals," p. 20.
5. Holtom, "The Meaning of Kami," p. 43.
6. Katō, *A Study of Shintō,* p. 163.
7. Sadler, *Saka's Diary of a Pilgrim to Ise,* pp. 10-11.
8. *Ibid.,* p. 48.
9. Holtom, *op. cit.,* p. 5.
10. Katō, "The *Warongo* or *Japanese Analects,*" p. 67. Hereafter this will be cited as *Warongo.*
11. Information in this paragraph was derived largely from DeVisser, *Ancient Buddhism in Japan.*
12. Coates and Ishizuka, *Hōnen, The Buddhist Saint,* p. vi.
13. On Nichiren see Anesaki, *Nichiren, The Buddhist Prophet.*
14. Nakai, *Shinran and his Religion of Pure Faith,* p. 111.
15. *Ibid.,* p. 119.
16. Fujimoto (trans.), *The Tannishō,* p. 22.
17. Waley, *The Way and its Power,* pp. 20-25.
18. Tachibana, *The Ethics of Buddhism,* p. 232.
19. *Ibid.,* p. 222.
20. Lloyd, "Developments of Japanese Buddhism," p. 461.
21. Satomi, *Japanese Civilization,* p. 181.
22. Ehara (trans.), *The Awakening to the Truth or Kaimokusho,* p. 39.
23. Naitō, "Shūkyō to Keizai Rinri, Jōdo Shinshū to Ōmi Shōnin," p. 273.
24. Eliot, *Japanese Buddhism,* p. 383.

25. Ishikawa, "On Kaibara Ekiken's Thought and Reasoning," p. 26.
26. Fisher, "The Life and Teaching of Nakae Tōju," p. 42.
27. Armstrong, *Just Before the Dawn,* pp. 175-176.
28. Fung Yu-lan, *A History of Chinese Philosophy,* vol. I, p. 130.
29. Eliot, *op. cit.,* pp. 284-285.
30. Fung, *op. cit.,* vol. I, p. 131.
31. *Ibid.*
32. *Ibid.,* p. 129.
33. *Ibid.,* vol. II, p. 520.
34. *Ibid.,* p. 521.
35. Katō, *Waronogo,* p. 12.
36. Hall, J. C., "Teijo's Family Instruction," pp. 139-140.
37. *Anon., Principle Teachings of the True Sect of Pure Land,* pp. 86-88.
38. Knox, "A Japanese Philosopher," p. 61.
39. Satomi, *op. cit.,* p. 108.
40. Kato, *Warongo,* p. 10.
41. Fisher, *op. cit.,* p. 40.
42. *Ibid.,* p. 41.
43. Knox, "A System of Ethics, An Abridged Translation of the Okina Mondō," p. 102.
44. *Ibid.,* p. 349.
45. *Ibid.,* p. 103.
46. Kirby, ''Ancestral Worship in Japan," p. 238.
47. *Ibid.,* p. 246.
48. *Ibid.,* p. 244.
49. Department of Education, *History of Japanese Education,* pp. 69-70.
50. Ehara, *op. cit.,* p. 61.

CHAPTER

IV

Religion and the Polity

THE RELATION OF RELIGION to political rationalization is a close one in Japanese history. We can only sketch in a few highlights of the historical developments before Tokugawa times, but some such background is necessary. In the Tokugawa Period we shall be especially interested in *Bushidō,* the Kokugaku school, the Mito school, and some tendencies among the popular movements.

Historical Background

All three of the great religious strands in Japan had close relations to the political sphere in the early periods of Japanese history. The earliest records we have of Shintō indicate the emergence of a state cult out of what is clearly a primitive tribal religion. The Yamato people consolidated their hegemony over central Japan in the early centuries of the Christian Era and apparently in connection with this political predominance, they managed to establish their own version of the mythology. This version incorporated the myth cycles of several areas in such a way as to establish the Sun Goddess, Amaterasu O-Mikami, the divine ancestress of the Yamato chief, as predominant over all the gods. The religious activities of the great shrine centers, notably Ise and Izumo, were brought into relation with the religious functions of the court. The Yamato chief was in the first instance a religious functionary, though he does seem to have divested himself of some of the more onerous sacred duties, which were transferred to the shrine centers, in order to obtain greater freedom of action. Nevertheless he remained in effect the high priest of the national cult. It is interesting to note that the earliest Japanese word for government is *matsurigoto,* which means religious observances or worship.[1] This would seem to indicate the lack of differentiation of function between the religious and the political spheres.

To what extent the above mentioned developments took place under Chinese influence is unknown. The direct influence of Confucian theories is clear, however, at least by the 17th century. The so-called Constitution of Shōtoku Taishi issued in 604 A.D., though it contains both Confucian and Buddhist elements, is especially Confucian with respect to its theory of government. It enunciates a theory of social harmony emanating from the acceptance by all of the supreme authority of the emperor. In Confucian theory the influence of the sovereign is not merely political but also ethical and indeed magical. All of these ideas were adopted with the effect of adding new ideological props, both sacred and secular, to the position of the ruling family. Now indeed for the first time it is possible to speak of an "emperor," rather than of a chief. Not only the religious and ethical theory of the role of the emperor and his government were borrowed but a whole complex of Chinese legal, administrative, property and other concepts and institutions were adopted at the same time. Though many of these institutions were fated to wither on barren soil, the fundamental concept of a central monarchy of Chinese type, fused it is true with the native ideas about the divine position of the ruling family, remained a permanent influence throughout all subsequent Japanese history.

The early history of Buddhism, too, is bound up very closely with political considerations. The earliest introduction of Buddhism was associated with the jockeying for power of the powerful families around the throne. Once the position of Buddhism was secure at court, it was rather closely integrated with the political aspirations of the ruling family. Here was a new and powerful influence which could aid in bolstering the position of the monarchy. Among the earliest sutras to receive repeated notice in ancient documents are those for the protection of the state, which have been noted in the preceding chapter. It is clear that various magical influences were being ranged on the side of the court which were beyond the control of any of the priests of the indigenous cult. Later the metaphysical formulations of several Buddhist sects were used for elaborate reinforcement of the position of the emperor. Such, for instance, was the doctrine of the Kegon sect which saw all the Buddhas as manifestations of the great Buddha Locana. The court perceived in this doctrine an analogy to the political hierarchy they wished to strengthen and thus gave strong support to this sect. In the mid-eighth century a large temple was erected to house a gigantic statue of Locana. "In the edict setting forth his reasons for the erection of the great Tōdaiji Temple, the Emperor Shōmu in 749 declared that the laws of the Buddhas and the Imperial edicts and legislation were to be regarded as identical, so that any one guilty of infringing either would surely, irrespective of rank and station, be visited by dire calamities."[2] Later the Tendai doctrines supplied another theoretical formulation which was used to bolster the position of the monarchy.

The net effect of these various developments was to lead to a conception of loyalty to the emperor which could override other religious and secular commitments. This clearly was a necessary step in overcoming the primitive traditionalistic objections to the rationalization of power. We may quote a single concrete example to illustrate this process:

> Under an imperial order to build ships, Kawabe-no-omi, disregarding admonishings by the people, felled trees on mountains sacred to the Thunder-Deity. Then it thundered very violently, but the Thunder-Deity—a deity in nature religion—could do no harm to Kawabe-no-omi, because he did what he ought to as a loyal subject under the command of the empress Suiko [reigned 593-629], who was a deity by far superior to the divine Thunderer.[3]

The progress of Buddhism was not entirely favorable to the advance of political rationalization. The increasing emphasis on ritual and magic at the court was certainly one factor in the weakening of the impulse to centralization of power which became apparent in the 8th century and continued increasingly until the rise of centralized feudalism at the end of the 12th century.

The influence of Confucianism, on the other hand, was still at work in the direction of political rationalization in these centuries. The *Classic of Filial Piety* (*Hsiao Ching*) was especially widely propagated. By the end of the 8th century it was taught in every school, and every child who knew how to read could recite it by heart. By the order of the Empress Kōken (reigned 749–758) a copy of the *Classic of Filial Piety* was required to be kept in every home, though it may be doubted if this command was literally fulfilled. Nevertheless, even in Kamakura times the *samurai,* high and low, even though they might have no other book, were apt to have a copy of this one. The importance of the book can perhaps be seen as a rough measure of the increasing importance the ethic it preaches was coming to have in Japanese society. As long as filial piety yields precedence to loyalty as the highest virtue, and as long as it is taught in a context of political values rather than integrative values primarily, and both these conditions seem to hold during the centuries under consideration, the increasing institutionalization of the Confucian ethic of filial piety can be seen as a step in the direction of political rationalization; the family itself is penetrated by political values and indeed becomes a miniature polity.

The Confucian teaching on the virtue of loyalty was also widely propagated and had a considerable effect on the evolving ethic of the warrior class: *Bushidō.* This will be discussed further in the next section devoted entirely to this status ethic. The point to be made here is that in the period after the failure of the attempt to establish a strong central monarchy in the 7th and 8th centuries political rationalization did not necessarily come to an end. The rationalization of power through an increase in extensive control certainly did come to an end. Rationalization did continue, however, in the form of an increase of intensive control within territorial units, namely the feudal domain. Thus the centuries from 1156 to 1600, though they did see considerable advances in central administration, were notable chiefly for developments at the intermediate levels. These were the centuries when *Bushidō* and much of the content of the later political values, even of those of modern times, was being formed.

It is remarkable that these centuries which saw the almost fanatical exaltation of loyalty, should also have seen the lowest ebb of the fortunes of the imperial family. This is largely explained by what has been said above. Loyalty was primarily to one's own feudal lord. No higher obligation had much meaning. Of course, this is not the whole story. There was a notable attempt to revive the central position of the monarchy in the 14th century, which elicited more than a little heroic devotion to the imperial cause before it finally was crushed. A notable side product of this struggle was a history of Japan written by the famous Kitabatake Chikafusa in 1340. This was a justification of the imperial cause and was strongly influenced by both Shintō and Confucian ideas. It foreshadowed many of the ideas which were to come into prominence again in the Tokugawa Period.

Bushidō

Bushidō, the Way of the Warrior, is of especial importance to any inquiry into the values and ethics of Tokugawa or modern Japan. This is because the *bushi* or *samurai* embodied or were supposed to embody the central Japanese values, and because in fact the ethic of *Bushidō* became in Tokugawa and modern times the national ethic, or at least a large part of it. Kawakami Tasuke has recently written that

> . . . Bushidō which had originally developed from the practical necessities of warriors, came to be popularized by Confucian moral ideas, not only as the morality of the warrior class but as the cornerstone of national morals.[4]

The samurai class was quite consciously seen as the embodiment and protector of morality. Tokugawa Mitsukuni (1628–1700), third prince of Mito, wrote in his instructions to his retainers,

> What, then, is the use of the *shi,* or *samurai,* class? Its only business is to preserve, or maintain, *giri.* The people of the other classes deal with visible things, while the *samurai* deal with invisible, colorless and unsubstantial things . . . if there were no *samurai,* right (*giri*) would disappear from human society, the sense of shame would be lost, and wrong and injustice would prevail.[5]

The term *Bushidō* used to describe the status ethic of the *samurai* class covers a wide range of ideas over a considerable span of time. The prevailing attitude ranges from an almost mystical preoccupation with death to a rather prosaic concern for the fulfillment of the duties of everyday life, from a primarily military outlook to a primarily civil outlook, from a close association with Zen Buddhism to a close association with neo-Confucianism. In each case the first tendency is generally earlier in time and the second becomes more important in the Tokugawa Period. But such a generalization cannot be pushed too far. Confucianism had an important influence from the start; militarism and a preoccupation with death remain important even in modern times.

Near the end of the preceding chapter, in discussing "the religion of loyalty" an incident was cited (pp. 81-2) to show the obligation to one's feudal lord taking a sort of religious ultimacy and overriding other religious considerations. The essentially religious aspect of the most intense form of *Bushidō* is well illustrated in the following quote from the *Hagakure,* an epitome of *Bushidō* compiled in the early 18th century in the fief of Nabeshima, province of Hizen, in Kyūshū:

> Wherever we may be, deep in mountain recesses or buried under the ground, any time or anywhere, our duty is to guard the interest of our Lord. This is the duty of every Nebeshima man. This is the backbone of our faith, unchanging and eternally true.
>
> Never in my life have I placed mine own thoughts above those of my Lord and master. Nor will I do otherwise in all the days of my life. Even when I die I will return to life seven times to guard my Lord's house.
>
> We have sworn to do four things: namely:—
> (1) We will be second to none in performance of our duty.
> (2) We will make ourselves useful to our Lord.
> (3) We will be dutiful to our parents.
> (4) We will attain greatness in charity.[6]

It is said, "*Bushidō* means the determined will to die," and the following quote from the *Hagakure* helps to explain this concern for death:

> Every morning make up thy mind how to die. Every evening freshen thy mind in the thought of death. And let this be done without end.
>
> Thus will thy mind be prepared. When thy mind is always set on death, thy way through life will always be straight and simple. Thou wilt perform thy duty; and thy shield will be stainless. When thou canst see thy way straight, with open eyes and free from obstructing thoughts, there can be no straying into errors. Thy performance of duties will be above reproof and thy name immaculate.[7]

I have seen it eye to eye: *Bushidō,* the way of the warrior, means death.[8]

That such intense expressions as these should be closely associated with the basic religious orientations discussed in the previous chapter is certainly to be expected. The background to the deep sense of devotion toward the lord is certainly to be found in a strong feeling of gratitude:

When you realize how for generations your family has served for the house of his lordship: when you remember how those who have gone before you served, and how those who are to come after you are to serve; you will be moved to a deep sense of gratitude. For you, there should be no thought but of service for the one who has claim on your grateful heart.[9]

The attitude toward death is closely related to a mystical state in which one is beyond life and death. Being determined to die, death has no sting. The self is eliminated. These attitudes are linked to the great interest the *samurai* showed in Zen Buddhism. For instance, Takeda Shingen (1521–1573), one of the great warlords of the 16th century, admonished his followers to practise Zen well and quotes to them the old saying, "The practise of the Zen has no secret, except standing on the verge of life and death."[10] Another manual of *Bushidō,* the *Budō Shoshinshu* compiled in the 17th century, gives us a further insight into the meaning of the *samurai's* concern for death:

. . . one who lives long in this world may develop all sorts of desires and his covetousness may increase so that he wants what belongs to others and cannot bear to part with what is his own, becoming in fact just like a mere tradesman. But if he is always looking death in the face, a man will have little attachment to material things and will not exhibit these grasping and covetous qualities, and will become, as I said before, a fine character. And speaking of meditation on death, Yoshida Kenko says in the Tsurezuregusa of the monk Shinkai that he was wont to sit all day long pondering on his latter end; this is no doubt a very suitable attitude for a recluse but by no means so for a warrior. For so he would have to neglect his military duties and the way of loyalty and filial piety, and he must on the contrary be constantly busy with his affairs both public and private. But whenever he has a little spare time to himself and can be quiet he should not fail to revert to this question of death and reflect carefully on it.[11]

Here we see that the meditation on death is for the purpose of purging one's self of desires and covetousness, in religious terms, of finding the true self. Lest he be misunderstood, the writer of this handbook takes pains to point out that he is not advocating meditation at the expense of ethical action. The latter, as is true in the dominant religious traditions, retains the ultimate primacy.

Death in the service of one's lord was considered the most appropriate end for a *samurai.* Indeed such a death had almost a "saving" quality, in the religious sense:

> As our Imperial Throne is endless from the beginning, so we should let this thought sink deeply, that our loyalty must be endless. According to the words of Ama-no-oshihi-no-mikoto, "He who dies for the sake of his lord does not die in vain, whether he goes to the sea and his corpse is left in a watery grave, or whether he goes to the mountain and the only shroud for his lifeless body is the mountain grass." This is the way of loyalty.[12]

Having described the religious underpinning of the *samurai* ethic, closely linked as it is with the basic religious orientations outlined in Chapter III, we may now proceed to a discussion of the moral qualities which are derived from and rationalized by this religious orientation.

First on the list of ethical qualities is of course loyalty, but closely linked to it is filial piety. Mitsukuni-sama said,

> Everybody is well aware that one who is ungrateful towards parents is also ignorant of a master's favors, even of humanity itself, and naturally is not an honorable *samurai.*[13]

The training of the child in filial piety is so that he may fulfill loyalty as an adult. Loyalty and filial piety tend to be very closely linked, almost identified with each other:

> And a *samurai* who possesses this spirit [filial piety] when he enters the service of a lord will thoroughly understand the Way of Loyalty and will show it not only when his master is prosperous but also if he meets adversity, and will not leave his side when his hundred horsemen are reduced to ten and this ten to one, but will defend him to the last, regarding his life as nothing in carrying out a warrior's fealty. And so though the terms "parent" and "lord," "filial conduct" and "loyalty" are distinct, they are in no way different in meaning. There is a saying of the ancients, "Look for a loyal retainer among the filial," and it is

quite unreasonable to think that if a man is unfilial to his parents he can at the same time be loyal to his master.[14]

Injunctions to be upright and fulfill one's duty are frequently met with, and absolute obedience is enjoined. These virtues when specified seem to have their expression in various forms of loyal or filial action, so perhaps do not need extended discussion in their own right. It should be noted that it was the obligation of a son or retainer to remonstrate with his father or lord if he thought the latter was doing wrong, but he was in no case to oppose or disobey him, and should in fact willingly accept an unjust death if it were so decreed.

The virtue of *jin* (Chinese, *jen,* translated as benevolence, humanity, love, etc.) was often highly praised but it is not always clear what was implied. At one extreme it seems to have meant an almost Buddhist compassion for all creatures. At the other it is more like courtesy or decency, merely a generalized obligation to be considerate. It is perhaps this latter meaning which is usually had in *Bushidō.*

Appropriate to the selfless devotion which we have seen as the highest duty and final fulfillment of the *samurai* is an almost ascetic style of life. Consequently the *samurai* was instructed to lead a sober, restrained, and frugal life. The following quotes from the *Hagakure* could be endlessly duplicated:

> Be sparing of speech. Where you would speak ten words, speak but one.[15]
>
> When you leave a festive place, take leave while you still desire to stay. When you feel you are satisfied, you have had more than enough. Enough is too much. Surfeit not yourself.[16]

Mitsukuni-sama advised his followers to live simply and without airs; avoid lewd talk at banquets; be simple in entertainments; be practical and simple in military clothing and equipment; have only what is necessary in clothes, food and dwelling and do not keep excess possessions; and be economical in expenditure though not failing to help relatives and friends in distress.[17]

Takeda Shingen advised that taste should not be overindulged; idle talk and gossip should be avoided; daily attendance on duty should not be neglected; discretion should be exercised in talking even among intimate friends; one should not associate with the ill-behaved; everything should be done with care.[18]

Yamaga Sokō in his primer for *samurai* (*Bukyō Shōgaku*) directed that the *samurai* arise early and go early to bed; use only correct words and not engage in frivolities; not ". . . be ashamed of simple food and clothing, nor . . . ever long for a comfortable life;"[19] keep occupied even when unemployed; maintain decorum and alertness on all occasions; and not spend more than his income.[20]

The following is a selection from the resolutions of Muro Kyūsō, a famous Confucian:

> I will arise every morning at six o'clock and retire each evening at twelve o'clock. Except when prevented by guests, sickness or other unavoidable circumstances, I will not be idle. If tempted to be indolent, I will call forth my right spirit to drive away my lazy spirit. I will avoid useless words even with inferiors. I will be temperate in eating, and drinking, merely satisfying my hunger and thirst. I will eat at regular times.[21]

If we can single out two features of this near ascetic style of life which are of especial importance, they are economy and diligence. Economy or frugality is the obligation to reduce individual consumption to a minimum and diligence is its obverse, the obligation to increase one's contribution to the lord's service to the maximum. Yoshida Shōin observed, "When I reverently look at my parents and uncle, I see how their conduct is based on diligence and economy and loyalty."[22] Diligence and economy are indeed close to loyalty.

The following is an interesting disquisition on economy from the house rules (*kakun*) of the *samurai* Ise Teijo. The word "profit" must be understood in the context of the whole passage.

> Throughout one's whole lifetime he must be spending gold or silver money, rice or copper cash. If in the way of spending it, he does not understand what is meant by economy, there will be useless waste and his family will become poor. To be economical, one must eschew the spending of so much as a single cash unprofitably, whilst, if a profit can be made, he may lay out a thousand gold pieces. The eschewing of unprofitable expenditure is for the very purpose of making a profitable outlay. Unprofitable outlays arise from being fond of too many delicacies in one's food, fondness for beautiful dress, constructing a

handsome residence, allowing one's wife or concubine to be extravagant, giving oneself up mainly to sensuality or amusement and other sorts of extravagance. Profitable expenditures include first of all those required in the course of one's attendance on your master (feudal lord), and for the discharge of government imposts, for the support of parents, brothers, wife and children, for the stipend of one's retainers, for the discharge of social obligations, for communication and correspondence, for house-repairs, for emergencies, and such like.[23]

Here we see that "unprofitable" expenditures are for personal consumption beyond what is necessary for an ordinary existence and "profitable" expenditures are those in fulfillment of one's obligations to lord and family or "necessary" if one is to be able to fulfill those obligations.

Diligence in the performance of duty was very highly regarded as it expressed the whole point of the *samurai's* existence. Muro Kyūsō said,

If one lives a day let him perform a day's duty and die; if he lives a month let him perform a month's duty and die; if he lives a year let him perform a year's duty and die.[24]

And Yoshida Shōin:

To take rest after death. This is a maxim, short yet charged with meaning. Perseverance, dogged determination. There is no other way.[25]

One last feature of the samurai ethic may be mentioned before summarizing. This is the very high regard for learning (*gakumon*). Almost all the *samurai* were literate and had acquaintance with at least some of the Confucian classics. But learning is not for its own sake. It has as its aim the cultivation of the self and the control of others. Learning and action are the same. The practice of learning and its results are not two but one.[26] Mitsukuni said that learning is not reading books for amusement, it is ". . . the Way in which we should walk, or the principle by which we should guide our daily conduct."[27]

The *Budō Shoshinshu* gives us a good summary picture of the brave *samurai:*

For he who is born brave will be loyal and filial to his lord and parents, and whenever he has any leisure he will use it for study, neither will he be negligent in practising the military arts. He will be strictly on his guard against indolence and will be very careful how he spends every penny. If you think this shows detestable stinginess you will be mistaken since he spends freely where it is necessary. He does not do anything that is contrary to the ordinances of his lord, or that is disliked by his parents however much he may wish. And so, ever obedient to his lord and parents he preserves his life in the hope some day of doing a deed of outstanding merit, moderating his appetite for eating and drinking and avoiding over-indulgence in sex, which is the greatest delusion of mankind, so that he may preserve his body in health and strength. For in these as in all other things it is rigid self-control that is the beginning of valor.[28]

It is interesting to put alongside of the foregoing a set of injunctions to *samurai* women which is quite parallel to the *Bushidō* code for men. It is indeed a *Bushidō* for women. The quote is from the *Onna Daigaku* of Kaibara Ekiken (1630–1714), which was the standard work used in the education of women.

A woman must be ever on the alert and keep a strict watch over her own conduct. In the morning she must rise early, and at night go late to rest. Instead of sleeping in the middle of the day, she must be intent on the duties of her household, and must not weary of weaving, sewing, and spinning. Of tea and wine she must not drink overmuch, nor must she feed her eyes and ears with theatrical performances, ditties, and ballads. . . .

In her capacity of wife, she must keep her husband's household in proper order. If the wife be evil and profligate, the house is ruined. In everything she must avoid extravagance, and both with regard to food and raiment must act according to her station in life, and never give way to luxury and pride.[29]

To the extent that the *samurai* lived up to their code as it can be reconstructed from various works such as those we have quoted above, they did indeed embody the Japanese central value system. The military emphasis is crucial. Military service is symbolically the best suited occupation for an embodiment of values primarily oriented to goal-attainment. It typifies selfless devotion to the collectivity and its head, even to the point of death. Death indeed in a military context can come to symbolize that very devotion. Again the achievement aspect of goal-attainment values is well symbolized by the heroic overcoming of difficulties, the execution of "deeds of outstanding merit" which is the essence of the life of the warrior. It is, then, to its symbolic importance for the central value system, I believe, that we can attribute in large part the very high valuation placed on the military in Japan even after two hundred and fifty years of peace. There can be little doubt that many *samurai* in the Tokugawa Period failed to live up to the ideal code as it has been portrayed above. But exemplars were never lacking and those who did not conform raised no other code as a legitimate alternative. Certainly the leaders of the Restoration were strongly moved by the "*samurai* spirit," and their ability to command the loyalty and obedience of the nation with so little opposition was in considerable part due to the fact that they did embody the ideal values not only of the *samurai* but of all Japan.

Though the *samurai* might best embody the ethical code which bears their name, it was by no means restricted to that class. It has been said, for instance, that during the Tokugawa Period the merchant class became *Bushidō*-ized. We shall see in the next chapter and in the treatment of the Shingaku movement that there is more than a little truth in that statement. Nor was the merchant class alone in such a development. Actually all the evidence available about popular sects and ethical movements indicates that they taught a virtually identical ethic. They all stressed loyalty and filial piety, obedience and righteousness, economy and diligence. All demanded selfless devotion to superiors, a minimum of personal consumption, and a vigorous prosecution of daily tasks and duties. They were at one with *Bushidō* in being "ethically activist" and "inner worldly ascetic." Such an ethic clearly reinforced the tendency to political rationalization in all classes and, what is especially interesting to this study, it had a clear implication for economic rationalization as well. But this is the subject of the following chapter. We will conclude this chapter with a discussion of certain tendencies toward political rationalization which cut across existing territorial and class boundaries, and led directly to the unification of Japan under the emperor as a modern state. Here too we will find religious motivation to have been of the utmost importance.

Sonnō and *Kokutai*

The Tokugawa Period saw the rise of new attitudes toward the emperor and a new politico-religious concept of the state, both of which were to have profound consequences for subsequent history.

The slogan *sonnō* (revere the emperor) typifies the new emphasis on the emperor and the term *kokutai* (literally national body), which will be explained later, expresses the new concept of the state. To speak of ideas which have their roots so deep in history as "new" may seem paradoxical, but within the context of the Tokugawa Period they can be seen as new, their rise and increasing influence can be traced and their dissolving effect on the Tokugawa synthesis observed.

Though these ideas were not restricted to any one or two intellectual movements, and were indeed widespread, especially near the end of the period, they can perhaps best be studied as they were developed by their most ardent advocates and propagandists, the Kokugaku School and the Mito School.

The Kokugaku School had its start in a revived interest in Japanese history, literature and religion which developed in the 17th century. The forerunners of the school, Keichū (1640–1701) and Kada Azumamaro (1668–1736), are chiefly known for their scholarly work on early Japanese poetry through which they laid the groundwork for an understanding of the early Japanese language. Such a knowledge was necessary if the early mythological accounts, histories, and rituals were to be fully intelligible and so was an important first step in a movement which aimed at the revival of the ancient Japanese culture and institutions.

From the start the movement had political and religious implications; it was not concerned with literature for its own sake. It was Kamo Mabuchi (1697–1769), however, who perhaps first formulated these implications in terms which were to be repeated with variations many times over by his followers. A number of key Kokugaku themes are contained in the following quote from Mabuchi:

> . . . while the Chinese for ages past have had a succession of different dynasties to rule over them, Japan has been faithful to one uninterrupted line of sovereigns. Every Chinese dynasty was founded upon rebellion and parricide.
>
> . . . In the 8th century the Chinese costume and etiquette were adopted by the Court. This foreign pomp and splendor covered the rapid depravation of men's hearts, and created a wide gulf between the Mikado and his people. So long as the sovereign maintains a simple style of living, the people are contented with their own hard lot. Their

wants are few and they are easily ruled. But if the sovereign has a magnificent palace, gorgeous clothing, and crowds of finely-dressed women to wait on him, the sight of these things must cause in others a desire to possess themselves of the same luxuries; or if they are not strong enough to take them by force, it excites their envy. If the Mikado had continued to live in a house roofed with shingles, and whose walls were of mud, to wear hempen clothes, to carry his sword in a scabbard wound round with the tendrils of some creeping plant, and to go to the chase carrying his bow and arrows, as was the ancient custom, the present state of things would never have come about. But since the introduction of Chinese manners, the sovereign, while occupying a highly dignified place, has been degraded to the intellectual level of a woman. The power fell into the hands of servants, and although they never actually assumed the title, they were sovereigns in fact, while the Mikado became an utter nullity.[30]

Here we see the extreme rejection of China which is so typical of this school. That Chinese doctrine is false and pernicious is amply proved by the history of that country, says Mabuchi. Its effects in Japan only confirm this fact. The Japanese in their pristine simplicity were truly natural men. Chinese influences are responsible for the subsequent decline and for all present evils. The clear implication is to do away with everything Chinese and return to that age of blissful simplicity. The great glory of Japan is her unbroken line of emperors. Therefore what is above all needed is a return to the true relation between sovereign and subject and an end to the corruptions of this relation which have resulted from Chinese influences.

Naturally both Buddhism and Confucianism were utterly rejected by the Kokugaku school. Motoori Norinaga (1730–1801), perhaps the greatest of the Kokugakusha, wrote,

In ancient times, although there was no prosy system of doctrine in Japan there were no popular disturbances, and the empire was peacefully ruled. It is because the Japanese were truly moral in their practice that they required no theory of morals, and the fuss made by the Chinese about theoretical morals is owing to their laxity in practice.[31]

Having rejected Buddhism and Confucianism, the Kokugakusha turned to the native religion, Shintō (though they disliked this "Chinese" term), for a religious underpinning. Motoori wrote,

Japan is the country which gave birth to the Sun, Amaterasu-o-mikami, which fact proves its superiority over all other countries which also enjoy her favors. The goddess, having endowed her grandson Ninigi no Mikoto with the three sacred treasures, proclaimed him sovereign of Japan for ever and ever. His descendants shall continue to rule it as long as the heavens and earth endure. Being invested with this complete authority, all the gods under heaven and all mankind submitted to him, with the exception of a few wretches who were quickly subdued.

To the end of time each Mikado is the goddess' son. His mind is in perfect harmony of thought and feeling with hers. He does not seek out new inventions, but rules in accordance with precedents which date from the age of the gods, and if he is ever in doubt, he has resort to divination, which reveals to him the mind of the great goddess. In this way the age of the gods and the present age are not two ages, but one, for not only the Mikado, but his Ministers and people also, act up to the tradition of the divine age.[32]

Motoori rejected all metaphysics as foreign importations and insisted on a literal belief in the ancient myths as contained especially in the *Kojiki*. He claims the Buddhist, Confucian, and Taoist explanations in logical terms are really all contradictory and can be refuted. He says in effect that to understand the world is beyond the power of man's reason and it is best to rely on revelation. The world is full of strange and inexplicable phenomena which we do not understand. Though the old myths may be hard to believe literally, they are no stranger than many things that happen in the world, and they have the weight of revelation behind them. For his final proof of Shintō he turns to the emperor:

The eternal endurance of the dynasty of the Mikados is a complete proof that the "way" called Kami no michi or Shintō infinitely surpasses the systems of all other countries.[33]

Hirata Atsutane (1776–1843), the last of the great Kokugakusha, did not make any considerable addition to the ideas of the school but is very important as a systematizer and propagandist. Through him and his disciples the ideas of Kokugaku became very widespread in the early 19th century and were certainly one of the major influences leading up to the Restoration.

The inclusion of a school whose ideas seem so regressive, both religiously and politically, in a chapter on religion and political rationalization may appear questionable. Kokugaku seemingly wished to do away with all the advances and rationalization which had occurred since the 7th century and return to a state of primitive simplicity. Nevertheless its effects were to bring about still further rationalization. How did this happen?

Kokugaku can be seen as a "millenial" religious movement. It had a clear religious goal which could be realized on this earth: the restoration of the emperor to actual sovereignty and purging of Japan of all corrupt influences. Once this had been done Kokugaku foresaw an era of harmony between subject and emperor, man and deity, in which peace and morality would naturally hold sway. The effect of accepting the Kokugaku message, then, would be to make men revere the emperor above all else and hope for or work for his restoration. Such a simple and effective message with its clear implications for action is, in our terms, religiously rational. No matter how much Motoori urged his followers to believe the *Kojiki* literally, the effect could not be the same as though they were steeped in the primitive magic there described. Belief in every superstition bcame for him a sign of devoted allegiance to the gods and the emperor. But it was the overriding allegiance which was important both for him and for us. This is the aspect of rationalization. Similarly the political implications of the Kokugaku doctrine were the establishment of a strong centralized monarchy toward which every Japanese owed absolute allegiance and the destruction of the shogunate or any other power which stood between sovereign and people. Under the objective circumstances of the day, both internal and external, it is clear that such a centralized monarchy could not be an idyllic tribal state like that which Motoori imagined to have held sway in 5th or 6th century Japan. Whatever the Kokugakusha intended, the result of what they preached in the political sphere could only be the enormous extension and rationalization of power.

The Mito school, which has strong resemblances to as well as differences from Kokugaku, takes its name from Mito, a town northeast of Tokyo, in which one branch of the Tokugawa family had residence as the ruling *daimyō*. Tokugawa Mitsukuni (1628–1700) may be considered the founder of the school. It was under his direction that the great history of Japan, the *Dainihonshi* was begun. This history was important because its meticulous scholarship proved beyond a shadow of a doubt that there had been a time when the emperor was not secluded but ruled directly. It showed in great detail the features of that era and the events which brought about its end. It was focussed largely on the person of the emperor and the court and written from a clearly loyalist point of view so that it could have but one import. Though it was no agitational production its careful scholarship did much to undermine the legitimacy of the shogunate and arouse feeling in favor of a return to the days when the emperor really ruled. Though this work was loyalist and nationalist, it was, interestingly enough, written in Chinese. This serves to mark off clearly the Mito school from the Kokugakusha who always wrote in the purest Japanese they could command.

Indeed the Mito school did not reject China in anything like the blanket terms which the Kokugaku school used. The Mito scholars placed Shintō first in their allegiance and they did criticize the Chinese for changing their dynasties, and Mencius for his advocacy of the so-called "right of revolution," and they certainly did feel that Japan was superior to all other nations, but they had the highest regard for the Chinese sages and explicitly taught the Chinese morality. They agreed with Kokugaku, however, in having no use at all for Buddhism. Their attitude can be summed up in a phrase from Tokugawa Nariaki: ". . . revere the 'Way' of the land of the gods (Japan) and use the teachings of China."[34]

What exactly the "Way" is that Nariaki had in mind is made somewhat clearer in the following quote from him:

> The eternity of the Imperial succession, the great relation between lord and retainer, father and child, together with heaven and earth do not alter themselves; this exactly is the "great Way" of heaven and earth.[35]

In this Way loyalty and filial piety are closely linked. Nariaki wrote, ". . . do not consider loyalty and filial piety as two different things."[36] As Hammitzsch has pointed out,[37] the high regard for the emperor when linked to this identification of loyalty and filial piety has some very interesting implications for the concept of the state. God, emperor, lord and father tend to be made into equivalents. The whole nation is a single family. The emperor is "divine," he is "lord" and he is "father" of the national family. The people are worshippers, retainers, and children. Loyalty is "the great filial piety" and devotion to parents is "the small filial piety" which exists only so that the great filial piety can be fulfilled.

What has been described above is one aspect of what is meant by *kokutai.* It is a concept of the state in which religious, political and familistic ideas are indissolubly merged. In the above formulation it approximates to a description of the first type of relation between man and the divine (described in Chapter III) and consequently action is governed by the concept of *on.* The emperor becomes the center of the national religion and the obligation to make return for his benevolence takes precedence over all other obligations.

But further, *kokutai* is conceived also in terms of the second type of the relation of man to the divine which we have found in Japan. In this case the emperor and the *kami* are identified and the people are identified with both. The emperor's will is the *kami's* will, and the people's will is the emperor's will. To be thus united in will with emperor and *kami* is what is meant by being "sincere," having a pure heart, etc. *Kokutai* then is an identification of the religious entity and the political entity. It has the dual aspect so characteristic of Japanese religious thought, and both of the major forms of religious action are involved in such a way that they are identical with political action.

We may perhaps turn to Yoshida Shōin (1830–1859) for a concrete expression of these ideas. He was strongly influenced by the Mito school and in turn was one of the most decisive influences on the leaders of the Restoration.

> All men born in our Empire should know the reason for its loftiness. After all, our Imperial Dynasty has continued uninterrupted from time immemorial. The vassals receive the fiefs from generation to generation. The rulers feed the people and in return the people have a great debt of gratitude toward them. Ruler and people are one body (*kunshin ittai*). Loyalty towards the ruler and piety of children towards their parents are one and the same. This is characteristic of our country alone.[38]

Shōin is only one of the more famous of the many who were spreading the teachings of the Mito school among the young *samurai* toward the end of the Tokugawa Period. Nor were they spread only among the *samurai* class. Popular preachers like Takayama Masayuki and Gamō Kumpei propagated them with great enthusiasm among the common people.

The idea of *kokutai* as formulated by the Mito school has the same general meaning as the teachings of Kokugaku. It is a little less "primitivistic" since it is willing to use ethical and theoretical notions derived from China in formulating the *kokutai* idea. It is, however, essentially just as utopian. The desire to make *kokutai* a living reality tends to put the goal-attainment dimension foremost. It acts to motivate a strong drive toward certain ends, at first the Restoration, then as it became a large part of the modern nationalistic ideology of Japan, toward building a strong country and finally toward imperialism. It tends to minimize the adaptive dimension: all obstacles are to be overcome at no matter what cost; those who wish to make personal profit from the adaptive sphere (the economy) are to be despised. It also tends to minimize the integrative dimension, by denying the existence of an integrative problem. All Japanese are "naturally" loyal to emperor and empire. Any who are not are not to be tolerated. The party politicians who represent different interest groups and try to balance out their different claims are despised, because the very existence of interest groups is considered treasonable. Such a trend as we have been describing represents the rationalization of power to the extent that the functional prerequisites of other spheres of the society than the polity are infringed on. There is a real sense in which Japanese militarism and totalitarianism in the modern period represents such a tendency. The ideological basis of these trends was indeed the complex of ideas centering around *kokutai* which have been discussed in this section. The most radical element in this movement, those who supported the idea of the "Shōwa Restoration" in the 1930's, conceived of a situation in which all economic and integrative functions would be under the direct control of the emperor, would be merged with the polity. They were violent in their denunciations of both "capitalism" and "politics." They represent the extreme and pathological limit to which absolute dominance of particularistic-performance values can be pushed. Short of this pathological extreme it would seem that there is a natural fit between some such ideology as that symbolized by *kokutai* and the dominance of particularistic-performance values. That these values in Japan are still strong would seem to be indicated in the fact that the "democratic" ideology of the post-war period is at the moment having difficulty holding its own against the resurgence of the old ideology in somewhat modified form.

However we evaluate the results, there can be little doubt that the effect of the *sonnō-kokutai* ideology has been to further the process of political rationalization in Japan. This chapter has attempted to show that this ideology is a fusion of religious and political ideas, and that at least in part its dynamism is attributable to religious motivation. How this political rationalization in turn effects the economic sphere is a matter which will be discussed in the following chapter.

Notes

1. Sansom, *Japan: A Short Cultural History,* p. 51.
2. Coates and Ishizuka, *op. cit.,* p. 15.
3. Katō, A Study of Shintō, p. 127.
4. Kawakami, "Bushidō in its Formative Period," p. 83.
5. Clement, "Instructions of a Mito Prince to His Retainers," p. 135.
6. Iwado, "*Hagakure Bushido* or *The Book of the Warrior,*" p. 37.
7. *Ibid.,* pp. 38-39.
8. *Ibid.,* p. 38.
9. *Ibid.,* p. 55.
10. Sakai, "The Memoirs of Takeda Shingen and the Kai-no-Gunritsu," p. 99.
11. Sadler, *The Beginner's Book of Bushido,* p. 5. Hereafter cited as *Bushidō.*
12. Coleman, "Life of Yoshida Shōin," pp. 158-159. Quote is from Shōin.
13. Clement, *op. cit.,* p. 130.
14. Sadler, *Bushidō,* p. 9.
15. Iwado, *op. cit.,* p. 44.
16. *Ibid.,* p. 45.
17. Clement, *op. cit.*
18. Sakai, *op. cit.*
19. Van Straelen, *Yoshida Shōin,* p. 94.
20. Koyama, "Yamaga Sokō and his Bukyō Shōgaku."
21. Armstrong, *Light from the East,* p. 85.
22. Coleman, *op. cit.,* p. 185.
23. Hall, J. C., *op. cit.,* p. 146.
24. Armstrong, *Light from the East,* p. 74.
25. Van Straelen, *op. cit.,* p. 84.
26. Nishi, *Tōyō Rinri,* pp. 12-13.
27. Clement, *op. cit.,* p. 119.
28. Sadler, *Bushidō,* pp. 20-21.
29. Takaishi, *Women and Wisdom of Japan,* pp. 40-41.
30. Satow, "The Revival of Pure Shintau," pp. 177-178.
31. *Ibid.,* p. 187.
32. *Ibid.,* p. 186.
33. *Ibid.,* p. 188.
34. Hammitzsch, "Die Mito-Schule," p. 68.
35. *Ibid.,* p. 70.
36. *Ibid.,* p. 68.
37. *Ibid.,* p. 50.
38. Van Straelen, *op. cit.,* p. 83.

CHAPTER

V

Religion and the Economy

IN THIS CHAPTER we will consider the economic ethic in Japan, the various forms it took in the different classes, its relation to the political ethic and to religion, and the effect of these relations on economic rationalization. For empirical illustration a number of the more important Tokugawa developments will be discussed, but a complete coverage of the relevant empirical data is beyond the scope of this study. Many interesting leads await further exploration.

One such lead is the relation of Zen Buddhism to the economic ethic. We know that Zen monks played a very important part in the trade of the Ashikaga Period (1392–1573).[1] We also know that the Zen sect puts a high evaluation on Spartan simplicity and frugality, and what is perhaps even more interesting, on productive labor. It is my impression that the Zen sect puts greater stress on work and less stress on mendicancy as a means of support than most other Buddhist sects. D. T. Suzuki tells us that, " 'A day of no work is a day of no eating' is the literal rendering of the first rule of Zen monastic life,"[2] and that, "Zen masters have . . . . always been anxious to see their monks work hard on the farm, in the woods, or in the mountains."[3] That work is sacred because it is seen at least in part as return for blessings received, is perhaps indicated by his further comments:

> . . . reverence for nature, together with the idea that a man should not eat his meal unless he had something accomplished for the community to which he belongs, forms the foundation of the Zendō life.[4]

Of course the frugality and lack of waste in a Zen community are proverbial. It would be most interesting to know if this Zen monastic ethic had any direct influence on the Japanese economic ethic. That it had an indirect influence by way of *Bushidō* is beyond question. A full exploration of this question awaits further research.

The present chapter will include a discussion of the relation of the polity and the political ethic to the economy and the economic ethic, and of the Japanese analogue of the "calling." It will conclude with a discussion of some manifestations of the economic ethic among the common people, the merchants and farmers.

Economy and Polity

The relation of economy to polity can only be understood in terms of the Confucian theory of the state which had a very great influence in Japan. The keynote of the Confucian thinking on the matter is "the unity of economy and polity." Indeed in the Tokugawa Period the word *keizai* translated in modern usage as economy meant, in the words of Dazai Shundai, "governing the empire and assisting the people."[5]

The Confucian thinkers saw a direct relation between economic well-being and morality and it was this above all which determined for them the political importance of economic life. Though the Confucians taught that morality should be adhered to regardless of economic conditions they were realistic enough to realize that this was hard of attainment for ordinary people. Mencius said:

> They are only men of education, who, without a certain livelihood, are able to maintain a fixed heart. As to the people, if they have not a certain livelihood, it follows that they will not have a fixed heart. And if they have not a fixed heart, there is nothing which they will not do, in the way of self-abandonment, of moral deflection, of depravity, and of wild license.[6]

If they have not a certain livelihood, then, the people are "ungovernable." This is a strong ideological basis for a concern with the economic life of the people which was characteristic of the Tokugawa rulers.

The core of the Confucian economic policy designed to ensure political stability is contained in the following often quoted statement from the *Ta Hsüeh:*

There is a great course [*tao*] for the production of wealth. Let the producers be many and the consumers few. Let there be activity in the production and economy in the expenditure. Then the wealth will be always sufficient.[7]

This then is the nubbin of Confucian economic policy, in its ideal expression: encourage production and discourage consumption.

The discouragement of consumption took two major forms, an inner and an outer. The inner form is the limitation of desires and the outer the limitation of expenditures, in other words economy or frugality. Hsün Tzu said with respect to the first:

. . . if man's desires are given rein, then their authority could not be endured, and things would not be sufficient to satisfy them.[8]

Mencius has an often quoted statement on this matter:

To nourish the heart there is nothing better than to make the desires few. Here is a man whose desires are few:—in some things he may not be able to keep his heart, but they will be few. Here is a man whose desires are many:—in some things he may be able to keep his heart but they will be few.[9]

Economy is urged on those both above and below. Its absence is seen to have direct political consequences. With respect to those below, Confucius says, "Extravagance leads to insubordination, and parsimony to meanness. It is better to be mean than to be insubordinate."[10] With respect to the ruler, Kaibara Ekiken (1630–1714) says in his *Kunshikun:*

If the ruler wants to govern his people with benevolence, he should practise economy. There are limits to the productive capacity of land and so, if the ruler is given to luxurious and spendthrift habits, the resources at his command will soon be exhausted and he will find it difficult to make both ends meet. This is especially so as agricultural crops sometimes fail. Should the ruler be reduced to financial straits, it would be impossible for him to perform acts of philanthropy, to provide against emergencies or to relieve the poor. Worse still, he will be forced to resort to extortionate measures, himself running into debt and placing his country in jeopardy. Benevolent government would be out of the question in such circumstances. All wise rulers have been thrifty. Economy is, indeed, a virtue essential to the ruler.[11]

From the above glimpse of Confucian thinking on political economy it can be seen that the main concern is for maintaining a balanced system. Production is in order to attain sufficiency and economy is to see that that sufficiency is not upset. There is no doubt that this sort of thinking was strong in Tokugawa Japan. On the other hand, this thinking was always joined more or less closely to another point of view perhaps more typically Japanese. Characteristically it finds its clearest expression in the economic ethic of *Bushidō*. As was shown in the last chapter diligence and economy were an important part of *Bushidō*. This diligence and economy were not, however, primarily motivated by a concern for balance and stability. Rather the primary motivation for them lay in their connection with selfless devotion to the lord's service. They were seen as means for goal attainment rather than primarily for system integration. Of course the *samurai* in the Tokugawa Period were not on the whole directly involved in the economy, that is, were not occupationally involved in business enterprises. But the *samurai* economic ethic is important for two reasons. In the first place, it did have an effect on the ethic of those directly involved in the economy in the Tokugawa Period. In the second place, it is important to the understanding of the behavior of the large number of *samurai* who took leading roles in business and industry in the Meiji Period.

What marks off the more "Japanese" view of political economy from the Chinese view is its stress on one-way dynamism in the attainment of goals and the selfless subordination of all collectivity members to the goal effort rather than on attaining a relatively static ideal of harmony. Of course in the Tokugawa Period these two views were inextricably intermixed and can only be separated analytically. What is especially interesting is that the stress on diligence in production and economy in expenditure is common to both. Partly for this reason the two types of thinking tend to shade into each other. It is my impression, however, that often concrete maxims such as those quoted above from the classics were interpreted in the context of "Japanese" ethical thinking and served to reinforce it. To the extent that this was true their meaning was quite different from what it would have been to a Chinese.

Thinking on political economy was not of purely theoretical interest but had a definite effect on government economic policy. A consideration of some of these policies may help to clarify the theories.

Moral exhortation was always an important part of government policy and this was true of the encouragement of production as elsewhere. Admonitions to work hard, not neglect one's business, not waste time, etc., were a standard feature of the regulations governing the *gonin-gumi* or five-family group which were issued by the government and periodically read to the people. The government, however, by no means confined itself to exhortation. The *bakufu* and many of the *han* took fairly vigorous action to encourage the opening of new rice fields by granting the remission of taxes and other privileges to those undertaking such ventures. Such action is undoubtedly part of the explanation for the fact that land under cultivation doubled from the beginning of the Tokugawa rule to the early 18th century and had perhaps trebled by 1868.[12] Further, the *bakufu* took an active part in introducing the cultivation of new plants, establishing experimental farms so that their culture could be studied and accurate advice given to the farmer. Among the plants introduced in this way were ginseng and sugar, both of which came to be cultivated in large quantity.[13] With this kind of thinking as a background it is perhaps not surprising that the *bakufu* took the initiative in establishing shipyards, arsenals and foundries in the last years of its existence.[14] How much the motivation for such policies was the desire to maintain a static equilibrium and how much the desire to build a rich and strong country for its own sake is, of course, impossible to determine, but both motives were unquestionably present. It should be noted that the *han* governments went even farther, if anything, than the *bakufu* in the encouragement of production. In many cases they were responsible for the development of strong industries such as papermaking, waxmaking, lacquer and silk within their boundaries and participated in the profits from the sale of these products on the general market.[15]

Government policy on the encouragement of economy was similarly strong on exhortation. The *gonin-gumi* regulations admonished strictly against amusements, luxuries, sports or gambling. Regulations inveighing against luxury were posted on every government notice board. Such admonitions were backed up by the law in the form of sweeping and systematic sumptuary legislation. Such regulations were indeed evaded by many clever dodges but were on occasion enforced with dire consequences to the offenders.

Every "reform" administration in the period took it upon itself to decrease government spending especially by cutting down on luxuries at the *shōgun's* court. At times various lines of luxury business were entirely prohibited and the theaters and amusement quarters put under severe restrictions. Perhaps the most drastic government policy was the confiscation of the entire estates of merchants who were being too lavish in their luxury spending. Such moves were meant to curb the power of the merchant class. It is questionable whether they succeeded in their aim. Takekoshi, commenting on the effects of perhaps the greatest of the confiscations, that of the Yodoya, writes:

> All the Ōsaka merchants were struck with terror and were very careful to show that they were of thrifty and economical habits, which helped to increase their wealth, and the eventual result of the confiscaion of the Yodoya property was that the power of wealth grew enormously. . . .[16]

Not only the bakufu had a developed economic policy; many of the *han* also had extensive economic programs. These are seen at their most developed in the policies of those great reforming lords who periodically arose in Tokugawa times. None is more famous than Uesugi Harunori, lord of Yonezawa. Entering his fief for the first time as a young man, he found the direst poverty and misery in all quarters. With the aid of his advisor, the Confucian scholar, Hosoi Heishū (1728–1801), he soon mapped out a policy to restore prosperity to his new fief. One of his first acts was to cut the salaries of the *samurai* in half and his own household expenses to a fifth of those of the former lord. He wore only cotton garments and ate the simplest of food. He adopted as his fundamental maxims "To have no waste places in his domains," and "To have no idlers among his people."[17]

As for positive policies, he undertook an extensive policy of land reclamation, which involved turning his *samurai* into farmers; he introduced mulberry trees and established a thriving silk industry; he required every family to plant a certain number of lacquer trees and established this industry as well. He carried out several astounding engineering feats in order to improve the irrigation system. As a result of such policies Yonezawa became one of the most prosperous fiefs in Japan.

An interesting feature of Uesugi's reform was the appointment of itinerant preachers for each district of the fief. They were to inculcate the virtues of industry, honesty and thrift as well as the Confucian ceremonies and properties. These preachers were held accountable for the moral lapses of their charges. Further, a Confucian university was established with Hosoi as provost. This school offered scholarships for those who were talented but poor. It early added a medical department where the new Dutch medical learning was taught.

However much reforms such as those in Yonezawa seem to resemble the Chinese Confucian model, one has the feeling that the rigor and discipline with which they were put through, the intensity of the control from the feudal lord to the poorest farmer, is related to the Japanese ethic expressed in *Bushidō* and related ideas discussed in previous chapters. The hardheaded rational Confucian ideas on economics (they were certainly far ahead of any native Japanese ideas on the subject) seem to take on a dynamism when united with Japanese values, which they usually lacked in China.

So far the relation between economy and polity has been discussed largely from the point of view of the state and state policy. We may now consider the same relation from the point of view of the economy and of economic and other social institutions.

A fairly orthodox version of the Confucian theory of social development can be obtained from Yamaga Sokō (1622–1685), who writes in his *Yamaga Gorui:*

Although all people are not the same in rank and class, they are of the same origin. It was inevitable that class distinctions should arise. In order to live people must have something to eat. This makes it necessary for them to raise agricultural crops. As farm work cannot be done properly by hand only, agricultural implements must be manufactured with bamboo, wood, metal, etc., and for their manufacture artisans are necessary. As manufacturers of articles cannot go about selling their goods to people in distant districts, people to act as intermediaries between these artisans and the consumers of their manufactures become necessary, and these middle men form the merchant class. It was under such circumstances that three classes of people—farmers, artisans, and tradesmen—came into being. If, however, each is bent on promoting his own interests, in utter disregard of the interests of others—the farmer trying to live an easy life without putting

> sufficient energy into his agricultural work, the artisan contriving to realize big profits by supplying goods of poor quality, and the tradesman devoted to profiteering by dishonest means—there will be no end to the unscrupulous practices and disputes that will arise and moral principles will be completely lost. It, therefore, becomes necessary for the Ruler to be set up from whom all shall receive necessary instructions. The Ruler so created exists for the good of all people, not for his own sake alone. Under his wise guidance, culture, public morals and order can be maintained throughout the country. As a Monarch rules where there is a people and as a State is formed where a Monarch rules, the people must be regarded as the basis of national existence.[18]

Here we see an organic or functional theory of society; status and functional differentiation are seen as based on objective facts and necessities. The thinking is rational, almost protoscientific. What is presented is a system in which each part is necessary to the others and indeed its justification is based on the functions it performs for the others. In this respect the monarch is no different from the other elements of society. We have here almost a foreshadowing of the "organ theory" of the emperor. It is interesting that Yamaga, one of the early important propagandists for *kokutai* and *sonnō,* should have expressed so baldly this Confucian theory.

This Confucian theory of society is essentially an equilibrium theory. If each part fulfills its function all will go well. If any part gets out of kilter the whole system is apt to be upset. Analogies with the workings of nature are common in Confucian thinking. The course of action which such a theory implies is to maintain the harmonious equilibrium by keeping each part in its proper role. A quote from Muro Kyūsō, another famous Tokugawa Confucian, may shed further light on this theory. After discussing the way in which the farmers, artisans and merchants are diligently to perform their duties, he says:

> Why are the farmers, artisans, and merchants like this? This is because they take as their mind the mind of heaven and earth; they take as their business the transformations of heaven and earth; they mutually see other people as one family; they love working for people and hate to cause other people work; they aid the Way of heaven and earth and perform the transformations of heaven and earth; and they do not give a thought to their own hardships. Because of this the farmers, artisans, and merchants have mutual concern for each other; they mutually work together; they mutually nourish each other. . . . But when they have greed for profit and damage the heavenly reason, because they

do not have mutual concern for each other and cause people work but do not work for people, the farmers do not cultivate for the empire, the artisans do not produce for the empire, the merchants do not trade for the empire, they steal the wealth of the empire, they rob the wealth of the empire, they obscure the Way of heaven, and break the transformations of heaven.[19]

Developing out of this theory of society is a very interesting concept of occupation. The word *shokubun,* which can be translated as occupation, has a somewhat different meaning than the English term. It implies that the occupation is not merely an end in itself but a part of society. One's occupation is the fulfillment of what one owes to society, it is the part one plays which justifies one's receiving the benefits of society. The term *tenshoku,* though not as common as *shokubun,* gives us a further insight into the concept of occupation. The first character in the compound is "heaven" and the implication is "heavenly occupation" or "heavenly calling." That is to say an occupation or calling ordained by heaven. This illustrates the gearing in of social and cosmic or religious thinking already implied in the quote from Kyūsō given above. In the pure Confucian thinking the implication is that this calling is a fixed and definite duty which demarcates each class and functional group in society. It is the duty of individuals to perform their callings in the appropriate manner and be tranquil and contented with their lot, which is after all determined by heaven. It is thus a rather static view of occupation somewhat comparable to that of Thomas and other medieval Scholastics in the West.

That the above theory of society and concept of occupation had a pervasive influence in the Tokugawa Period is beyond question. We have, however, seen in the last chapter a concept of the national polity which does not fully coincide with what we have just described. Often the purely Confucian theory was expounded by ardent advocates of *Bushidō* and *kokutai,* as, for example, in the case of Yamaga Sokō. This being the case it is advisable to look at the two views in conjunction to see whether the meaning of the Confucian theory may have shifted in a new context.

What we have in mind is the fusion of the concept of occupation as described above with the idea of the obligation to make return for limitless *on*. The occupation of *samurai* offers a prototype of this fusion. The duties and tasks of his office are seen as fulfilling his obligation to his lord. They must be fulfilled with utmost devotion and without consideration of self. But in Tokugawa times this notion was not held exclusively in the *samurai* class. All classes were expected to be loyal and to make return for *kokuon* or the blessings of the nation. Occupation as a means of fulfilling one's endless obligations to one's superiors came more and more into prominence as we shall see below. Instead of viewing society as a harmonious equilibrium whose balance must be maintained, this idea tends to see society as moving in a single direction, that of fulfillment of obligations to superiors. As the period progressed the focus of these loyalties became more and more unified in the person of the emperor until Tachibana no Moribe (1781–1849) could write:

> Beginning with the Gracious Personage who headeth the Government officials right down to the lowest—though there may be differences of high and low—since every one of them is a servant of the Sovereign, to write a thing is for His Majesty, to cure an illness is for His Majesty, to cultivate a field is for His Majesty, and to trade is for His Majesty.[20]

In spite of this shift in emphasis, many features of the Confucian view remained. One still owed obligations to society in general as well as to superiors, and superiors owed obligations to inferiors for benefits derived from them. But the overriding obligations implied in the idea of *kokutai* gave the concept of occupation a dynamic open-ended potentiality which it lacked when viewed purely in terms of Confucian harmonistic thinking. Again Confucian ideas have a new significance in the Japanese context. The idea of a social organism and of the necessity of harmony between its parts is maintained, but all the parts are seen as subordinate to a single end. Here again we may see goal-attainment values taking precedence over system-maintenance values.

If we can summarize the tendencies discussed in this section we can perhaps use the phrase "the penetration of the economy by political values." It is important to remember that the political values in question are closely integrated with religious concepts, as was pointed out in the last chapter. Though many features of this penetration had economically irrational results, especially when the political motives were purely in the direction of maintaining the *status quo* and keeping a rigid system of social control in effect, to the extent that the result was the encouragement of production, the encouragement of economy, and the development of a dynamic concept of the calling, this penetration must be seen as having a strongly favorable effect on economic rationalization.

In the remaining sections of this chapter the preceding discussion will be made more concrete by a consideration of the economic ethic of the merchants and farmers. Consideration of the relation of filial piety and the family system to the economic ethic will also be undertaken.

Economic Ethic of the Merchant Class

The economic ethic of the merchant class as reflected in and influenced by the Shingaku movement will be the subject of the next chapter. This section, then, will be confined to general remarks and to a discussion of the influence of Jōdo Shinshū on one section of the merchant class, the Ōmi merchants, a subject carefully studied by Naitō Kanji.

The Jōdo Shinshū was widely disseminated among the common people of Japan, both farmers and towndwellers, so that it is likely that the implications discovered by Naitō of this ethic for the Ōmi merchants were fairly general. This is a problem for further research.

In Chapter III some background of the early period of this sect has been given and Rennyo Shōnin (1415–1499), the so-called second founder of the sect, was mentioned. Rennyo is chiefly of interest to us because of the fact that he made important advances with respect to the religious ethical regulation of everyday life. For Rennyo occupational life was like food and clothing, indispensable to the religious life, but still something alien to it. The fervor for the "other shore" took precedence for him over any everyday concern. Nevertheless, his view of the occupational life as integrated with the religious life is shown by his remark that, "If we engage in business, we must realize that it is in the service of Buddhism."[21] His stress on *on* and his inner-worldly asceticism are revealed in the following description:

Although in the midst of poverty, he always felt grateful to Amida Nyorai, by whose grace he believed that he was living. Whenever he sat down to dinner, he would say, "how happy I am to be able to take this meal, while there are so many in the world starving without anything to eat." He would then express, his hands clasped, his heartfelt gratitude in reciting Amida's Holy Name. He always told his family members and followers not to waste anything necessary for everyday life, because by doing so one would commit a sacrilege to creation. Once he found a piece of paper thrown away in the hallway. He picked it up and, reverently, raising it before his forehead, observed with a sigh, "How can they be so sinful as to waste what has been given in blessing!"[22]

In the early period Shinshū stressed salvation by faith alone and paid little attention, relatively, to ethical demands. The early literature is full of statements that anyone can be saved no matter how wicked. Rennyo raises the ethical demand to a very important place in Shin thought but it remains something separate from the religious demand. By middle Tokugawa times, however, salvation and ethical action came to be indissolubly linked. No more was heard about the wicked being saved. Ethical action had become the very sign of salvation. The following is a quote from a Shinshū tract of the period:

A person who lacks faith can easily do unreasonable evil deeds. Therefore, although he should not expect the complete atonement of his inborn evil qualities, it would be well for him daily to improve his bad heart as a sign of his having attained a believing heart (faith).[23]

Naitō in referring to this attitude says:

That a person who wishes for rebirth in the Pure Land dares to commit religious evil deeds, is not only inappropriate but indeed reveals his own lack of faith.[24]

Ethical behavior in the world was then both a return to Amida for blessings received and a sign of one's inner faith. Diligent work in one's occupation came to have the central place among the ethical duties so required. A Shin priest describes the everyday attitudes which believers should have:

. . . externally to obey the government laws and not forget the way of the five (Confucian) virtues, internally to believe deeply in the original vow (of Amida), to entrust the good and evil of this world to the causes of the past, whether *samurai,* peasant, merchant or artisan, each to have his family occupation as his highest intention, then they will be called good pilgrims of the Pure Land.[25]

It is through work in the world, most especially in one's occupation, that religion is best expressed.

> When engaged in meditation, all kinds of bad thoughts arise and do not stop for a minute, consequently our breasts are more disturbed than when we do our work in the world, and it is appropriate to compare it to tying a mountain monkey to a post.[26]

Not only is work in the world stressed, but an ascetic attitude toward consumption is also present. A rather extreme example of this is contained in the following story of a devout Shinshū believer of the Edo Period:

> In one of his epistles, Rennyo Shōnin warned his followers against drinking. Gozaemon thought at first that he had nothing to do with the same warning, because he took no liquor. But in reading the epistle with keener insight, he found that Rennyo's real intention was to warn them against anything that might stand in the way of listening to the Buddha's teaching. He at once gave up chess-playing which had been his only hobby.[27]

We may summarize the sort of teachings found in Shin tracts by quoting a few of the maxims frequently found in them:

> Always think of the divine protection.
> Cheerfully do not neglect diligent activity morning and evening.
> Work hard at the family occupation.
> Be temperate in unprofitable luxury.
> Do not gamble.
> Rather than take a lot, take a little.[28]

The great stress which the Shin teachings place on labor in the calling in the Edo Period leads one naturally to inquire as to the view taken with respect to profit. The traditional Confucian attitude was that profit was at best dubious. Confucians often claimed that the worthy man keeps righteousness (*i*) and throws away profit (*li*), whereas the merchant keeps profit and throws away righteousness.

For Buddhists, greed was one of the cardinal sins, and greed had been closely linked to the merchant's quest for profit. How then did the Shin teachers reconcile their raising labor in the calling, including that of the merchant, to a sacred obligation with the fact of profit? As might be expected, dishonest profit or excessive profit were strongly inveighed against. Their thought, however, went beyond this rather negative attitude, and with the doctrine of *jiri-rita,* profiting both self and others, justified business profit in religious terms:

> In merchandising we receive remuneration for supplying the consumer with manufactured goods. The artisans receive their remuneration by producing the goods and supplying them to the consumer. What the world calls this remuneration is profit. But the basis of receiving this profit depends on profiting others. Thus both the business of merchants and of artisans is the profiting of others. By profiting others they receive the right to profit themselves. This is the virtue of the harmony of *jiri-rita.* The spirit of profiting others is the Bodhisattva spirit. Having a Bodhisattva spirit and saving all beings, this is called Bodhisattva deeds. Thus Bodhisattva deeds are just the deeds of merchants and artisans. In general the secret of merchants' and artisans' business lies in obtaining confidence through Bodhisattva deeds.[29]

The above very interesting doctrines and ethical injunctions taught widely by Jōdo Shinshū in the Edo Period lead one naturally to the question of what influence they had on actual behavior. Fortunately we do have excellent evidence from at least one quarter. We know that the merchants of Ōmi province were strong believers in Shinshū from such facts as the great concentration of Shin temples in the primary merchant towns, the large number of merchants on the temple registers, and the frequent pious statements in the biographies of various of these merchants. What then was the character of these Ōmi merchants?

Though many of them started as pedlars traveling far through the mountains districts of central Japan, they often came to amass large fortunes and established branch shops in the three principal cities of the empire. Their behavior was proverbial and the following are typical of contemporary comments on them:

They make diligence the flesh and patience the bone.

> They go out early in the morning and return late at night. They do not avoid the elements nor do they dislike hardship and misery. They cover their body with cotton clothing and fill their mouths with vegetable food. They do not dare to throw away a piece of thread or a scrap of paper, nor do they waste a farthing or a half-pence.[30]

The great Ōmi merchants in most cases did not move their residence to one of the large cities but continued to maintain their headquarters in the merchant towns of Ōmi Province from which they conducted their nationwide business. They spent their years austerely pursuing their callings or devoting themselves to Buddhist matters. The following excerpt from the biography of one of these merchants, Takata Zenemon, written by his son, gives a good portrait of the type:

> At the beginning about the age of 16 or 17, having no capital, he borrowed three to five ryō, and carrying lampwicks and bamboo hats, he went out into the mountain districts. . . . He diligently for over fifty years exerted himself practicing strenuous economy. But with honesty as a basis, he worked without minding labor that was hard to endure, and was answered with heavenly considerations and since we descendants have received his blessings we must strongly warn against extravagance and, immersed in a sense of deep gratitude, we must not for a moment neglect the family business.[31]
>
> As for the nature of the old man, he was frugal and simple. He had faith in people and he never spoke of their errors. Though he did not read books he was attached to the way of doing good. He was happy only with the business of the house. In not neglecting it several decades were like one day and he had no other pleasure. Becoming old he handed the house on to his eldest son, studied Buddhism and took the tonsure. . . . In addition to this he should be called a blessed man who served the Buddha morning and evening and reverently spent his leisure time.
>
> Thus when he was old he admonished his children saying, "From the time I was young I determined to raise a family through commerce. When I went selling in Kishū I passed over mountains and through fields, I worked without minding heat or cold, rain or wind. All during these decades I have not once thought of wanting to make money excessively and moreover have not done so. Because wealth is accumulated by means of honesty and frugality, sons warn yourselves and daughters also admonish your husbands."[32]

Besides giving a picture of a hard-working and pious merchant, the above quote may serve as an introduction to a consideration of the merchant class in general and the relation between the family system and economic motivation within it. Before continuing this discussion perhaps a few concluding remarks on Shin are in order.

The present example is a case of rather direct influence of religious motivation in the economic sphere. The intermediate importance of the polity and political values seems to be largely lacking. There are, it is true, frequent injunctions in Shinshū tracts to be obedient to superiors and carefully observe the laws, but occupation is seen chiefly as a return for obligations to Amida rather than to one's feudal lord. There is an interesting story which sheds some light on the relation of political and religious values in Shinshū. A feudal lord, hearing that one of his retainers was a devout Shin adherent, decided to test the latter's loyalty by demanding that he renounce his faith. This command the retainer could not obey so he prepared to die, after explaining to the lord that he could not be untrue to his religious obligations. The lord, impressed with his sincerity, replied:

> You have spoken very well. Now I fully understand the teachings of Shinran Shōnin, to which I think no other teaching is preferable. He who is taught to break his bones for the grace of his spiritual teacher is most trustworthy because he also understands the grace of his lord and holds himself always in readiness to sacrifice himself for the lord's interests. Blessed am I who have a Shinran's follower like you.[33]

In spite of the fact that in this Shinshū story the two obligations are reconciled through the gracious change of heart of the lord, it is clear that the religious obligation has retained primacy. In *Bushidō,* Shingaku, Hōtoku, many of the Shintō sects, etc., the political and religious obligations are really completely merged and inseparable. To the extent that this is not true for Shinshū, it represents a somewhat deviant type, but a most interesting one, because it actually is the closest Japanese analogue to Western Protestantism and its ethic most similar to the Protestant ethic.

Shin was, however, only one of many influences on the moral life of the merchant classes. Further, even among devout Shin believers, other elements played an important part in their ethical thinking, witness the stress on family values in the passage on Takata Zenemon. In order to get a broad view of the ethic of the merchant class a brief survey of the materials contained in the merchant house rules will be undertaken. The practice of making house rules was copied from the *samurai,* who began making them in the Middle Ages. It was not till the Edo Period that the practice became widespread among the merchants and it may be considered as part of that general process of formaliztion of status ethics which characterized the era. The material here presented is based largely on the researches of Miyamoto Mataji who has made a study of large numbers of these documents.

The house rules (*kakun*) were usually rather brief documents. They contained clauses on inheritance and relations with branch families, but were largely given over to general moral injunctions. They contained the ideal pattern of what a merchant's life should be. Usually a second document, a set of shop rules (*tensoku*), was devoted to concrete details of management and was somewhat longer than the *kakun*. The two were not rigidly separated, however, and were not infrequently combined.

All *kakun* and *tensoku* contain some mention of faith (*shinkō*). For example they may contain the injunction to "work diligently for the care of Buddhist matters," or "Worship and revere morning and evening gods and Buddhas and do not neglect faith in them."[34] There is seldom mention of any particular sect; it is a generalized piety which is enjoined.

One of the first clauses in all *kakun* has to do with strict obedience to all laws and notices from the government of the *shōgun*. For example, the second clause of the Mitsui *kakun* is as follows: "All laws and ordinances issued by the government should be faithfully followed by all, from master to the lowest of employees."[35] This is one aspect of *hōkō* or service which was seen as a return for the blessings from one's country (*kokuon*), and especially as gratitude for the peace which the Tokugawa government had brought. A further extension of the idea of *hōkō* is a concern for the welfare of the whole society, and not just that of one's one house. The Nakamura family *kakun* says, "When traveling on business in another province do not think only of your own affairs; have regard for all in the province and do not covet selfish advantage," and the Ichida family code says, "Do not make an unjust profit from merchandise."[36] Finally this concept of *hōkō* or service merges with the idea of *shokubun* or occupation (calling). Labor in the world is seen as an appropriate return of gratitude to country and society, an analogue to the Western concept of the calling which we have already discussed in the first section of this chapter. This stress on the obligation of *hōkō* or service in the merchant class shows the importance of "political" motivation in the economic sphere.

Most interestingly the idea of *hōkō* is not just used with respect to the larger political entity. It is a very important concept governing conduct within the merchant house itself. The house is itself a sacred entity and demands, when symbolized in the idea of the ancestors, the gratitude and service of all members including the living head. For example, the first clause of the Mitsui *kakun* is, "We all live in happiness today owing to our ancestors, and for this we should all be thankful."[37] Another code says, "We ought to think of ourselves as the clerks of the ancestors," and yet another, "It is scarcely thirty years until I transfer the house to my child; the time is short and I must think of myself [entirely] as a servant."[38] We have seen similar sentiments above in the extracts from the biography of Takata Zenemon: ". . . immersed in a sense of deep gratitude, we must not for a moment neglect the family business." This idea of *hōkō* within the merchant house naturally also involved the filial service of children to parents and the loyal service of clerks to their superiors and to the master. The standards of this service were often very high and rivalled in strictness those of the *samurai*. In this concept of family service, then, we have another very interesting reinforcement of economic motivation. It makes labor in the family business an almost sacred obligation because it is seen as a requital for the favors of the ancestors. The head of the house is under this obligation no less than any other member. This is a case in which religious and secular motivations are completely merged. Obligation to the family as a polity-like collectivity and obligation to the ancestors, the symbols of the family religion, turn out to be identical. It is to this phenomenon that Watsuji Tetsurō and other writers are pointing when they stress that the merchant class economic motivation was not self-interest, not "self-profitism," but rather "family-profitism" and that the latter is compatible with and indeed requires the most diligent, abstemious and selfless action on the part of the individual merchants.[39] Lazy, extravagant or dishonest behavior was condemned largely because it was an abrogation of family obligations and indeed endangered the continuance of the family. For example, the Mitsui *kakun* says, "Self-indulgence and self-importance will always lead one's house to ruin. Be strict in self-discipline, be kind and helpful to those who are related with your family, and be industrious in your business."[40]

Another consequence of the semisacred character of the family was the high regard for family honor and the obligation not to sully the family name. One must not injure the reputation of the house or let the business decline as this would bring shame on the ancestors. Such an attitude was used to reinforce high standards of honesty, quality and credit. It undoubtedly helped reinforce universalistic standards in the business world and helped create the sort of confidence between business houses which led to the widespread use of credit billing and the like.

There is little doubt that this stress on the family as a semisacred entity, though it acted to motivate a formidable intensity in economic action, also had another aspect which tended to counteract economic rationalization. Devotion to family precedent apparently often acted to stifle initiative such as the expansion into new fields of commerce. Concern for maintenance of the family business intact also often led to an extremely conservative business policy. The concept of *shokubun* could be interpreted not in terms of a dynamic idea of the calling, but as one's humble lot with which one's ancestors were satisfied and with which one also should be content. Which aspect took precedence again seems to be a matter of the balance between system-maintenance and goal-attainment values. It is important to remember that the family structure in Japan had been sufficiently penetrated by "political" values that it could act as a strong motivational reinforcement for such values in the society as a whole or in the economy in particular. However, in periods or situations in which goal-attainment values were relatively weak the family on the whole might tend to reinforce traditionalism and system-maintenance values. The motivational significance of the family, then, must be understood in relation to the total social situation. Even with this qualification I think it can be said that the family system acted as a powerful motivating factor in the direction of economic rationalization in the Edo Period, and that this influence became even more marked with the general political and social changes of the Meiji Period.

Japanese cities of the Edo Period offered many temptations in the way of luxuries and amusements. There can be little doubt that the merchant class supplied many purchasers of luxuries and many devotees of the gay quarters, but the dangers of such behavior were very much apparent to many and the house rules almost universally take the sternest attitudes toward it. For example, the Mitsui code says,

> Life in the countryside is simple and frugal but in urban places like Edo, Kyōto and Ōsaka there is a tendency to luxury. *Chōnin* are apt to become less attentive in business and more indulgent in luxury: this is the reason why their houses fall in the second or third generation. Of this point one should be always wary.[41]

In general the house rules prescribe an economical and orderly, almost ascetic everyday life. The Taniguchi family code says, "Always be economical and avoid unprofitable expense."[42] There are many provisions which prohibit the light accomplishments such as playing the *samisen,* singing or dancing. Collecting curios, costly furniture or ornaments is often strictly forbidden. Oversleeping is severely condemned and "early to bed, early to rise" is often preached. Injunctions to personal cleanliness and keeping a clean house and shop are frequently included.

Much more on the merchant ethic will be included in the next chapter on the Shingaku movement but perhaps even this brief survey of the material contained in the house rules is enough to give a general impression of it. Its stress on diligence and economy, on an inner-worldly asceticism which is strikingly reminiscent of early Protestantism, all in the context of and rationalized by a concept of labor as a service demanded by some "higher" entity, society or family, would seem to mark it as an ethic peculiarly favorable to economic rationalization.

The Peasantry and the Hōtoku Movement

Hard work and frugality would seem to be virtues common to the peasantry the world around, but perhaps they were present in excess among the Japanese farmers. Though in part such virtues among a hard pressed peasantry are the product of sheer necessity, this is certainly not the whole explanation in Japan. The economic virtues were strongly backed by the sense of obligation to society and to the family in a way quite similar to that discussed above in the case of the merchant class. The peasantry were also influenced by a number of ethical movements which tended to reinforce their inner-worldly asceticism. The Shin sect was strong in many areas and it is of note that many of the Ōmi merchants began life as peasant lads. Shingaku was largely urban in its influence but it did have some effect on the countryside and it should be remembered that Ishida Baigan, its founder, was of the farmer class by birth. The popular Shintō sects which had an ethical content similar to that of Shingaku were very strong among the peasantry. And Hōtoku, which we shall shortly discuss, was an important ethical movement originating from and largely directed to the farmer class. The scope for economic rationalization was not terribly great in the village and here the effect of the peasant ethic on economic life is perhaps open to question. There is no doubt, however, that a more diversified and efficient agriculture did develop in the Edo Period, partly with governmental aid and encouragement, and that a number of "cottage" industries were started which had fairly high standards of quality and uniformity. Perhaps the greatest importance of this ethic, however, lies in the fact that a steady stream of peasants left the countryside and entered the merchant or artisan class in the cities all through the Edo Period, and in the fact that a large part of the new labor force which came into being after the Restoration of 1868 was drawn from the peasantry. In moving into other sections of the economy these peasants usually kept the economic ethic which they grew up with so that the economic motivation it implied became harnessed in the service of economic rationalization in general.

The Hōtoku movement is of interest partly because it is a reflection of the peasant ethic, and partly because it represents a sharpening and intensification of that ethic. It was founded by Ninomiya Sontoku (1787-1856), a farmer who conceived it as his duty to raise the level of morality of the farmers and at the same time to improve their economic production. For his ideas he drew from Confucian, Shintō and Buddhist sources but he united them in a practical and simple teaching. From his youth Sontoku was a model of industry and frugality and many are the stories of his deeds. As a youth he began to see that labor itself had a larger meaning. He wrote,

> I began to see that even an insignificant person like myself might contribute materially to the general welfare and prosperity of his country. From that time I saw how homely daily labor, which most people

think of only as a disagreeable task, might be made to have a high meaning in it, and I determined to devote all my energies to the service of others.[43]

The basic theory of Sontoku, one he never tired of elaborating, was implied in the very term which designates the movement: *hōtoku. Hōtoku* means essentially the same thing as *hōon,* which we have discussed often before; return for blessings. One aspect of this *hōtoku* is closely tied in with the family system and the duty of filial piety:

> The origin of the body lies in the nurture of the parents. The succession of descendants depends on the painstaking efforts of husband and wife. The wealth of our parents depends on the industry of their ancestry, and our wealth depends upon the accumulated good deeds of our parents. Our descendants' wealth depends on us and our faithful discharge of duty.[44]
>
> Speaking of making return for the blessings we receive, we must say it is the interest on borrowed money, thanks for favors received, value for articles bought, wages for the laborer's toil. We must look on the benefits we have received in this way, and make return to heaven, earth and man for them. If we do this we shall be able to accomplish anything we wish. This is a joy to God, and gives our fellow men pleasure in our conduct and confidence in our words.[45]

What he means by returning blessings in the highest sense is indicated in the following passage which directly follows the passage which has already been quoted above on page 73:

> Everyone who is, according to his heavenly gift, living within his means, by industry and economy, by saving his surplus money as a fund for restoring and developing deserted wastes, paying debts, rescuing the poor, helping villages and provinces, by saving home after home, village after village, until all Japan having become prosperous, the prosperity shall extend to foreign countries, is making return for the blessings he has received from heaven, earth and man.[46]

This passage is interesting on several counts. From it one gets the impression that salvation in the religious sense and economic recovery seem to be conceptually fused. There is indeed an almost millenial expectation that not only Japan but the whole world will be saved through such return of blessings. The stress is certainly on the collectivity rather than on the individual or even the family. It is perhaps most significant that Sontoku was preaching in the last years of the *bakufu* in the same atmosphere in which the

Kokugaku and Mitogaku ideas discussed in the last chapter were being propagated.

Another aspect of Sontoku's teaching is of great interest. Unlike most Japanese thinkers he seems to have had a "man over nature" orientation rather than a "man in nature" orientation. Correlated with this is a rejection of the cyclical theories of Buddhism and Confucianism, and the espousal of a view close to that of one-way progressive development:

> Confucianism teaches the law of circulation, Buddhism teaches transmigration. And to escape the tyranny of transmigration they teach Nirvana, the peaceful kingdom. Confucius teaches us to obey the will of heaven and thus live a life of peace. My teaching is different, it is intended to enrich the poor and give prosperity to those who need it. Escaping both the law of circulation, and transmigration, we may live in a place of prosperity. Fruit trees naturally bear well one year and rest the next. My idea is to prune and nurture them so they will bear well every year. It is natural for the rich to become poor, but I would overcome nature and make prosperity permanent.[47]

Other passages also emphasizing the idea of man over nature may be quoted:

> The success of human life depends upon our ability to plan and scheme. . . . To sow our grain is natural, but if we wish to make the grain profitable, we pull up the weeds around it, to give it a better chance. It is not natural to pull up weeds. So following natural desire, we must labor, but when natural desire clashes with duty, it must be restrained.[48]
>
> Human life is strenous and opposed to nature. The human way is to repair deserted places and fertilize sterile plains. Few understand the difference between the human way and the way of nature.[49]

Another passage may seem to contradict those quoted above, but in effect it says the same thing. It manages to save the idea of the harmony of man and nature but develops a special idea of nature for the purpose:

> If we rely upon Nature we need have no fear for the recovery of our country, for she constantly heals and repairs. Yet we look to Nature, the parent of us all, not as an idle boy looks to his father, but as an industrious boy looks to his father, kind, yet severe in punishment, and eager to recognize the boy's merits. Nature will give no benefit without labour.[50]

It is interesting that in this view nature is "father" and not "mother."

As might be expected, Sontoku never tires of urging diligence and economy. Here again is that inner-worldly asceticism which seems to be such an important part of the Japanese ethic:

When you cultivate many acres of land, you do so spadeful by spadeful. When you walk twenty-five miles, you do so step by step. If you build a great mound, you do so basketful by basketful. In the same way, by being diligent in little things you may accomplish much.[51]

Work much, earn much, and spend little. Gather plenty of fuel, and burn as little as possible. This is the secret of making a country wealthy; it is not miserliness. Since human life is opposed to nature, we must save and provide for the future by industrious effort, the earnings of this year providing for the necessities of next year. Saving is the virtue of self-denial.[52]

Sontoku is noteworthy not only as a religious and ethical teacher but also as a practical man of affairs. On several occasions he was put in charge of feudal estates which were in a sad state of decay and in a few years' time had transformed them into prosperous and economically sound districts. His policies were many but consisted chiefly in insisting on the strictest economy and on the extension of the amount of cultivated land, development of irrigation, etc., by means of the money saved. One of his most important principles was *bundo* which meant that more should be accumulated in one year than would be spent in the next, the reserve being kept for emergency or capital improvement. He urged the establishment of credit societies in the villages which made interest-free loans for capital improvement. (The borrower was expected to make a "voluntary" gift to the association on returning the loan, but the rate was much lower than that of the usurer.) These credit ascociations were often called Hōtoku Societies and were half religious, half economic in character. An extract from the general rules of such a society governing the admission of members may be of interest. These particular rules were drawn up in the Meiji Period:

Anyone wishing to enter the society must fulfill the following conditions:

(1) He must show by his good deeds gratitude to the gods, the Emperor, his parents, and his ancestors for their grace.

(2) He must be industrious and economical, living according to his means, and holding up a standard of conduct that will tend toward his own and his country's prosperity.

(3) He must sow good seed, plant good roots, and thus he will enjoy eternal happiness.[53]

The direct encouragement of capital improvement and accumulation which Hōtoku fostered is indeed a striking example of the influence of religion on economic rationalization. But the significance of Hōtoku as such is limited due to the fact that it had influence in only a few rather limited areas. Its importance lies rather in its expression of parts of the peasant ethic which were very widespread and as an indication of what potentialities for economic rationalization were contained in that ethic.

In this chapter I have tried to show the influence of religion on the economy both directly and through the religiously influenced ideas of the polity and the family. I have tried to define an economic ethic characterized by strong inner-worldly asceticism and an analogue to the concept of the calling through which labor becomes a "sacred obligation" which is rooted in these religious, political and familistic ideas. Certain essential features of this ethic seem to be held in common by each of the major groups in the population, the *samurai,* the *chōnin,* and the farmers, though differences between them can be noted. *Bushidō,* Shinshū, and Hōtoku have been singled out for fairly extensive discussion as examples of ways in which religious considerations tie in with the economic ethic and as expressions of that ethic among the classes which these movements respectively influenced. In the following chapter I will undertake a detailed analysis of one religious-ethical movement, Shingaku, in an effort to define even more sharply that economic ethic and its underpinnings.

Notes

1. Sansom, *Japan, A Short Cultural History,* p. 354.
2. Suzuki, *The Training of the Zen Buddhist Monk,* p. 23.
3. *Ibid.,* p. 24.
4. *Ibid.,* p. 38.
5. Azuma, *Kinsei Nihon Keizai Rinri Shisō Shi,* p. 5.
6. Legge, *Chinese Classics,* vol. II, p. 23.
7. *Ibid.,* vol. I, p. 243.
8. Dubs, *The Works of Hzüntze,* p. 65.
9. Legge, *op. cit.,* vol. II, p. 373.
10. *Ibid.,* vol. I, p. 71.
11. Honjō, "Economic Ideas in Tokugawa Days," p. 5.
12. Smith, N. S., "Materials on Japanese Social and Economic History," p. 19. These figures do not seem to harmonize with the generally held view that Japanese population in the Tokugawa Period remained relatively constant at a level somewhat under 30 million.
13. Horie, "An Outline of Economic Policy in the Tokugawa Period."
14. Smith, T. C., "The Introduction

of Western Industry to Japan during the Last Years of the Tokugawa Period."

15. Horie, "The Encouragement of *Kokusan* or Native Products in the Tokugawa Period."

16. *Takekoshi, The Economic Aspects of the History of the Civilization of Japan,* vol. III, p. 255.

17. Murdoch, *A History of Japan,* vol. III, p. 386.

18. Honjō, Economic Thought in the Early Period of the Tokugawa Era," p. 4.

19. Azuma, *op. cit.*, p. 4.

20. Hall, R. K., *Kokutai no hongi,* p. 86.

21. Reischauer, A. K., "A Catechism of the Shin Sect," p. 384.

22. Nakai, *op. cit.*, p. 143.

23. Naito, *op. cit.*, p. 269.

24. *Ibid.*, p. 279.

25. *Ibid.*, p. 277.

26. *Ibid.*, pp. 264-265.

27. Nakai, *op. cit.*, p. 208.

28. Naitō, *op. cit.*, p. 275-6.

29. *Ibid.*, p. 285.

30. *Ibid.*, p. 254.

31. *Ibid.*, p. 255.

32. *Ibid.*, p. 256.

33. Nakai, *op. cit.*, p. 246.

34. Miyamoto, "Sekimon Shingaku to Shōnin Ishiki," p. 22.

35. Mitsui, "Chōnin's Life under Feudalism," p. 71.

36. Miyamoto, *op. cit.*, p. 17.

37. Mitsui, *op. cit.*, p. 71.

38. Miyamoto, *op. cit.*, p. 18.

39. Watsuji, "Gendai Nippon to Chōnin Konjō," pp. 320-324.

40. Mitsui, *op. cit.*, p. 72.

41. *Ibid.*, p. 73.

42. Miyamoto, *op. cit.*, p. 20.

43. Droppers, "A Japanese Credit Association," p. 83.

44. Armstrong, *Just Before the Dawn,* p. 177.

45. *Ibid.*, p. 178.

46. *Ibid.*, pp. 175-176.

47. *Ibid.*, pp. 208-209.

48. *Ibid.*, p. 213.

49. *Ibid.*, p. 214.

50. Droppers, *op. cit.*, p. 82.

51. Armstrong, *Just Before the Dawn,* p. 232.

52. *Ibid.*, p. 232.

53. *Ibid.*, p. 185.

CHAPTER

VI

Shingaku and its Founder, Ishida Baigan

SHINGAKU IS A MOVEMENT which began when Ishida Baigan (1685-1744) hung out his shingle and gave his first public lecture in 1729. After Baigan's death the movement grew decade by decade until by the early 19th century there were many scores of Shingaku lecture halls all over Japan. Its chief appeal was to the city classes, thousands of whom thronged its halls for over one hundred years, but it also made inroads among the peasantry and *samurai*. Many Japanese scholars consider it to have been one of the greatest influences on the morality of the common people in the Tokugawa Period. Its influence was spread not only through its public lectures, but through the sermons and tracts which were printed in vast numbers and very widely read, through the house codes (*kakun*), many of which were drawn up by Shingaku preachers, and through charitable acts which the movement undertook. In this chapter I will try to outline the religious thought and ethical teaching of Shingaku as well as its forms of organization and method of instruction. I will focus on Ishida Baigan, founder of Shingaku and perhaps its most original thinker. Familiarity with the corpus of his writings allows a more comprehensive treatment of his thought than of that of some of the later figures. His work is, of course, the basis of all later developments; the life of the founder of any important religious movement has an intrinsic interest. Following a discussion of Baigan's life and thought there will be a discussion of the spread and development of the school in later years. Many of the most important organizational principles and teaching methods of the school were introduced after Baigan's death and so will not be discussed until this concluding section.

Ishida Baigan[1]

Ishida Baigan was born in the village of Higashi Agata in Tamba province on the 15th day of the 9th month of the year 1685. Higashi Agata was a farming village about 16 miles from Kyōto, and it was there that Baigan spent his youth engaged in work on his father's farm. The father was a strict and upright man and seems to have made a profound impression on the growing boy. He was not the eldest son and since he could not expect to inherit, some provision for his livelihood had to be made, so he was apprenticed to a Kyōto merchant at the age of eleven, a normal age for apprenticeship to begin. Thus though of peasant extraction, Baigan had entered the merchant class. Even beginning at the bottom rung he could expect gradual promotion and, if his services were sufficiently outstanding eventual establishment of himself in an independent business. The organization of merchant houses has been discussed in Chapter II and this description may be referred to for an idea of the situation Baigan found himself in.

At the age of 15, however, Baigan left his apprenticeship in mid-course and returned to his village, for reasons that are by no means clear. Elsewhere he says, "My natural disposition was argumentative and I was from an early age disliked by friends. I was often unkind but at about 14 or 15 I suddenly came to my senses and regretted this." Whether this sudden awareness had anything to do with his decision is not known. At any rate the step was a momentous one. Just at the point when he was becoming thoroughly indoctrinated into the *chōnin* life of Kyōto and beginning what might have been the most ordinary of merchant careers, he threw it all over and returned to his native village, where he was to spend the next eight years, the very crucial years from 15 to 23. In doing this he ruined his chances for a normal merchant career—as was pointed out in Chapter II, only through a normal apprenticeship could a man hope to rise. One hired as an adult, the so-called *chūnen,* was always under a basic handicap and could not hope for much in the way of a merchant career.

Baigan, however, may not have been worrying very much about his career, but rather, as the above quotation indicates, he may have been concerned with his own inner problems. In these years spent at home, perhaps in response to his inner need, he became interested in Shintō. The Ise priests, who at that time had built up throughout the country a large organization of societies for the Ise pilgrimage, were especially successful in Kyōto and neighboring areas and it is most likely that Baigan was influenced by them. At any rate, when Baigan returned to Kyōto at the age of 23 it was not with the intention of reviving his career as a merchant but with the express purpose of propagating Shintō.

He took service with a certain Kuroyanagi house in the upper city, probably as a *chūnen,* but his real interest was in preaching Shintō. Listeners were few and so he took to patrolling the city ringing a bell in order to attract them. His desire was to become a model of the human way. Seeing that his first efforts were rather unsuccessful he turned to study. He would take a book with him when going on an errand and read it if he had a spare moment. In the mornings he arose before others were awake and read near the window; in the evenings he read after others were in bed. In spite of his devotion to study he did not neglect his master's business in the least. His intention in study was not to amass knowledge for its own sake but to cultivate his person so that he would be an example for all men.

He continued to work in the Kuroyanagi house for a number of years, becoming a trusted employee and an especially close friend of the master's mother during her lifetime. Eventually he was made a *bantō* or chief clerk, his job being probably to supervise the *chūnen.* All through these years he continued to study and develop his ideas.

When he was 35 or 36 he began to feel that he had mastered the theoretical knowledge of the nature (*sei,* Chinese *hsing*), but in spite of his intellectual certainty, his feelings were still assailed with doubts. In order to correct this he sought a teacher who could help him allay all doubts. Though he searched widely for several years he could find no one suitable until finally he had an interview with an old teacher by the name of Oguri Ryōun. Ryōun had been a high official to a *daimyō* but for some reason had resigned and retired to Kyōto as a teacher. He was learned in the Sung nature philosophy (*seiri,* Chinese *hsing li*) and was adept in Buddhist and Taoist teachings as well. Baigan was profoundly impressed by his interview with him, decided to become his follower, and from that time forward devoted himself exhaustively to the practice of contemplation (*kufu*). When about a year and a half had passed in this way Baigan had his first experience of enlightenment. At that time he was about 40 and was called to his home village as his mother was sick.

> It was in the first third of the first month, while nursing his mother, he opened a door and suddenly the doubts of former years scattered. The way of Yao and Shun is only filial piety and brotherliness (*kōtei,* Chinese *hsiao-t'i*). Fish swim in water and birds fly in the sky. The Way is clear above and below. Knowing the nature (*sei*) to be the parent of heaven and earth and of all things, he greatly rejoiced.[2]

When he returned to Kyōto he discussed this experience with his teacher. Ryōun felt apparently that it was only a partial illumination. Baigan and the nature were still separate. He was still "observing" nature. If he would know the truth it was that "there must be the nature but without the eye." Having progressed thus far Baigan devoted himself even more assiduously to meditation and continued it intensely for more than a year longer. At last his efforts were rewarded.

> Late one night he lay down exhausted and was unaware of the break of day. He heard the cry of a sparrow in the woods behind where he was lying. Then within his body it was like the serenity of a great sea, a cloudless sky. He felt the cry of that sparrow like a cormorant dividing and entering the water, in the serenity of a great sea.[3]

After that there was not a difference between his self and his nature.

This experience had a profound and determining effect on Baigan. It brought him great happiness.

> If there were a person who wished to draw my extreme happiness, he would have to draw a person suddenly opened, forgetting to move his hands or lift his feet.[4]

It brought him an entirely new feeling of self-confidence and freedom from doubt. From now on he could accept every situation without wavering and could face the world head-on. It brought him a strong desire to help others attain the happiness and certainty which he now enjoyed. Twenty years of seeking had borne fruit. He had found his heaven and earth and now he was ready to help others do the same.

His intention was fixed and he moved slowly in the direction of carrying it out. When he was forty-three he left the service of the Kuroyanagi family and began to lecture privately in various homes. In 1729 Oguri Ryōun died at the age of 60 and it is perhaps not entirely coincidental that it was also in 1729 that Baigan, age 45, at last took up a permanent residence and for the first time opened a lecture hall. Posting his famous notice before his house,

> On a certain month, and a certain day, there will be a lecture. There is no admission charge and even though uninitiated, persons who wish to may listen freely.[5]

he began to lecture, and month in, month out, continued to do so until the time of his death.

At first the attendance was very small and at times though there was only a close friend present, he sat face to face with him and lectured. One night only one pupil appeared.

> This pupil said, "Tonight there is no other audience and since it would trouble you to lecture just for me, please rest tonight."
> Our teacher replied, "When I began to lecture, expecting to face only the reading stand, I was satisfied if there was an audience of one," and he lectured.[6]

These incidents indicate the intensity of Baigan's conviction and his unwavering determination to carry through his intention no matter what discouragements arose.

Gradually his attendance increased and he began to lecture in various parts of Kyōto and often also in Ōsaka. Disciples began slowly to collect themselves. His audience was largely of the merchant class and the lectures were timed so as not to interfere with business. He lectured every morning and every other evening. For his disciples and those especially interested he held three meetings a month in which a mutual questioning took place. Baigan addressed questions to his pupils and also answered their inquiries.

Though he encouraged his disciples to know the nature through the practice of meditation (*kufu* or *seiza*) at first they were dubious as to whether it could be done. One of his pupils, Saitō Zemmon, was convinced and rigorously practised mediation. One night he unexpectedly heard the sound of a drum and suddenly knew the nature. The other disciples still doubted until Kimura Shigemitsu while covering *shōji* one winter suddenly knew his nature. After that many believed and attained knowledge.

Baigan developed the lecture, the question and answer meeting and the practice of meditation as three methods for his teaching, each useful for a somewhat different purpose. They remained the three basic teaching methods of Shingaku throughout its history.

He also began the acts of charity which became a characteristic of the movement by such deeds as taking food to a village which had burned down in the dead of winter, and organizing the distribution of alms in a period of widespread distress.

At the age of 55 he published his first book, *Toimondō,* literally "City and Country Dialogues." It was composed on the basis of rough drafts he made in reply to inquiries from people from day to day, and contains most of what we know of his philosophy. His only other book, *Seikaron,* literally "Essay on Household Management," was published in 1744, the last year of his life. As the title implies, it is concerned with concrete injunctions on prudent and ethical behavior.

On the 23d of the 9th month of the year 1744 Baigan ate a stew containing some large mushrooms. That night he fell ill of indigestion and never rose on the 24th. He died at about noon of that day in his home, being in his 60th year. He was buried at Toribe-yama southeast of Kyōto.

> After his death the things which remained in his house were only three boxes of books, the drafts of his replies to the daily questions of people, his reading stand, his desk, his inkstone, his clothes and the utensils of his daily use.[7]

The above chronicle gives the bare bones of Baigan's life. It will now be necessary to fill it out with a description of his character, of the society in which he lived and of the reaction of that society to this new religious teacher.

Baigan himself gives us an interesting summary of his character and its development, the beginning of which we have already quoted:

Our teacher said, "My natural disposition was argumentative and I was from an early age disliked by friends. I was often unkind but at about 14 or 15 I suddenly came to my senses and regretted this, and though I thought that by about 30 I had in general corrected this, still it showed in the edges of words, and at 40 I felt there was still a little sourness like burnt plum pickle, but by about 50 I felt my bad disposition was quite gone."

Till about 50 when our teacher was in someone's presence and there was something on which their minds differed, it seemed that he showed a sour face, but at about 50 he did not show the slightest sign whether there was something on which they differed or not, and at about 60 he said, "Now I have become completely at ease (*raku*)."[8]

These statements indicate a lifelong effort to gain control over his own feelings, perhaps especially his aggressive impulses, and attain a state of tranquility. Baigan was reputed to be sharp and stubborn in debate and *Toimondō* is said to reflect this, though from the point of view of a Westerner he seems almost always to have been polite and considerate. Nevertheless, he seems to have felt otherwise and also to have felt that such qualities were not admirable but in need of control. Perhaps the significance of the passage would be enhanced if we compare it with the statement in the *Analects* of Confucius on which it is obviously modeled:

The master said, At fifteen I set my heart upon learning. At thirty, I had planted my feet firm upon the ground. At forty, I no longer suffered from perplexities. At fifty, I knew what were the biddings of Heaven. At sixty, I heard them with a docile ear. At seventy, I could follow the dictates of my own heart; for what I desired no longer overstepped the boundaries of right.[9]

Baigan's statement is perhaps more personal and more poignant, but both illustrate essentially the same process, the gradual attainment of a state in which one's natural feelings and one's moral obligations are in perfect harmony.

Baigan, then, as we have seen, was engaged in a lifelong struggle to overcome what he felt was his bad disposition. His seeking the way must be seen in this context—it was "throwing away the self and practicing the way." This throwing away self and practicing the way helps to explain a number of features of his personality. When taxed with his failure to marry he replied, "My aspiration is to propagate the way. Encumbered with a wife I fear I would lose the way, so I live alone."[10] This may be partly interpreted in terms of the financial and other difficulties involved in setting himself up as an independent teacher in which having a family would be a great burden, but I think more basically it is a renunciation of certain needs of his personality which Baigan perhaps identified with his bad disposition or selfish desires and which stood in the way of his attaining the way.

This need to renounce certain features of his personality is reflected in the asceticism which characterized his life. He did not normally go to theaters or go sight-seeing, he slept only the necessary minimum, for many years he ate only two meals a day and these of the simplest fare. His frugality, as reflected in a number of incidents in his biography, may seem to be pathologically compulsive. He could not, for example, bear to waste anything and devised uses for such things as worn-out mats, *shōji,* and old ink. Though this certainly fits in with his personality as we know it, we must remember that he was raised in the country and was steeped in peasant attitudes toward frugality. It is therefore impossible to disentangle how much to attribute to culture and how much to personality but certainly both elements were involved. However extreme some of his habits may seem, he does appear on the whole to have kept his balance. When one of his pupils chided him on eating only two meals a day, he considered the matter and came to the conclusion that he was indeed perhaps endangering his health and henceforth ate three meals a day. Asceticism does not for him seem to have been an end in itself. When it reached the point where it endangered the carrying out of his actual worldly obligations it had to be curtailed.

Another aspect of his personality which may be seen as related to his inner struggles is his excessive concern for the welfare of others. This can be viewed as an attempt to compensate for the excessively hostile impulses he felt for others, and which he so strongly regretted. For example, when he was head clerk, instead of taking the warmest spot on cold winter nights he took the coldest one for his bed and left the warmer places for his inferiors. And again,

> Our teacher when coming and going on the road in summer left the shade to others and himself walked in the sunshine. In winter he left the sunshine to others and himself walked in the shade.[11]

He showed great concern lest he unnecessarily kill living beings and even tempered his hot water with cold when throwing it out so as not to boil any small creatures. Similarly his concern with charity may be seen in this context. Of course these attitudes were closely linked with Buddhist ideas and with the Confucian teaching on humanity (*jin,* Chinese *jen*) which he greatly stressed. Also in this aspect as well Baigan did not go to extremes but maintained a balance. Once when criticized for going on a moon-viewing party with his disciples during a period when severe floods ravaged neighboring provinces, he replied that though he lamented the floods he did not see that anything would be gained by sitting around being mournful. The correction of floods was not within his competence. Rather he felt his concern should be with the instruction of his pupils.

Both asceticism and brotherly love have an important part in Baigan's religious teaching. The above attempt to delineate psychological bases for these attitudes is by no means an effort to impugn his sincerity. Rather I wish to show that he was motivated by inner needs and sought a religious solution for those needs. He was not in the first instance a conscious social ideologist. His social teachings were of course influenced by his social milieu but they were primarily motivated by his religious concerns. This is an important point which we shall return to later as there have been those who have viewed Baigan as an apologist for the merchant class who merely used religion as a convenient means. This would make his religious interests mere window dressing, mere epiphenomena. The evidence of his life and character which has been presented above refutes this motion.

The argument could be made that Baigan himself may have thought his interests were primarily religious but being a typical *chōnin* it was inevitable that his thought should be merely a reflection of *chōnin* consciousness. The evidence again is strongly against this view. He was never a typical *chōnin.* In the first place he was not by birth a *chōnin* at all but a farmer and his formative years were spent in the country. In the second place his position in the *chōnin* social structure was the somewhat anomalous one of *chūnen.* He could not have had a typical *chōnin* career even if he had wished. There is abundant evidence that he did not wish. The years he spent in service were devoted to study and self-cultivation. He performed his tasks well but his life-work was otherwise. Finally he spent the last years of his life as an independent teacher, hardly a typical *chōnin* occupation. His teachings were closely related to the *chōnin* ethic but they were not merely an unconscious reflection of it.

Those writers who have seen Baigan as primarily an apologist or ideologist for the merchant class have in some cases attributed to him an important political motivation. They have seen him as the enemy of "feudalism" and as the champion of political freedom for the city classes. Such an opinion seems to me wholly unsupported by the facts. He never criticizes the *bakufu* or in any way questions the fundamentals of the contemporary class system. He says in many places that government is the duty and responsibility of the *samurai* class and never, it seems to me, could even have conceived the merchants and artisans as playing a political role. His attitude toward the emperor is one of religious awe, toward the nobility almost sacred veneration, and toward the *samurai* the deepest respect. He reserves some of his sharpest attacks for merchants who aspire to *samurai*-like pretentions. The passages which such writers always cite are those in which Baigan asserts the universality of moral obligations and the indispensable and honorable function of the merchant class. In the following section we will discuss these passages in the context of his total thought. Even out of context they do not by any means make him into an incipient social revolutionary.

If, then, we have shown that Baigan's motivation was primarily personal and his interest primarily religious, what forms did that interest take? The summary of his life has already indicated the main lines of development. His initial interest was in Shintō. This remained important, being expressed in a high veneration for the emperor, for the Sun Goddess and for her shrine at Ise. He gives expression to the *kokutai* idea in outline, saying that Japan is a land of the gods superior to all other lands and that other doctrines are merely helps and aids to Shintō. Nevertheless, it cannot be said that his teaching was primarily Shintō. Rather Confucianism seems to have been the greatest influence on his thinking. The concepts of heart (*kokoro,* Chinese *hsin*) and nature (*sei,* Chinese *hsing*) which are at the basis of his system are directly taken from Mencius and the explanations of them are derived largely from Sung neo-Confucianism. During his years of study in the Kuroyanagi household he seems to have mastered the classics and the Sung commentators. Finally under the influence of his teacher Ryōun he became familiar with the doctrines of Lao Tzu and Chuang Tzu and of Zen Buddhism. These influenced his thinking on enlightenment and meditation though the Sung Confucians who themselves were influenced by Buddhism and Taoism had ideas on these subjects and may have pushed him in the same direction. Much in Baigan's thought seems to resemble that of Wang Yang Ming but there is no evidence that he read Wang and he does not quote him or his disciples so that any influence is purely conjectural. We may get some idea of the major influence on his thought by considering those books which he frequently expounded. Of the Confucian classics there were the *Four Books,* the *Classic of Filial Piety,* the *Book of Changes,* and the *Book of Poetry*. Several works of the Chu Hsi school were included: the *Diagram of the Supreme Ultimate Explained,* the *Small Learning,* the *Kinshiroku* and the *Seiri Jigi.*[12] In addition to these there were the *Lao Tzu* and the *Chuang Tzu* and two works written in Japan, the *Japanese Analects* (*Warongo*) and the *Tsurezuregusa.*[13] The last two are syncretic works, the former primarily Shintō, the latter primarily Buddhist.

Baigan's approach to these various books and doctrines was not, as we have seen, that of abstract interest. He was seeking a Way which could answer to his own inner needs. But in finding his way, in reaching his personal solution, he universalized his own problems and transcended them. From a seeker he became a giver. He freely utilized the religious thought of his day to construct a relatively simple doctrine which brought meaning and harmony into his own life and into the lives of many others as well. He taught a method of attaining enlightenment within and he taught that such enlightenment must be expressed in ethically rigorous action without. In doing so he reworked traditional religious ideas in accordance with his own needs and the needs of his time. Once it became his intention to bring others to the same happiness he had attained, Baigan thought carefully about the sort of people to whom he was appealing and their spiritual and ethical needs. He was not an original thinker if one thinks of basic religious ideas. His originality rather lay in the sphere of adapting these ideas to the people of his own time.

What, then, were the characteristics of his time and of the people among whom he lived? He came to Kyōto in the fourth year of Hōei (1707). The year period preceding Hōei was Genroku (1688-1704). Though we tend to think of Genroku as a period of high cultural achievement, it was also a period of extravagant license. It was a period in which the "*daimyō* spirit" seized many merchants and also it was a period when more than one merchant met an untimely ruin thereby. There is reason to believe that the merchant class in general was in a state of reaction against the excesses of Genroku at about the time Baigan was entering service. Diligence, economy, and morality were receiving greater stress than before.[14]

In 1716, less than ten years after Baigan entered service, Yoshimune became the *shōgun*. He was to rule until the year after Baigan's death, 1745, and the effects of his rule on the merchant class were many. Yoshimune inaugurated a powerful reaction against those tendencies which were undermining the *samurai* class and the *bakufu* rule. He wished to revive the martial and Spartan spirit among the *samurai* and one of his means to this end was to urge the practice of economy. He took the lead himself by cutting down the shogunal household expenditures, discharging a large percentage of the ladies-in-waiting, living on simple fare and wearing cotton garments. This policy had severe repercussions on the merchant class, especially in the Edo where government contractors and purveyors of luxury goods were very hard-hit. The effects of Yoshimune's policies were less severe in the Ōsaka and Kyōto area because the economy of these cities was geared to the normal needs of the nation and not so closely tied in with government spending and the luxury trade as was Edo. Even so business declined, the number of failures of houses was not few, and work for laborers decreased.

The *bakufu's* prohibition of suits between *samurai* and merchants over loans was an especially hard blow to the Kyōto-Ōsaka financial world and many merchants were ruined thereby. Partly as a result of such failures Mitsui Takafusa wrote a book counseling economy and urging merchants not to engage in loans to *daimyō* or *samurai.*

At the same time that business conditions were relatively poor the intensity of the *bakufu* administration was increased. Laws were more rigorously enforced and the sort of admonitions on the subjects of diligence and economy which had long flowed from Edo were given even more pointed significance.

Such, then, were the special characteristics of the time when Ishida Baigan was seeking the way and beginning to expound it. Weaknesses in the Tokugawa system had made themselves felt. The real power of the merchant class was rising rather than declining as the *samurai* became more and more helpless economically even in spite of Yoshimune's reform. But the immediate effect was not one of dissolution of the old structure. Rather it was in a period of retrenchment and temporary rejuvenescence. For the merchant class it was not an easy time. Rather tensions and strains must have been considerable. At the same time the reaction of the city classes, partly under governmental pressure but largely as a result of their own experience, was to carry through their own retrenchment policy, to tighten their own morality and to apply themselves even more vigorously to legitimate business. It is in this situation, with both its negative and positive aspects, that Baigan began to preach, and neither his teaching nor the response to it can be understood without considering this situation.

Perhaps it is not entirely accidental that it was in Kyōto rather than in Edo that Shingaku arose. We have already noted that the Edo merchants were closely involved with the government and with the luxury trade. Opportunities for graft were enormous and this encouraged a speculative political capitalism which in turn was reflected in an extravagant style of life. The economy of the city was based largely on the consumption needs of the thousands of government officials, direct retainers to the *shōgun,* and the further thousands of officials and *samurai* connected with the dozens of *daimyō* residences in the city. The Edo spirit was proverbially spendthrift and extravagant. "Do not have any money on which the sun has set," was said to have been the motto of the *Edokko.*

The economy of Kyōto and Osaka had quite another basis, however, and this was reflected in a somewhat different spirit among the merchants of those towns. Ōsaka was the great trade center of Japan. Products from many provinces—rice, oil, cotton, *sake,* medicine, etc.—passed through its houses of commerce. It was indeed "the kitchen of the empire." Kyōto was a great center of fine handicrafts and its products were sold all over Japan. The merchants of the Kyōto-Ōsaka area were noted for their methodical, steady and honest way of life in contrast to the merchants of Edo.[15]

The differences in the economies of the two areas are real enough and if the differences in popular stereotype reflect some actual differences in attitude, then it can be seen that the Kyōto-Ōsaka area was a more favorable ground for the inauguration of such a movement as Shingaku than Edo would have been.

If, as indicated above, the objective conditions of Baigan's era and locality were not unfavorable for the inauguration of a new religious movement which stressed an intense piety and ethical rigorism, it must not be concluded that he met with no difficulties. To many people the very idea that an old *bantō* of a merchant house would suddenly call himself a philosopher and start lecturing to all and sundry was ludicrous in the extreme. Baigan was the disciple of no recognized teacher and belonged to no known school or sect. He was not a priest nor did he have either wealth or position. He humbly claimed to be unlearned and poor in literary style and there were many who leaped to agree with him. He himself tells us in the opening pages of *Seikaron* that many people criticized him, some praised him to his face but laughed at him behind his back, many said that such an unlearned person was not fit to teach others. Further, he tells us that there were those who said he did not compose his own lectures but merely repeated without understanding lectures that he had heard previously.[16] We may even detect a lingering echo of sarcasm from the modern writer Watsuji Tetsurō when he refers to Baigan as a *bantō* of a clothing shop who believed he had been able to grasp the meaning of the sages directly through his own experience.[17] The world largely viewed him as a madman, heretic or ignoramus or else they ignored him as a person without merit and with no following.

In spite of such difficulties and abuse Baigan persevered. Forsaking any desire for fame or fortune he stood by his intention to teach the Way, even if he had to stand on the street corner to do it. Gradually, as we have seen above, he began to gain a hearing and attract disciples but it is clear that had he not had the greatest perseverance the discouragement of his first reception would have overwhelmed him. He had, as we shall see in the next section, a doctrine peculiarly attractive to the city classes of his time. But without the greatest efforts on his part no one would ever have heard it. His success was no easy victory but earned at the greatest cost, and we must admire his fortitude in being willing to pay the price.

On the other hand, it would be difficult to call his life tragic or heroic. He avoided politics and so never brought on himself the ire of the *bakufu,* as did, for example, Yamaga Sokō or Kumazawa Banzan, both of whom were exiled in their later years. Though meeting in many ways a hostile reception at first, he never underwent the savage persecution which has been the lot of so many founders of religions. His life, as it were, is painted in subdued tones. It is largely free of the more intense hues. But if one is willing to look closely there is much to respect and not a little to admire.

The Thought of Ishida Baigan

Any discussion of Baigan's thought must depend largely on the two books which he published, the *Toimondō* and the *Seikaron.* Some additional information may be derived from his biography, the *Ishida Sensei Jiseki* compiled by his pupils, but this is largely given over to an account of his life, his habits, and various anecdotes. Neither *Toimondō* nor *Seikaron* give anything like a connected exposition of doctrine. *Toimondō* is really a collection of dialogues, as has been noted above, and doctrinal matters are always treated in the special context of the question at hand. *Seikaron* is almost entirely concerned with practical matters and, though of great interest for his ethical teaching, is only occasionally revealing as to his philosophical and religious ideas. As a result of this situation an attempt to discuss Baigan's thought at all systematically is extremely difficult. One must rely on very short remarks scattered through a mass of quite concrete conversation, often contradictory, and not infrequently obscure. In addition to the textual problems some of the difficulty must be attributed to Baigan's thought itself. It tends toward a monism in which everything—heaven, earth, man, mind, things, nature, principle—is equated. Terms are difficult to pin down and seem to keep slipping into each other. Discourse often proceeds by association of words rather than by logical progression. And in the final analysis words, for Baigan, cannot transmit the truth anyway and his advice to the perplexed was to go quietly and meditate. Nevertheless we shall attempt to give as coherent an explication of his thought as possible.

A consideration of the concept of *gakumon* will project us into the center of Baigan's system. Literally the word means study or learning or scholarship, but here the meaning is much broader. This broader meaning was already present, as we shall see, in Mencius, and it is relatively clear that the most profound single influence on Baigan's thought was Mencius.

We may distinguish two main directions of process covered by the term *gakumon*. One is that leading to enlightenment (*kenshō*), to "knowing the nature" or "knowing the heart." The other is the ethical practice following from that enlightenment or knowledge. There is a sense in which the first, to use Tillich's term, "vertical" direction is primary and the second "horizontal" direction is consequent, and quotes can be extracted to support this view. However, there are also other interpretations of the relations between these two processes which can be supported from the text. One of these makes knowledge and action (Chinese *chih* and *hsing*) identical. The two processes are not really two but one. The other makes ethical behavior a condition for and part of the process of gaining enlightenment. Though logically these various positions may seem contradictory, I do not think they would have been felt to be so by Baigan or his disciples. Each position is an aspect of the truth. Each is true and yet the others are also true. There is a sense in which his mission was to bring other men to the happiness of enlightenment, of union with heaven and earth. There is also a sense in which practice, ethical action, always retained primacy.

Let us first examine *gakumon* in relation to the "vertical" process. Baigan says, "Knowing the heart (*kokoro,* Chinese *hsin*) is the beginning of *gakumon,*" and "Knowing the nature (*sei,* Chinese *hsing*) is the essence of *gakumon,*"[18] and "Attaining (*uru*) the heart is the beginning and end of *gakumon.*"[19] This view may be seen as based on Mencius, whom Baigan quotes,[20] "The way of *gakumon* is nothing other than seeking the lost heart."[21]

Gakumon, which is so closely linked with the vertical or religious-mystical process, is just as closely linked with the horizontal or practical-ethical process. "The *gakumon* of the sages is to know that action (*okonai*) is the basis (*moto*) and literature (*bungaku*) is the trimmings (*shiyō*)."[22] For a rather complete spelling out of the practical action implied above we have the following:

> As for the way of *gakumon,* firstly behave prudently (*mi o tsutsushimi*), serve your lord with righteousness and serve your parents with love, treat your friends with faithfulness, love men at large and have pity on poor people. Though you have merit, do not be proud. Maintain economy with respect to such things as clothing, furniture and the like and do not seek elegance. Do not neglect the family business, and as for wealth, measure what comes in and be aware of what goes out. Obey the laws and govern the family. The way of *gakumon* is roughly thus.[23]

Though Baigan stresses spiritual or ethical action as the meaning of *gakumon,* he does not entirely ignore the more narrow meaning of study or scholarship. He compares the heart to a mirror and considers writings as a polisher to polish the heart. He very often used classical texts as the basis of his lectures. However, when asked whether *gakumon* were anything other than reading books he replied,

> Indeed it is in reading books. However, if one reads the books and does not know the heart of the books, it is not called *gakumon.* The books of the sages contain their own heart. Knowing their heart is called *gakumon.* However, one who only knows the characters, because this is a skill, is called a person skilled in characters [rather than a scholar (*gakusha*)].[24]

It is the heart of the sages which one must unite with. In the last analysis their words are but the dregs which may even obstruct the effort to know their heart. The knowledge of the heart is not something that can be transmitted in words but must be discovered for oneself. This is true *gakumon.*

Taking this view of *gakumon,* even the illiterate can attain it. In *Seikaron* he gives examples of illiterate peasants who performed heroic acts of filial piety.[25] These peasants who cannot read are more truly scholars (*gakusha*) in Baigan's sense than are the learned Confucian specialists in characters who do not know the heart.

We have frequently used the phrases "know the heart" or "know the nature," but what do these terms really mean in Baigan's thought? He says, "The highest aim of *gakumon* is to exhaust one's heart and know one's nature. Knowing one's nature one knows heaven."[26] The seventh book of Mencius opens, "He who has exhausted his heart knows his nature. Knowing his nature, he knows heaven."[27] Knowing heaven, at least for Baigan, means that one's own heart is united with the heart of heaven and earth. He tells us that heaven and earth create all things and all things are in their hearts united with heaven and earth.

> However, being darkened by human desires, this heart is lost. Consequently when we speak of exhausting the heart and returning to the heart of heaven and earth, we are saying to seek the lost heart. If one seeks and attains it, one becomes the heart of heaven and earth. When one says, "becomes the heart of heaven and earth," one says, "without a heart (*mushin*)." Though heaven and earth are without a heart, the four seasons progress and all things are produced. The sage attains the heart of heaven and earth and is entirely without his own heart. Though it is as though there is no heart, benevolence, righteousness, propriety and wisdom all operate. When one is suddenly penetrated doubts are cleared up at one stroke.[28]

It is clear from the above that the union of one's own heart and the heart of heaven and earth is a phrase indicating some sort of mystical experience. We have already seen that Baigan and many of his pupils went through such an experience. As in mysticism generally, what is indicated is some dissolution of the boundary between self and nonself, one becomes united with the universe. This union is accompanied by a feeling of great happiness and tranquility but also with a great feeling of power.

> The good person (*jinsha*) makes his heart united with heaven and earth and all things. There is nothing which can be said not to be

himself. If he makes heaven and earth and all things himself, there is nothing which he cannot attain. If one does not know the heart, there is a difference between oneself and heaven and earth. . . . This is like a sick man with paralyzed hands and feet. The sage penetrates heaven and earth and all things with his own heart.[29]

The experience in question after all cannot be conveyed in words so we may rest content with the dim idea of it which may be derived from the above quotes. It is possible to say more, however, about the process by which one comes to this experience. In essence this process involves getting rid of that which obscures the heart which is identical with the heart of heaven and earth. What is doing the obscuring is called the human heart or the selfish heart or the desirous heart. Baigan uses simply the one word heart (*kokoro,* also translated "mind") on most occasions to indicate what is being obscured, which leads to some terminological complications. Teshima Toan, his pupil, solved this difficulty by using the term *honshin,* which means basic heart or original heart or true heart in contrast to the selfish or desirous heart. One can then say that it is one's true heart which is being obscured by one's selfish heart. At any rate the point is to eliminate the selfish heart. The selfish heart which contains human desires is constantly being aroused by external things. These desires keep the true heart clouded and it cannot be known until they are eliminated. There are several ways to eliminate them.

First, and the most formal, is the practice of meditation. One "exhausts the heart" and then one "knows the nature." This exhausting the heart had with the Sung Confucians already become a clearly defined technique. Baigan calls it *kufu* or *seiza. Kufu* implies the expenditure of effort and *seiza* simply means quiet sitting. What is involved is a sort of concentration of the will. Words and all external things are as much as possible abandoned. Baigan's technique of meditation was, in fact, strongly influenced by that of the Zen sect of Buddhism.

A second way in which the selfish heart and its desires can be eliminated is through the practice of asceticism. As we have already noted, Baigan did not go in for extremes in this respect. He did, however, live with a good deal of what one could safely call austerity. He tells us that he ate sparingly and did his own cooking for many years in an effort to exhaust his heart and eliminate a desirous heart.[30] Whereas the practice of meditation was clearly a religious exercise divorced from daily life, it is obvious that asceticism as advocated by Baigan blended easily into and reinforced the practical frugality which characterized the merchant and peasant ethics.

Finally, the selfish heart was to be eliminated by devotion to one's obligations and occupation. Here it is clear that the religious drive toward the elimination of the selfish heart and the attainment of the true heart served to reinforce loyalty, filial piety and a devotion to hard work in one's calling. The emphasis here is on the elimination of selfishness, of putting self before others.

Here then we have a "this-worldly mysticism." Though the practice of mediation might seem a retreat from the world, Baigan did not mean it to be so. He himself continued to live a busy life in society and expected his pupils to do so. One did not retreat to the wilderness to practice meditation, one simply utilized one's spare time and retired to the rear of the shop. Further, one's daily practice of economy and frugality and one's devotion to diligent work were not alien to the religious life. Rather they were aids in the attainment of enlightenment. The this-worldly, practical, ethical nature of this apparently mystical doctrine of "knowing the heart" becomes apparent when we examine what the results of such knowledge were suposed to be.

> Sometimes the mind of man is enlightened. By means of this the Way is propagated. The comprehending heart is the substance (*tai*). The great relations of man are the function (*yō*). The substance is established and the function operates. These functions are the relation of lord and follower, father and child, man and wife, older and younger brother, friend and friend. The good heart of benevolence, righteousness, propriety and wisdom is the heart which puts into practice these five relations.[31]

Here we see that the result of knowing the heart is that one knows intuitively the complete naturalness of the received morality. We may recall Baigan's feelings at the time of his first enlightenment: "The way of Yao and Shun is only filial piety and brotherliness. Fish swim in water and birds fly in the sky." Enlightenment is "knowing nature" and it is becoming clearer what nature is:

> When we speak of nature (*sei*, Chinese *hsing*) it is that principle which everything from man to the birds and plants receives from

heaven and whereby they develop. . . . Observing the progressions of last year's seasons, we know those of this year. Looking at the things of yesterday, we know today. This so-called looking at the past is what we call knowing the nature of the world. When we know the nature [we see that] the way of the five virtues and the five relationships are contained within it. The *Chung Yung* says, "What heaven has decreed is called the nature. Following the nature is called the way."[32] To follow the nature without knowing the nature cannot be.[33]

Nature is that which makes everything what it is. It is the nature of grass to be green. It is the nature of man to have the five relations. "If one knows the nature, then the way to act is easy."[34] Knowing the nature can partly be taught from books and from observing the past. But this is not the knowledge that really counts. When one knows not externally but intuitively then one becomes united with the heart of the sages and of heaven and earth. One knows intuitively that the received morality is inherently natural, and one can act in accordance with it without the least hesitation or doubt. Thus action is the result of Baigan's mysticism. The result of enlightenment is not nirvana or any form of withdrawal from the world. Rather it is complete whole-hearted and unconflicted action in accordance with morality. It will be the task of the rest of this section to determine what Baigan understood that morality to be. Only when we have a clear idea of that will all the implications of the religious teachings become clear. But before moving to that discussion I would like to underline with a couple of quotes just how clearly Baigan saw the relation of his mystical teaching to his ethical teaching.

Mr. Yukifuji asked, "In instructing your pupils, do you teach making the mind (*kokoro*) the whole of it?"

Our teacher replied, saying, "It is not thus. I teach by means of conduct."

Mr. Yukifuji inquired, "If it is thus, then do you teach making the five relations the whole of it?"

Our teacher replied, "It is so."[35]

Here we see the ethical concern taking clear primacy. The following quote indicates that Baigan realized that the mystical aspect of his teaching could become an end in itself and divert away from morality:

Our teacher, speaking to a pupil who had come to know his nature, said, "What learning (*gaku*) creates is that one reflects on righteousness and unrighteousness so that one will only follow righteousness. To cultivate the nature without accumulating righteousness is not the Way of the sages." He often made his point.[36]

The discussion up to this point, I think, is sufficient to show that Shingaku as taught by Ishida Baigan is an excellent example of the second type of religious action discussed in Chapter III. As opposed to *Bushidō,* Shinshū, and Hōtoku,[37] all of which have a primary emphasis on *on* and thus are examples of the first type of religious action, Shingaku has a primary emphasis on union with deity, or with the "ground of being." In Chapter III it was suggested that Mencius was the source of that long tradition of "ethical mysticism" in the Far East and it is clear that Shingaku belongs squarely in that tradition. If a case is to be made for the motivation arising from religious action of this type being favorable to economic rationalization, as is being done in these pages, the reader may well ask, "Then why not in China?" This is not the place to go fully into this question, but here we may suggest two differences from China which may help to explain the contrast. In the first place, this religious tradition in China was the almost exclusive property of the literati, the gentry official, class. Even within that class it was probably not cultivated seriously except by rather small circles of intellectuals. Shingaku in Japan, however, adapted this religious tradition to the needs of the merchant class and gained for it a wide currency there. To my knowledge there was no development in China even remotely comparable to this. It is clear that the possibilities for effects on the economy of a religious ethic are very different if that ethic is held by broad sections of the merchant class or if it is the property of a small group of intellectuals. Secondly, and I think more basically, the actual content of the ethic to which one is committed by religious action of the Mencius tradition is treated largely as given, and therefore has a certain degree of independence from the specifically religious framework. But it is clear that what is assumed as given in China is not necessarily the same as what is assumed as given in Japan. There may be overlap of terms and concepts between them, but there are also important differences of emphasis and even of basic values. In a word, Japanese ethical values, when receiving the reinforcement of religious motivation, may have quite different implications than Chinese ethical values receiving the same religious reinforcement.

Though Shingaku can safely be categorized in the second type of religious action, this is not to say that the concept of *on* is absent. In strictly ethical passages it occurs frequently. It is not, however, often found in a specifically religious context. That is, religious action is not seen as a requital of the *on* received from heaven and earth, as for example, Hōtoku tends to view it. Religious action is rather the attempt to destroy the selfish heart and unite with the heart of heaven and earth.

At times Baigan abandons the Confucian terminology of "heaven and earth," the "nature," etc., and speaks directly of the worship of Amaterasu. He says she should be venerated as the ancestress of Japan and that her decrees should be submitted to.[38] However, this Shintō aspect of his teaching is integrated into his religious thought at the philosophical level. He sees the good person as united with the heart of Amaterasu, which I am sure was not for him different from the heart of heaven and earth. Baigan tended to put the worship of Amaterasu first and to consider Buddhism and Confucianism as secondary aids. This is interesting from an ideological point of view, but philosophically it has little meaning. Basically his thought is Confucian and when he compares the different religious traditions it is, in fact, to find them united on philosophical fundamentals. Shintō was by no means the source of those fundamentals, however much of them it had absorbed by Baigan's day.

Keeping the above discussion of his religious position in mind we may now turn to a discussion of Baigan's ethical thought. As a basis for this we must consider his views on the nature of society and particularly of Japanese society.

> The gods of our land have received it from Izanagi no Mikoto and Izanami no Mikoto. From the sun, moon, and stars to the ten thousand things, they rule over all. Since nothing is omitted, it is a unity and we call it the land of the gods. Here is a matter which should be meditated on. In China it is indeed different. In our country the line of the Sun Goddess continuously succeeding, holds the throne. Consequently one worships the Shrine of the Sun Goddess as ancestress. Since she is the ancestress of our heavenly ruler, even the common people make pilgrimages to her, calling it "*sangū*." In China it is not so.[39]

Here are, in rather clear form, the essentials of the idea of *kokutai,* of that politico-religious structure of Japan which sets it off from China and all other countries. Elsewhere he compares *kokuon* (blessings from the nation) to heaven and earth and says the brush is inadequate even to describe them.[40] He considers maintaining one's station, respecting superiors, governing the family, being economical and avoiding luxury, attending to the family business as ways in which one can return this *on*. These ideas of *kokutai* and *kokuon* provide the basic structure within which Baigan views society.

Before proceeding to discuss more specifically Baigan's ethical views, it might be of interest to summarize a conversation he had with a Zen Buddhist priest on the subject of killing living things, as it brings out certain general orientations of his.[41] The priest upholds the prohibition on killing living things but Baigan tells him this is a Hinayana rule and not a Mahayana rule and that many priests, especially Zen priests, have killed things. The priest asserts that it most definitely is a Buddhist law and furthermore it is a Confucian precept as well, namely the Confucian virtue of benevolence (*jin,* Chinese *jen*). Baigan replies by defining benevolence as the virtue of love (*jiai*) and being without a selfish heart. Cutting off the self is one of the chief teachings of Buddhism. It is a law of the world that some things must be cut off so that others can strive. The strong feed on the weak. Baigan asserts that even monks eat rice, which is living, and pests must be killed if rice is to grow. If the priests really adhered to their rule they would starve. In summary he says, "The heavenly way (*tendō*) produces all things, and nourishes its living things with its living things."[42] "It is the way of heaven that the noble eat the humble."[43] "You should know to use the humble for the sake of the noble. For example, the lord is the noble and the retainer is the humble. The humble retainer gives himself for the noble lord and accepts death."[44]

Here we see the broadest metaphysical underpinning to the idea of selfless devotion. Natural law and the doctrine of the destruction of the selfish heart are both mobilized to support it. A somewhat more detailed picture of the role of the "retainer" is given in the section on the Way of the Warrior (*bushi no michi*) in *Toimondō:*

> First of all a person serving a lord is generally called "retainer." "Retainer" is explained as "pulled." His heart is always pulled to the lord.[45]
>
> The retainer's rice and soup is a stipend granted by the lord. Without it how could he sustain life? Therefore he substitutes his own body for the body of his lord and does not reflect on his own person as much as dew or dust. This is the Way of the retainer.[46]

This description of the "retainer" takes on pointed significance when we consider Baigan's famous idea that not the *samurai* alone are "retainers." Farmers are the "retainers" of the countryside and merchants and artisans are the "retainers" of the city streets. All alike are to serve with equal devotion. Each fulfills his appointed task for the common end. Here indeed is the organic view of society discussed at the beginning of the preceding chapter, but here it is clearly not an organic view in which system maintenance is primary. Rather it is that specifically Japanese view of society in which goal-attainment values are dominant.

The function of the *samurai* is to help the ruler to govern and to serve as a prototype of the retainer, as is indicated in the above quote. As for the farmer,

> . . . he goes out to the fields in the morning before dawn and returns home in the evening by starlight. . . . In spring he ploughs, in summer he weeds and in the fall he harvests, never forgetting to produce as much as possible from the fields, even to a single grain of rice.[47]

The artisan produces his handicrafts and the merchant carries on trade. Each exhausts himself for the sake of all. In this respect all classes are alike.

> Although the *samurai,* farmers, artisans and merchants differ in occupation, since they all appreciate the same principle (*ichiri*) if we speak of the Way of the *samurai* (*samurai no michi*), it goes for the farmers, artisans and merchants, and if we speak of the Way of the farmers, artisans and merchants, it goes for the *samurai.*[48]

Basing himself on this conception of society Baigan makes an impassioned defense of the merchant class which is so famous and so important that it must be quoted at length:

> If there were no trade, the buyer would have nothing to buy and the seller could not sell. If it were thus, the merchants would have no livelihood and would become farmers and artisans. If the merchants all became farmers and artisans, there would be no one to circulate wealth and all the people would suffer. The *samurai,* farmers, artisans and merchants are of assistance in governing the empire. If the four classes were lacking, there would be no assistance. The governing of the four classes is the role of the ruler. Assisting the ruler is the role of the four classes. The *samurai* is the retainer (*shin*) who has rank from old. The farmer is the retainer of the countryside. The merchant and artisan are retainers of the town. To assist the ruler, as retainers, is the Way of the retainer. The trade of the merchants assists the empire. The payment of the price is the stipend (*roku*) of the artisan. Giving the harvest to the farmer is like the stipend of the *samurai.* Without the output of all the classes of the empire, how could it stand? The profit of the merchant too is a stipend permitted by the empire. To call this, which is only the profit of your own trade, greedy and immoral is to hate the merchants and wish for their destruction. Why hate and despise only the merchants? As for your saying not to give a profit for trade, if one pays and deducts the profit it will destroy the laws of the empire. As business is ordered from above, profit is received. Thus the profit of the merchant is like a permitted stipend. . . . As for the Way of the *samurai* also, if he does not receive a stipend, he is not fit for service. If one calls receiving a stipend from one's lord "greedy" and "immoral," then from Confucius and Mencius on down there is not a man who is moral [knows the Way]. What sort of thing is it to say, leaving *samurai,* farmers and artisans aside, that the merchants' receiving a stipend is "greed" and that they cannot know the way?[49]

In this statement Baigan is clearly assimilating the merchants to the model of the *samurai.* He insists that their function is to be of assistance to the empire and that the profit they receive is but the just reward for their services, comparable to the stipend of the *samurai.* It is this statement and others similar to it that those writers who have seen in Baigan an "antifeudal" tendency usually cite. Actually it is clear that the statement implies not a rejection of the *samurai* class or the *samurai* ethic but an insistence that the merchant class model itself on that ethic. Clearly Baigan is claiming a status honor for the merchant class which many contemporaries were denying it, and doing so in intense emotional terms. But he is claiming it on the basis of the fact that the merchants did embody a *samurai*-like ethic, the Way of the retainer. Baigan was an ardent champion of the merchant class, but his advocacy was based entirely on a strong affirmation of the dominant values of his society, not on a rejection or even a criticism of them.

I do not mean at all to underestimate the importance of Baigan's defence of the merchant class. The insistence that the merchant class had a legitimate place within the *kokutai,* that it could embody the central values of loyalty, selfless devotion, and so forth, was of the greatest importance in helping to remove the stigma from economic activity. Though it was not until Meiji that this stigma was effectively removed, the arguments used then are exactly those of Baigan: the pursuit of trade and industry is a form of loyalty to the realm and thus honorable for *samurai* or anyone else.

It might be well to see what Baigan was up against by quoting a few Tokugawa writers on the merchant class. Yamagata Hantō (1746–1821) wrote:

> It should be the first aim of administration to treat townspeople badly and to treat the farmers with special favor. . . . It is good government to encourage agriculture and discourage commerce and industry, with a view to causing the decline of urban districts. When towns are prosperous, the provinces decline and vice versa. This is the natural order of things.[50]

Hayashi Shihei said, "The *chōnin* are quite useless; they simply batten on the stipends of the *samurai.* They are indeed a good-for-nothing lot."[51] Takano Shōseki had this to say: "Merchants deserve the name of idlers. They are people who live on foodstuffs produced by others and they wear clothes manufactured by others. They are like parasites."[52]

Other writers were not so extreme in their condemnation, but still considered the merchants as of low moral standing. Yamaga Sokō, for instance, felt that merchants were indispensable, but not worthy of respect because, "They only know profit and do not know righteousness. They only care about profiting themselves."[53]

Though such writers as those quoted above do represent an important trend in Tokugawa thought and one that Baigan did a valuable service for the development of the economy in combatting, they by no means represent the only attitude on the subject. Many other writers, some of them Confucians of *samurai* origin, were closer to Baigan in their views than they were to the detractors of the merchants.

For example, Miura Baien (1723–1789) wrote:

> Farmers produce millet, rice, mulberry and hemp to feed and clothe others as well as themselves. Artisans manufacture articles necessary in daily life, thereby mitigating the discomforts of existence. Merchants distribute rice, barley, fabrics, etc., produced by farmers and the articles and tools manufactured by artisans so that all the people may have their wants supplied.[54]

Motoori Noringa, who was himself of merchant stock, wrote, "Merchants are indispensable in trade. The more merchants there are, the better for the state and the public at large."[55] And finally we may quote Kaihō Seiryō (1755–1817) who, if anything, goes Baigan one better:

> To sell rice is nothing more or less than a commercial transaction. It may therefore be said that all the people, from the feudal lords of the great provinces down, are in a sense engaged in commerce. . . . Commerce is absolutely indispensable in daily life, hence it is wrong to despise money or hold commerce in contempt.
>
> There is nothing shameful about selling things. What is shameful is the conduct of men who fail to pay their debts to merchants.[56]

Baigan, as has been noted above, takes as a model for the *chōnin* ethic that of the *samurai*. He is quite explicit on this point: "He who ought to be the model for the men of the world is the samurai."[57] "For everything, as a shining model, one should make the samurai a law."[58] Out of such thinking comes a very important principle embodied, for example, in the following quotation:

> When one says "the way of the merchant" how can it differ from the way of the *samurai*, farmer or artisan? Mencius said, there is only one way. *Samurai*, farmer, artisan and merchant are each creatures of heaven. In heaven are there two ways?[59]

In such a statement it is not hard to see a strong element of universalism. Of course Baigan would say that it is in principle (*ri*, Chinese *li*) that all are the same while in form (*kei*, Chinese *hsing*) they differ. Form means concretely occupation and Baigan does not question the principle of inherited occupational classes (though he indeed moved from one to another). Even with these limitations the universalistic element remains considerable. It is an important aspect of his teaching on profit, honesty and frugality.

As we have already seen, Baigan refuses to allow any special stigma to be attached to the profit of the merchant. For example, he says,

> Obtaining profit from sale is the Way of the merchant. I have not heard selling at cost called the Way. . . . The merchant's profit from sale is like the *samurai*'s stipend. No profit from sale would be like the *samurai* serving without a stipend.[60]

Not taking a profit is not the Way of the merchant.[61] The merchant's function from of old has been "to take what is in excess and exchange it for what is lacking,"[62] and it is thus a service for the empire. "The master of wealth is the people of the empire."[63] The merchants are merely the clerks for the empire. The wealth is not theirs, they are but stewards. A just reward for their services is, however, perfectly permissible. By assimilating merchants to the role of retainer and equating profit to the stipend of the *samurai* Baigan gave a moral justification to the merchant occupation and to the profit derived from it. His theory served to tie the economy in to the central political values in a peculiarly close way. The implications of this step for economic rationalization were enormous though the full effect of them would not be felt until after Meiji. With respect to this developing ideological position Baigan must be seen as only one of many contributors, even if an important and symptomatic one.

Though Baigan gives a powerful justification to the idea of profit he at the same time has very strong ideas as to what is a just profit and as to the evils of unjust profit. It is with respect to this problem primarily that he discusses the importance of honesty (*shōjiki*), though this universalistic value had the widest significance in his thought. While taking an honest profit will lead to prosperity, taking an unjust one will lead to ruin:

> Merchants, if they are ignorant of the Way of the sages, in making money make it unrighteously, and will cause their descendants to be

cut off. If they really love their descendants they will study the Way, and cause them to prosper.[64]

Here it is apparent that Baigan was not unfamiliar with the idea that honesty is the best policy. This is even more evident in the following:

> Trickery, even though it may bring immediate profit, will inevitably bring on the punishment of the gods. As for honesty, though there may be no immediate benefit, it is Amaterasu's reward that it will receive heaven's compassion in the end. If you become a criminal to the gods, you will have no place to live. You will be unable to live in the broad world, and to live confined is a sad thing. . . . But if one practices honesty and is not disjointed in heart, one can live in the broad dwelling space of the limitless world, and have profound happiness. What I teach is to cause you to escape the difficulties of the cheat and thief, and cause you to be called an honest man. If you become responsive to the mirror-like mind of the gods will it not be joyous?[65]

We may quote the following to give an idea of the sort of dishonesty Baigan was inveighing against. This is concerned with "double profit" which he strongly condemned:

> If a piece of silk or a strip of *obi* is short an inch or two the weaver will mention that it is short and lower the price. However, the merchant sells it at the price of a regular piece disregarding the inch or two short and takes the profit of the reduced price himself. Taking the profit just as if the size were accurate is taking a double profit. . . . Moreover, if a piece of goods is misdyed the merchant makes a small thing large and reduces the price thus hurting the dyer. He receives the full price of the goods from the one who has ordered it, but he does not pass this on to the dyer. This is even worse than a double profit.[66]

Honesty for Baigan not only means taking a just profit, it also means paying one's debts and having respect for property. In *Seikaron* he recounts the advice he gave to a Kantō merchant who was nearly wiped out in a bad flood.[67] The merchant asked Baigan's advice. His own records were lost so he could not collect the debts owed him. What should he do about the debts he owed? Baigan advised him to sell everything he still possessed even to stripping himself naked, and repay his debts. Such an exemplary display of honesty would cause his debtors to respect him and take pity on him, aiding him to re-establish himself. With such a reputation for honesty he would be sure to prosper. Stated somewhat more abstractly and with a strong universalistic underpinning, here is Baigan's theory of property and debts:

> Since the people have been sent down from heaven, they are all children of heaven. Because of this an individual is a small heaven and earth. Being a small heaven and earth he basically lacks selfish desires. For this reason my things are my things. Another's things are another's things. What is lent is received and what is borrowed is returned. Unselfishly doing what one ought, even to the smallest hair, this is honesty. If this honesty is practiced, the world would be harmonized in unity. All within the four seas would be like brothers.[68]

Baigan's conception of economy is closely connected to and in a sense based on honesty:

> How can one talk of economy with respect to the four classes separately? What one calls economy is not a special matter. It leads back to inherent honesty.[69]

In its broadest sense "honesty" (*shōjiki*) means for Baigan correct and upright behavior, and especially behavior in accordance with one's situation. Extravagance is always relative to one's position but it is always wrong, whether practiced by ruler or merchant. "Economy" (*kenyaku*) is always in accordance with one's proper situation and thus is an expression of honesty. He recounts how the last ruler of the Yin dynasty in China ruined himself and lost his kingdom due to his excessive extravagance and luxury.[70] Drawing the moral from this he says,

> Although there are high and low, the principle which raises up families and destroys families is one. Extravagance easily grows with time. It is something one must fear and be cautious about.[71]

Though economy is a universal principle Baigan is chiefly interested in its application to the merchant class. He says,

> In looking over conditions in the world in general, there is nothing which decays so easily as a *chōnin* family. If you seek the cause of this, it is an illness called foolishness. This foolishness quickly becomes extravagance. Though foolishness and extravagance are two, we must say that they are hard to distinguish.[72]

He advises strong measures to cut down on expenditures for food, clothing, furniture and the like in *chōnin* families. Someone accused him of spreading contention in the world by upsetting people's customary habits and causing arguments and bitterness within families. To this Baigan replies that contention is sometimes necessary and not inevitably bad. He points out that one administers moxa cautery to a misbehaved child, though the child screams and writhes. The institution of rigid economy in the family may cause disputes but it also will have a good effect in the end.[73]

Baigan places economy in the largest moral context and praises it as the basis of benevolence (*jin,* Chinese *jen*). If one is poor one cannot help other people. Only if one has a sufficiency of material goods can one be really charitable.

One of the themes on which Baigan is most insistent is knowing one's occupation and practicing it diligently. For example, he says, "If you do not know occupation, you are inferior to birds and beasts. The dog protects the gate and the cock informs us of the time. . . . If as merchants we do not know our occupation, we shall come near the destruction of the family which our ancestors have transferred to us."[74] Again he says, "If we know righteousness (*gi,* Chinese *i*) how can there be an inclination to neglect our occupation?"[75] One's occupation is what heaven has decreed. It is the basis of one's service to one's nation and its ruler and it is the basis for continuing the family. It is within the context of occupation that a just profit, honesty and economy have meaning.

It is quite clear that the idea of occupation (*shokubun*) is closely linked to the central values of loyalty and filial piety. It is in Baigan's ethical thought perhaps the primary means by which loyalty and filial piety are expressed. We need not quote here the many remarks Baigan has to make on the subject of loyalty and filial piety as they do not differ substantially from the general Tokugawa thought on these subjects, which by now should be quite familiar to the reader. We may only note here that Baigan quite explicitly equates the polity and the family in ways which have been already discussed in detail in this book. For example, he compares the head of the family among the common people to the *samurai,* the governing officials of the nation.[76] And in *Toimondō* he says the following: "From the point of view of the wife and children, the head of the house is like a lord. Thus both you and your mother are like retainers."[77] He goes on to say that it is correct for retainers to exhaust their bodies in the service of the lord.

Thus our discussion of Baigan's social and ethical teaching has brought us full round. It was with a description of society as based on the lord-follower relation that we began and it is with that relation as fulfilling the sum of moral virtues that we end. Here then is the kernel of the received morality which the enlightened person who is free from selfish desires and united with the heart of heaven and earth will find perfectly natural and will perform without the least hesitation or doubt. In understanding the social implications of the Shingaku movement we must emphasize both the religious and the ethical aspects. Each is necessary if we are to really understand the meaning of the other. If we looked only at Baigan's mysticism we would not see the great implications for social action which become clear when we view the ethical imperatives which that mysticism implies. If we looked only at the ethical teaching, we could say that it was an interesting sort of exhortation but we would understand little of the intense motivation to fulfill these exhortations which the religious teaching aroused. It is the religious aspect which appealed to all the deep inner needs of troubled people for salvation from their misery. This religious appeal reaches to the profoundest depths of human motivation. It is the linking of such motivation as this—of the weary for succor, of the troubled for repose, of the guilty for absolution—to the fulfillment of certain practical, ethical duties in the world which gives that ethic a dynamism which it could never have if it were mere exhortation.

Although my knowledge of the later Shingaku movement is fragmentary and I cannot speak with the assurance that I feel about Baigan, it is my strong impression that the later movement remained quite close to the teaching which we have discussed in this chapter. There have been those who have claimed that Baigan was primarily concerned with enlightenment and ideology whereas the later teachers were concerned with indoctrination and religion. I have tried to show above that Baigan's chief motivation was always religious and not ideological so that this contrast is meaningless to me. What is meant by enlightenment as opposed to indoctrination seems to be that later writers were not as explicit in their defense of the merchant class and its profit, but talked in general religious and ethical terms. This is an important but I think not a basic difference as I shall try to show below.

The Later Shingaku Movement

We may here briefly survey the institutional growth and history of Shingaku as a social movement and discuss the teaching of the school in the later period.

It is to Teshima Toan (1718–1786)[78] that the Shingaku[79] movement was indebted for that great leadership and organizational ability which are necessary if a new religious movement born out of the inner struggles of its founder is to find institutional stability. Baigan himself is reputed to have called Toan the "Mencius" of his school, but we might even more accurately compare him to Paul. He was born in Kyōto of a wealthy merchant family. His father had literary interests and encouraged his son in like pursuits. At the age of 18 he became a pupil of Baigan and in a little over two years, in 1738, Toan attained enlightenment. He studied under Baigan for 10 years until Baigan's death when Toan was 27. Not long after this he married and set up his own household.

Toan was a famous preacher, gathering crowds of great size so that his lecture room was always overflowing. In his writing he made considerable contributions to the development of Shingaku thought, mostly by giving a somewhat clearer explanation of Baigan's central ideas. We have already noted that the concept *honshin* (basic heart), which became a hallmark of later Shingaku teaching, was developed by Toan. But it is perhaps in his organizational efforts that he made the greatest impression on Shingaku. In his later years he dominated the entire movement, so much so that it was often called Teshima-gaku. In reviewing below Toan's contributions to the organization of Shingaku, we will also be sketching the formal structure of the movement as it was to continue from Toan's time on down.

Toan began to lecture in 1760. In 1765 he changed his residence and using part of his new residence as a lecture hall, he called it Gorakusha. This was the first Shingaku *kōsha,* and was to be followed by more than 180 others. Toan and his pupils founded in Kyōto three other *kōsha,* the Shūseisha in 1773, the Jishūsha in 1779, and the Merinsha in 1782, which came to be known as the *sansha.* These three *kōsha,* with the Meirinsha at their head, became the center of the later Shingaku world, and it was necessary to acquire the seal of the three *sha* (*sansha inkan*) if one was to reach the highest orders of the movement.

By the time of Toan's death there were 22 *kōsha* in 14 provinces. The organizational structure of these institutions was largely determined by him and it might be well to sketch that structure at this point.[80] We may first give a brief physical description of the *kōsha* itself. The *kōsha* was usually a rather simple building 25 to 30 mats in width. A large part of it was taken up by the lecture hall. In the center of this was a *tokonoma* usually containing some auspicious motto. Above and to the right of this was a small shrine to Amaterasu, and above and to the left the likeness of the master of the *kōsha,* the *shashu.* The preaching (*kōshaku* or *dōwa*) took place in these halls and when there were a great many people present it was customary to have men and women sit separately with a screen separating them. Each *kōsha* without exception had a two-character name, usually drawn from some classical text.

The master of the *kōsha* usually lived in the building and managed its affairs as well as teaching. There were usually a number of students (*shonyu*) who lived in the *kōsha* practicing meditation and studying and receiving the guidance of the *shashu.*

Next to the *shashu* were a number of persons ranging from two or three to six or seven with the position of *tokō.* These officials had the job of assisting in the business of the house and aiding the *shashu* in teaching. They were chosen on the basis of the following qualifications: 1) permission of lord and parents; 2) not weighed down by the family business; 3) without family difficulties; 4) as many friends as possible; 5) an admirable character. This office did not require exceptional learning or saintly virtue, but could be held by any person who was devoted to meditation (*seiza*) and had common sense enough to carry on the business of the house. This post was in many senses the key administrative post in the movement and served to train those who later became prominent leaders in both administrative and educational tasks.[81]

The *hojinshi* and *kaiyūshi* were essentially assistants to the *tokō*. Their number was more variable than that of the *tokō* but the qualifications for the post were similar. Just as the *tokō* was an office which served as a training ground for higher posts, these offices provided training for those who would become *tokō*.[82]

The *kōshi* was a person who had the right to lecture and directly teach the more serious students. He had to be a person of wide learning and exemplary virtue. In selecting a *kōshi,* both his ability as a lecturer and his daily words and actions were very critically evaluated. These preachers were usually selected from the *tokō* or the *rōyu,* whom we will discuss shortly. They had to be persons who had attained enlightenment, and as proof of their rank were given seals (*inkan*) entitling them to preach in any *kōsha*. The *shashu* would ordinarily be a *kōshi,* but there were many *kōshi* who were not masters of *kōsha* but either attached themselves to one headed by another, or preached itinerantly. The *rōyu* was an official without fixed duties. He was rather an advanced and trusted student who might substitute for any of the other officials, even in preaching, if need be and aided the *shashu* in plans for the expansion of activities. As has been mentioned, this position could lead to that of *kōshi*. It might also be mentioned that the *tokō* likewise could substitute for the preacher on occasion.[83]

Though it is unlikely that either the very richest or the very poorest *chōnin* often entered the various offices of the Shingaku *kōsha,* nevertheless they were open to a broad stratum of people and drew from many occupations and levels of prosperity. The officials were supported by contributions from pupils and interested laymen often on the occasion of some religious festival. The standard of frugal living set by Baigan was maintained by his later disciples so that not a great deal was required. The Shingaku movement did not lack the support of very benevolent patrons who might be so generous as to supply a house and grounds for a *kōsha*.

Baigan laid down the essential teaching methods of the school, the lecture (*kōshaku* or *dōwa*) drawing alike from classical texts and everyday life and strongly ethical in tone; the question and answer meeting (*kaiho*) in which the more serious students aired their doubts and were questioned as to their understanding; and meditation (*seiza, kufu*), which consisted in moral self-examination and the attempt to attain enlightenment. The first two of these almost always took place in the *kōsha* (except for the lectures of itinerant preachers which might be held anywhere) and the last, meditation, was an important part of the training of the students living in the *kōsha*. All of these were continued and developed by Toan and his disciples and certain additional methods were adopted.

The *rinkō* and *kaidoku* were essentially reading circles.[84] A number of students gathered around one of the *kōshi* or *tokō* and undertook to read from a certain book. Each passage was in turn discussed by the pupils until an adequate idea of its meaning, with the help of the teacher, was reached. Further innovations of this period were the *zenkun* and *jokun*.[85] The *zenkun* was a class of instruction for young boys and girls between the ages of seven and fifteen. The *jokun* was a lecture for adult women. Both of these became very popular in later Shingaku. In the later period each *kōsha* came to celebrate three annual days of remembrance. These were the anniversary of the death of Baigan (9th month, 24th day), the anniversary of the death of Toan (2nd month, 9th day), and the anniversary of the death of the founder of that *kōsha*. On these days the picture of the man being remembered was displayed and a few simple offerings made. Though not elaborate these celebrations were taken with great seriousness.[86] In addition to its religious and educational activities, the *kōsha* was a center for charitable services. It helped to provide medicine for the sick, wet nurses for women who could not suckle, and in case of emergencies such as fire or flood, helped to organize relief for the destitute.

One interesting feature of Shingaku organization which is directly attributable to Toan is the issuance of a paper (*dansho*) which indicates that he who bears it has attained enlightenment.[87] At first these papers had to come from Kyōto and have Toan's signature to be valid. They were given out only three times a year and the occasion became a minor celebration in the *kōsha*. Very early Nakazawa Dōni (1725–1803) began to issue a similar paper from

Edo. Later, as the movement grew larger and began to suffer organizational splits such papers were issued from various centers. This practice began in the early 1780's and Ishikawa Ken tells us that from that time until about 1880 over 36,000 people received such certificates.[88] This is a most interesting figure as these certificates were not lightly issued but were given out only under the strictest supervision. To attain enlightenment required several years of intense study and meditation. Yet it was no small coterie who reached this rarified state. There is no way of estimating the number of interested students who failed to attain this advanced aim, and of course no way of judging how many people were more or less casually influenced by occasionaly attending a Shingaku lecture, but we may be safe in assuming that it was a large multiple of those who persevered to the end. All statements about the influence of Shingaku on the people must be based on inference, but here is a solid fact on which inference can be based. The *inkan* or seals which were issued to those authorized to teach in Shingaku *kōsha* and which have been mentioned above, were also issued from the same centers as the *dansho*. The maintenance of a monopoly of the issuance of these two kinds of certificates was certainly the strongest means whereby some sort of centralization was maintained in the movement.

After the time of Toan, when the organizational forms and teaching methods which have just been described were fully worked out, the movement continued to grow with great rapidity. By 1789 there were 34 *kōsha,* by 1795, 56, and in 1803 there were 80 in 25 different provinces. A number of preachers of great ability arose and commanded large audiences. One of the foremost of these was Nakazawa Dōni (1725–1803).[89] He became a pupil of Toan rather late in life and was sent by him to Edo in 1780. In 1781 he founded the Sanzensha in Edo, which was to be one of the most famous and most influential *kōsha* in Shingaku history. He was descended from a family of weavers and was in his early years a devout adherent of the Nichiren sect, and later studied with Zen masters. It is to this that the large influence of Buddhism in his teaching is attributed. Here we see an example of the fact that Baigan's syncretism tended to be somewhat unstable. While Dōni emphasized Buddhism some of the other later teachers emphasized Confucianism or Shintoism or even Taoism. Officially, of course, the school always respected all the three teachings and used them for its own ends. Returning to Dōni, we must regard him as perhaps the most active and vigorous preacher the movement produced. He traveled extensively, from the far north of the main island to Shikoku in the south, always addressing large crowds. He attracted many *samurai* to his audiences and even interested a number of *daimyō* in Shingaku. He and his disciples established educational institutions in many of the great fiefs, often with the encouragement of the feudal lord.

One very interesting tendency in later Shingaku was well illustrated in the work of Dōni. This was the close association with the *bakufu* and the use of Shingaku lectures to expound government edicts. In 1793 Dōni published his *Gokōsatsu Dōwa,* or lectures on government notices. Several writers, among them Miyamoto Mataji,[90] see in this a betrayal of Baigan's position and the transformation of the Shingaku teachers into "ruling class robots." Nevertheless, when one considers the content of these government notices one must wonder if there was really such a betrayal. These notices were full of exhortations to loyalty and filial piety; they urged the people to tend strictly to their business and avoid amusements or gambling; they stressed the importance of the utmost frugality in consumption; they warned against quarreling or public disturbance and demanded strict obedience to officials. It is hard to see what in Baigan's teaching is contradicted by these exhortations and easy to see how one trained in Shingaku thought could use these statements as texts as well as any other. I, at least, have failed to detect in Baigan that note of opposition to the central values and the *samurai* class which Dōni was supposed to have betrayed. On the other hand, too close an association with the *bakufu* may well have hindered the influence of Shingaku in the last years of the Tokugawa Period when public sentiment was recoiling from that institution.

The first half of the 19th century was a period of continued growth for Shingaku as a movement, but perhaps also a period of some weakening of its inner spirit. By 1830 there were 134 *kōsha* in 34 provinces and more were added even after that time. As has been mentioned, we have evidence for the existence of at least

180 *kōsha* in all. However, though the movement grew, it lost in cohesion. The Kantō (Edo area) split off from the Kansai (Kyōto-Ōsaka area) and Hiroshima became an independent center in the west. Teachers of great note became fewer though the quantity of Shingaku literature printed in the last years of the Tokugawa was prodigious. The tendency for a close relation with the *bakufu* grew gradually stronger. On the occasion of the reforms of Tempō (1830–1844) all public performances (theater, etc.) were banned with the exception of four cases: Shingaku, Shintō lectures, lectures on military works, and *mukashi-banashi* (tellers of old tales). Beginning in 1845 and continuing until the end in 1867, the *bakufu* annually issued orders on the 11th day of the first month to the effect that the Teshima Shingaku was a very worthy movement and deserved the support of the merchant class.[91]

Though it continued to survive here and there for a few years, the Restoration of 1868 was a deathblow for Shingaku as a movement. As we have seen, it had been more and more closely allied with the *bakufu* and this was perhaps one cause of its rapid loss of popular favor. It is not hard, however, to discover others. The first years of Meiji witnessed a great attempt to cut all ties which had bound Shintō and Buddhism for so many centuries. A syncretic movement like Shingaku was bound to be affected by such a tendency. It had maintained from the beginning the unity of the three teachings (*sankyō itchi*) but now it was faced with a national revulsion against such fusions. There were those who wished to drop the Confucian and Buddhist elements and apply to the government for the status of a Shintō sect. Clearly this would have destroyed the essence of the Shingaku teaching and it is not surprising that such a solution was not adopted. Shingaku was very largely an urban movement and it was the cities which were most quickly affected by westernization and industrialization. One of the great sources of Shingaku prestige and influence had been in connection with its educational facilities and the fact that its officials were learned. It has been pointed out that merchant families came to Shingaku teachers to have them draw up house rules, etc. But now the kind of education which Shingaku represented was no longer so respected. The government was building up a school system which would meet the needs of the city classes which the *bakufu* had largely ignored. Thus Shingaku, tainted by its association with the *bakufu,* uncertain as to its doctrinal base, and displaced as an educational facility, rapidly lost ground as an organization. In a sense, however, its dissolution was more victory than defeat. The ethical content which it had held to be so important was not forgotten but continued to be propagated even more widely than before. In particular the ethics textbooks of the new public school system read much like a Shingaku lecture. The popular Shintō movements which arose in late Tokugawa and early Meiji times in many cases leaned heavily on Shingaku materials for their ethical teachings. Though its techniques of meditation may have been forgotten, its ideal of uniting one's heart with the heart of heaven and earth continued to exist in popular thought in such attenuated forms as "making one's heart sincere" and "making one's heart like a shining mirror."

With this rapid survey of the history of later Shingaku in mind, let us glance briefly at the thought of the later period. Though a number of interesting minor developments were made in the religious thought, they did not signify any major change of direction and we will confine ourselves here to the ethical teachings. We may begin with a concrete set of admonitions from Wakizaka Gidō (17 ? –1818), a pupil of Toan, who is famous for having preached to the inmates of the Kyōtō prison.

1. Revere Shintoism, Buddhism, and Confucianism and cherish sincerity in all.
2. Obey the law, accept your social position and cherish thrift.
3. Make your household harmonious and cherish your trade, your calling.
4. Cherish loyalty, filial piety and forbearance.
5. Cherish compassion, secret charity, caring for one's body and caring for one's family.
6. Make your conduct good and cherish the education of children and retainers.
7. Know that blessings are to be found in work and cherish your work of today.[92]

Here is the stress on piety and loyalty, on thrift and diligence, and on the family which we might expect from a follower of Ishida

Baigan. Abstracting from a great many such sets of admonitions Miyamoto Mataji has made a general characterization of the ethical teachings of later Shingaku and we will rely on his summary, which is organized in three categories: family harmony, responsibility toward society, and ideas about business:

> I Do not forget the words "filial piety." Practice strict economy, and practice hygiene, and be careful about both food and wine and be not excessive. Selfish and unreasonable words and deeds are forbidden. Work hard for the family business and do not complain about insufficiencies. Have patience and quickly rectify mistakes. Have a sympathetic heart. Do not forget the achievements of the ancestors and be kind to relatives and old people. Have faith in the gods and Buddhas.
>
> II You must be honest (*shōjiki*). Have respect for superiors and sympathy for inferiors. Strictly obey the laws of the nation. Be gentle and avoid quarrels and brawls. Do not break promises. Act so that you do not forget your debts of gratitude to others. Do not throw up the mistakes of others.
>
> III In all the world there is nothing that is called one's own. The family is handed down by ancestors and passed on to descendants. Money does not belong to just one individual. If money belongs to society as a whole it is not to be spent by one person for his own sake. If small it must be spent for the whole family, if large for the public benefit. Trade should not have for an object only the acquiring of money. Always think of the prosperity of the family.[93]

Here, I think, the basic ethical view of Baigan is most clearly to be seen. Selfless devotion to the collectivity and its goals is what is required. Hard work, frugality and a reasonable disposition are all aspects of this devotion. For later Shingaku as for earlier the person who has attained religious enlightenment, the state of selflessness, is the one who can perform the ethical duties described above spontaneously and without doubt or hesitation. This being the case it is hard for me to see a difference in the earlier and later movements with respect to their relation to economic rationalization. The later movement did not continue Baigan's vigorous defense of the merchant class nor did it attempt to rationalize the merchant's profit as he did. And yet it seems to me that the ethic which has just been summarized implies that same attitude toward the merchant class. Certainly the merchant role is seen as a legitimate context for the performance of loyalty and filial piety. Perhaps the later Shingaku teachers lacked the taste of burnt plum pickle and the willingness for controversy which characterized Baigan, but in the essentials of either religious or ethical teaching it is hard to see a difference.

In this chapter, confined as it is to the study of a single movement, it has been possible to give a more detailed analysis of the relation between religion and the polity and economy than was previously possible. We have studied a movement largely confined to the city classes, and even with respect to them it is hard to estimate just how much influence it actually had. What evidence there is indicates that it was considerable. It is probably not possible to say more than that. Enough has been said in earlier chapters, however, about the general ethical background and about other movements of the period to allow us to say that Shingaku is not only of importance for its own specific influence, but as an example of religious and ethical developments of which it was but a part.

As a religion it taught enlightenment and the selfless devotion which was both a means toward it and a consequence thereof. Politically it reinforced rationalization and the extension of power by emphasizing the great importance of loyalty and the selflessness of the retainer. Its emphasis on the emperor is important, in spite of its close ties to the *bakufu,* in preparing the popular mind for the Restoration. Though a merchant class movement, it sought no direct political power for the merchants but accepted the *samurai* as policy leaders and attempted to assimilate the merchants to a *samurai-like* role in the economic field. The significance of this kind of thinking for the Restoration and the Meiji Period will be commented on in the next chapter. Economically it reinforced diligence and economy, it valued productivity and minimized consumption. Further it advocated universalistic standards of honesty and respect for contract and gave them religious underpinnings. In these ways it must be seen as contributing to the growth of a disciplined, practical, continuous attitude toward work in the world among the city classes, important for both entrepreneurs and workers in an economy entering the process of industrialization. In doing all this it utilized one of the oldest and most powerful religious traditions in the Far East, that going back to Mencius. By fashioning this tradition to the needs of the city classes of its day Shingaku brought meaning into the lives of the harried and troubled merchants and channelled their energies in directions which were to have the profoundest consequences for their society.

Notes

1. The chief source for the life of Ishida Baigan is the *Ishida Sensei Jiseki,* a memoir of Ishida written by his pupils and translated as an appendix to this book. Some additional information was obtained from Kachibe, "Sekimon Shingaku Shiron."

2. *Ishida Sensei Jiseki,* in *Shingaku Sōsho,* vol. 6, p. 292. Hereafter these will be cited as *Jiseki* and *SGSS.*

3. *Ibid.,* p. 292.

4. *Toimondō, SGSS,* vol. 3, p. 169.

5. *Jiseki, SGSS,* vol. 6, p. 294.

6. *Ibid.,* p. 295.

7. *Ibid.,* p. 316.

8. *Ibid.,* pp. 307-308.

9. *Analects,* II, 4. Waley, *The Analects of Confucius,* p. 88.

10. *Jiseki, SGSS,* vol. 6, p. 314.

11. *Ibid.,* pp. 302-303.

12. The *Diagram of the Supreme Ultimate Explained* (J. *Taikyoku Zusetsu,* Chinese, *T'ai-ch'i T'u-shuo*) was written by Chou Tun-yi (1017-73), one of the early neo-Confucians. The *Kinshiroku* (Chinese, *Chin Shih Lu*) and the *Small Learning* (J. *Kogaku,* Chinese, *Hsiao Hsüeh*) are books of instruction written by Chu Hsi himself and were very popular in Japan. The *Seiri Jigi* (Chinese, *Hsing-li Tzu-i*) by Ch'en Ch'un (1151-1216), a disciple of Chu Hsi, is a small glossary of philosophical terms.

13. The *Warongo* is a *Shintō* work compiled in the 17th century. The *Tsurezuregusa* is a miscellany written by the Buddhist monk, Yoshida no Kaneyoshi (1283-1350).

14. For a discussion of the conditions of the day and their relation to the merchant class see Hasegawa, "Chōnin Seikatsu to Shingaku Shisō," pp. 37-44.

15. For a discussion of the contrast between Edo and Kyōto-Ōsaka see Hasegawa, *op. cit.,* pp. 13-18.

16. *Seikaron, SGSS,* vol. 1, pp. 135-136.

17. Watsuji, *op. cit.,* p. 325.

18. *Toimondō, SGSS,* vol. 3, p. 91. A helpful analysis of Baigan's thought, and especially of *Toimondō,* is contained in Kachibe, "Sekimon Shingaku Shiron."

19. *Ibid.,* p. 176.

20. *Ibid.,* p. 90.

21. Legge, *op. cit.,* vol. II, p. 414. I have somewhat altered Legge's translations.

22. *Toimondō, SGSS,* vol. 3, p. 92.

23. *Ibid.,* p. 111.

24. *Ibid.,* p. 192.

25. *SGSS,* vol. 1, p. 137.

26. *Toimondō, SGSS,* vol. 3, p. 138.

27. Legge, *op. cit.,* vol. II, p. 448. I have somewhat altered Legge's translation.

28. *Toimondō, SGSS,* vol. 3, pp. 189-190.

29. *Ibid.,* p. 114.

30. *Jiseki, SGSS,* vol. 6, p. 305.

31. *Toimondō, SGSS,* vol. 3, p. 162.

32. Legge, *op. cit.,* vol. I, p. 383. I have somewhat altered Legge's translation.

33. *Toimondō, SGSS,* vol. 3, pp. 90-91.

34. *Ibid.,* p. 97.

35. *Jiseki, SGSS,* vol. 6, p. 313.

36. *Ibid.,* p. 307.

37. Hōtoku, though it stressed *on* primarily, did include teachings quite similar to those of Shingaku. For example, Sontoku said, "From the god-given soul in man comes the true heart, —our conscience; from the flesh comes the selfish heart,—the human mind. Bad grass growing in the fields must be taken out by the roots, or it will destroy the good plants. The selfish mind (literally 'human mind') will hurt the true mind, therefore we must root out all selfishness, and nourish the virtues

of charity, righteousness, propriety and wisdom." (Armstrong: *Just Before the Dawn*, p. 230.) Here again the influence of Mencius is obvious.

38. *Toimondō, SGSS*, vol. 3, p. 188.
39. *Ibid.*, pp. 121-122.
40. *Seikaron, SGSS*, vol. 1, p. 154.
41. *Toimondō, SGSS*, vol. 3, pp. 123-127.
42. *Ibid.*, p. 125.
43. *Ibid.*
44. *Ibid.*
45. *Ibid.*, p. 106.
46. *Ibid.*, p. 107.
47. *Ibid.*, p. 96.
48. *Seikaron, SGSS*, vol. 1, p. 158.
49. *Toimondō, SGSS*, vol. 3, pp. 149-150.
50. Honjō, "Economic Thought in the Latter Part of the Tokugawa Era," p. 12.
51. *Ibid.*
52. *Ibid.*
53. Watsuji, *op. cit.*, pp. 326-329.
54. Honjō, *op. cit.*, p. 11.
55. *Ibid.*
56. *Ibid.*, p. 15.
57. *Toimondō, SGSS*, vol. 3, p. 158.
58. *Ibid.*, p. 157.
59. *Ibid.*, p. 158.
60. *Ibid.*, p. 145.
61. *Ibid.*, p. 148.
62. *Ibid.*, p. 109.
63. *Ibid.*
64. *Ibid.*, pp. 109-110.
65. *Seikaron, SGSS*, vol. 1, p. 162. The symbolism of this passage seems to be derived from the analogy of sanctions in the social system, notably disinheritance. The threat is of a cosmic disinheritance.
66. *Toimondō, SGSS*, vol. 3, p. 152.
67. *Seikaron, SGSS*, vol. 1, pp. 159-162.
68. *Ibid.*, pp. 158-159.
69. *Ibid.*, p. 158.
70. *Ibid.*, pp. 138-139.
71. *Ibid.*, p. 139.
72. *Ibid.*, p. 143.
73. *Ibid.*, p. 142.
74. *Toimondō, SGSS*, vol. 3, p. 131.
75. *Ibid.*, p. 113.
76. *Seikaron, SGSS*, vol. 1, p. 159.
77. *Toimondō, SGSS*, vol. 3, p. 133.
78. Biographical material on Teshima Toan was derived from Ishikawa's monumental *Sekimon Shingaku Shi no Kenkyū*, p. 269 ff.
79. The term Shingaku was actually not used by Baigan, who referred to his teaching as *seigaku* (nature learning). Shingaku (heart or mind learning) was first used by Toan in 1778, and it was in common use by 1779. The term Sekimon Shingaku (Shingaku of the school of Ishida) was used to differentiate the movement from Buddhist and Confucian *shingaku*. This term was in use by the 1790's. The word *shingaku* was originated by Chinese Buddhists but it was later used by Confucians of both the Chu Hsi and the Wang Yang-ming schools, especially the latter. The term was first used in Japan in a book published in 1656 and was a common term by the 18th century. See Ishikawa, "Shingaku Gaisetsu," pp. 1-5.
80. On the *kōsha* organization see Shiraishi, "Shingāku Kyōka no Hōhō," pp. 6-7.
81. On the *tokō* see *ibid.*, p. 10.
82. *Ibid.*, p. 11.
83. *Ibid.*, p. 12.
84. *Ibid.*, pp. 42-43.
85. Ishikawa, *Sekimon Shingaku Shi no Kenkyū*, p. 263.
86. Shiraishi, *op. cit.*, pp. 33-34.
87. Ishikawa, *op. cit.*, p. 242.
88. *Ibid.*
89. Biographical material on Nakazawa Dōni was derived from Ishikawa, *op. cit.*, p. 304 ff.
90. Miyamoto, *op. cit.*, p. 28.
91. *Ibid.*, p. 28.
92. Quoted in Kōno *Kokumin Dōtoku Yoron*, p. 250-51.
93. Miyamoto, *op. cit.*, pp. 30-31.

CHAPTER

VII

Conclusion

I WOULD LIKE to take up two or three questions which are relevant to our argument but whose full exploration lies outside the scope of this book before making my final comments on the relation of religion to the rise of modern Japan.

By limiting the analysis arbitrarily to the Tokugawa Period two major aspects of the problem of the relation between religion and the rise of industrial society in Japan have had to be left out. The first of these is a historical study of the formation of what we have called the central value system, which we believe to have existed in its essentials at least by the beginning of the Tokugawa Period. The second is an analysis of the modern period, especially Meiji, with respect to the way in which the values and motivations we have been discussing actually did contribute to the rise of an industrial society. Both of these studies would have to be undertaken in at least as much detail as this one if our conclusions were to be fully convincing. Since that is not at present possible, here we can only suggest some of the ways these gaps might be filled.

The central value system, as we have used the term, is meant to designate the most generalized orientations toward human action, especially in defining role expectations, which are found in a society. Relatively little is known about the processes leading to the formation of such central value systems, though Weber's comparative work points to the important role of religion in their development. Since we have not dealt with the formation of the central value system but have taken it as given for the period we were primarily concerned with, no contribution to the problem of the relation of religion to the formation of the central value system has been made here. We have, however, dealt with two other types of relation between religion and the central value system. Every central value system seems to imply or require certain concomitant religious beliefs and actions. That is, there must be some metaphysical grounding, some view of the world, which makes that value system meaningful in the largest context, and thus motivates people to adhere to it; and there must be forms of religious action which will allow people to meet the threats of death, guilt and meaninglessness, of basic alienation, in such a way that the integration of their personalities is maintained and their commitment to the central values stabilized. In Chapter III we attempted to set forth the basic forms of religious belief and action which seem to be concomitant with the Japanese value system. Though some historical remarks were made, we essentially ignored the historical dimension and discussed the general religious orientations that were in existence at the beginning of the Edo Period. Finally, the last type of relation between religion and the central value system with which we are concerned is that between the central value system and what we may call "pietist" movements. Such movements arise usually as intense forms of the basic religious tradition and attempt to inculcate a more strict adherence to the central value system, especially in times of moral laxness or among classes somewhat deviant in their devotion to the central values. Chapters IV, V and VI have given an ample selection of such movements from the Tokugawa Period. We have attempted to show that such movements, starting from a primarily religious interest nevertheless made important contributions to political and economic rationalization. But there is a sense in which all the intensification which the religious movements brought about was merely the development of tendencies inherent in the central value system. Looking at it from this point of view it is the central value system which is the most important variable and which is most in need of explanation. Though this has not been the subject of this study, during the course of the work a number of observations on this subject have come to mind which it might be well to include at this point.

From the earliest period of Japanese history we have evidence for a very high regard for loyalty to one's lord. Many incidents in the *Kojiki* and *Nihongi* indicate as much. For example, the *Nihongi* recounts that a follower of Jimmu Tennō in his voyage across the inland sea sacrificed himself by jumping into the water in order to quell a storm and save his lord.[1] This was a society in which there was endemic warfare and the relation of lord and follower, especially in a military context, came to have a pre-eminent importance. From a somewhat later period (7th century), we may quote from a long poem written after the death of Prince Takechi, which, after recounting his military prowess, says,

> Because of our lord who has gone
> To rule the Heavens above
> In what endless longing we live,
> Scarce heeding the days and months that pass!
>
> Like the water of the hidden pool
> On the bank of the Haniyasu Lake
> They know not whither to go—
> Sore perplexed are they, the servants of the prince![2]

The emphasis on loyalty to one's lord in a society of this general type is not restricted to Japan, nor is the intense personal loyalty implied in the poem we have just quoted. We need but to look to the Anglo-Saxon poem, *The Wanderer,* for a close parallel:

> All joy has departed. Truly does he know this who must long forgo the advice of his dear lord. When sorrow and sleep both together often bind the wretched lonely man, it seems to him in his mind that he embraces and kisses his liege lord, and lays hands and head on his knee, as sometimes in days of yore he enjoyed the bounty from the throne. Then awakens the friendless man; he sees before him the dark waves, the sea-birds dipping, spreading their wings, frost and snow falling, mingled with hail. Then are the wounds of his heart the heavier, the sore wounds after his dear one; his sorrow is renewed.[3]

This society of the Anglo-Saxons had the same high regard for loyalty that the ancient Japanese had. It was a disgrace to live if one's lord had died in battle. A warrior was to give his life for his lord, if need be, in return for all that he had received from the lord. Whitelock tells us that "when the claims of the lord clashed with those of the kindred . . . the duty to the lord should come first."[4] She points out that such attitudes were by no means new among the Germanic peoples and quotes Tacitus:

> Furthermore, it is a lifelong infamy and reproach to survive the chief and withdraw from the battle. To defend him, to protect him, even to ascribe to his glory their own exploits, is the essence of their sworn allegiance. The chiefs fight for victory, the followers for their chief.[5]

Nor did they cease to exist under Christianity and she quotes Cnut's laws, probably from the pen of Archbishop Wulfstan:

> For all that ever we do, through just loyalty to our lord, we do to our own great advantage, for truly God will be gracious to him who is duly faithful to his lord.[6]

In both Japan and the West these semitribal conceptions of the lord and follower relation persist in the Middle Ages and form one source of the "feudal" values of the respective cultures. In each case this period sees a transition away from purely personal loyalty to loyalty to a status. From this point on the two cases are not parallel. The intense values of warrior loyalty continue to play some role in the West in various transformations and with varying significance in the different national groupings, but in late feudal and early modern times other values become much more important. In Japan on the contrary these values continued to hold primacy and to be elaborated for classes and situations far removed from the tribal battle field.

In the West universalism in many contexts transformed or replaced the ethic of warrior loyalty. For example, the old particularistic loyalty was replaced by the new impersonal ideology of nationalism which emphasized a more universalistic loyalty. In Japan, on the contrary, particularism remained unchallenged. Japanese nationalism remained peculiarly particularistic due to its focus on the imperial family, reigning for ages eternal, the main family of which all Japanese families are branch families. In the West in spite of various uneasy alliances the universalism inherent in Christianity ultimately acted as a solvent on most relations of particularistic loyalty outside the nuclear family. In Japan national Shintō was hardly more than an expression of particularistic loyalty and Confucianism acted as strong reinforcement of it rather than a solvent. Buddhism had its greatest effect on the ethic of warrior loyalty in the ideas of selflessness and asceticism which strengthened rather than dissolved it. The ideal of the Japanese warrior was by no means the carousing hedonistic robber baron of the late Middle Ages in Europe. The separation of the warrior ideal from hedonism or desire for plunder which have characterized the warrior ethic in so many times and places is of the greatest importance in making possible the adaptation of that ethic to classes other than the warriors. The Buddhist monk in his selfless devotion to his religious duties has been taken as an ideal for the warriors, as for instance when Minamoto Yoritomo writes to Sasaki Sadashige in December of 1191:

> *Samurai* warriors should take responsibility for safeguarding the Ruler and the country in the same devoted way as Buddhist priests obey to Buddha's precepts. Seeing that the country is now under the civil and military rule of the Kamakura *shōgun,* all the *shōgun's* retainers, irrespective of the relative extent of fiefs granted to them, should serve their supreme lord with the uniform spirit of devotion and at any moment be prepared to lay down their lives in repayment of the favours received. They should not regard their lives as their own.[7]

Confucianism also had a profound effect on the Japanese warrior ethic. It should be remembered that the character frequently used to write the word *samurai* was the Chinese *shih. Shih* as used in the Confucian classics is translated by Waley as "knight."[8] The society of pre-Ch'in China has often been called "feudal" and whether or not this term is appropriate, there were certain similarities between it and Japanese society which were not shared by the later imperial China. For example, the *shih* of the classics could more easily be related to the Japanese *samurai* than could the scholar-gentry official of the later period. What is important is that, though certain elements of a warrior status remained part of the ideal of the *shih,* Confucius and Mencius had already gone far toward universalizing this ideal. Learning, virtue, and responsibility for the governing of the people were all important components of it. This ideal also had an element of asceticism or at least frugality and distaste for profit. Loyalty ranked very high in the values of the *shih,* which served to make a convenient link with the *samurai* ethic, but the important thing about the influence of this Confucian thinking on the Japanese ethic was that it tended to broaden it beyond purely military concerns to include intellectual, economic and governmental interests. The partial development of a military warrior stratum into a class of bureaucratic officials, as occurred in the Tokugawa Period, is made more understandable if these transitional aspects of the Confucian ethic are taken into account. Another consequence of the transformation of the warrior ideal into the ideal of a "good man" is that it contributes to the possibility of the generalization of that ethic to classes other than the warriors. The great difference from China is that whereas there the military aspect tended to atrophy and particularistic loyalty to one's lord, though important, was not primary, in Japan the military aspect remained important even if it had to be only symbolic and the idea of loyalty to one's lord continued to override all other ethical concepts. Another important influence of Confucian thinking in Japan was its emphasis on filial piety which helped to rationalize the Japanese idea of the family in terms of "political" values without at the same time being able to make familistic values as central as in China.

To summarize these speculations on the development of the Japanese value system, we may say that its roots go far back into the tribal past but that it took its definite form during the troubled centuries of the Middle Ages. Basically the ethic of a warrior class, under the influence of Confucianism and Buddhism it became sufficiently generalized so that it could become the ethic of an entire people. The continuity of the imperial line and of the national religion served to symbolize an almost "primitive" particularism. The high evaluation on military achievements and the fulfillment of one's lords commands became generalized beyond the warrior class into a high valuation of performance in all spheres. These, at any rate, are the hypotheses I would make after a cursory survey of the problem. If they turn out to be correct it is apparent that religion and religiously based ethics played a great part in this development.

We may now turn just as briefly and just as hesitantly to a consideration of the relation between the ethic which has been analyzed in this study and the development of the Meiji and modern periods. We might begin with a consideration of the 1868 Restoration itself. It was, as we have noted in Chapter II, carried through largely by the lower *samurai*. In Chapter IV we discussed the ideology of *sonnō* and *kokutai* which gave legitimation to the movement for the overthrow of the *bakufu* and the restoration of the imperial monarch, and noted that this ideology was not in conflict with the *samurai* ethic, *Bushidō,* but entirely consonant with it. The specific historical cause leading to the Restoration was the problem of how to deal with the encroachments of the Westerners. The battle cry of the Restoration was *sonnō-jōi,* revere the emperor and expel the barbarians, which implied that the *bakufu* had been lax in allowing foreigners to encroach upon Japan, and that all loyal Japanese would join in getting rid of the *bakufu* as the first step in getting rid of the foreigners. The point I am trying to make is that the Restoration was carried through by the *samurai* for at least explicitly political reasons. Of course economic causes had some part: in Chapter II a number of the economic weaknesses of the Tokugawa system were pointed out. But the *bakufu* did not fall because of a financial crisis, it was not unable to function economically. The ideology of the Restoration was not motivated by economic considerations and had no economic demands.[9] Moreover, although the merchant classes had been affected by the proimperial propaganda and may well have wished the end of the *bakufu,* they did not take an active part in its overthrow. True, they supplied money to the loyalist cause, but so did they to the *bakufu,* and it is to be doubted if this implied much concerning their political thinking one way or the other. They were accustomed to accommodating political superiors when they demanded money, whoever those superiors might be.

There is little doubt that the increasing disparity between performance and reward had a great deal to do with the movement for the Restoration, but this disparity built up pressures primarily in the lower *samurai* class, not in the "bourgeoisie." The 1868 Restoration, as has been pointed out before, cannot be understood as a "bourgeois revolution," as the attempt on the part of an economically restricted middle class to overthrow "feudalism" and win economic freedom. It would be difficult to find a trace of such a desire on the part of the *chōnin.* E. Herbert Norman, who combed the Tokugawa Period in an effort to find anyone who expounded a democratic-liberal political ideology, was almost forced to give up the attempt when he discovered Andō Shōeki, who did make a rather sweeping attack on the feudal system and its ideological base. But this man was not a merchant, he was an isolated thinker, without influence, whose works were not even published. Of course there were many complaints from the merchants about particular policies of the *bakufu* and covert lampooning of the government was common. But there was no crystalization of this into any ideological form, much less organizational. The merchants were basically loyal to the old government or the new. They were hard-working, frugal, and in most cases honest, but, as we have seen in the discussion of Shingaku and elsewhere, they were oriented to receiving directions from the rulers, to whom they relegated policy-determining functions. The fact that the merchants were not the spearhead for change and were not oriented to taking initiative in new and challenging circumstances is of the first importance in understanding the process of the modernization of Japan. If the merchants were not so, certainly neither were the farmers or artisans. Only one class was in a position to lead the nation in breaking new ground: the *samurai* class. From the nature of its situation, its locus of strength was the polity, not the economy. Thus both the Restoration and the subsequent modernization of Japan must be seen first in political terms and only secondarily in economic terms. I am insistent on this point because the tendency to regard economic developments as "basic" and political developments as "superstructure" is by no means confined to Marxist circles but permeates most current thinking on such matters.

Modernization, however, though it includes the notions of modernization of government, as well as education, medicine, etc., is so heavily dependent on economic factors that it is almost synonymous with industrialization. It is poor logic to draw from this the conclusion that the motivation for modernization must be primarily economic. Actually it seems clear that a great deal of the motivation for modernization in Japan was political rather than economic, concerned with the increase of power, for which the increase of wealth was but a means. The fact that it was the new Meiji government which took the lead in the introduction of new industries and carefully fostered the beginnings of the *zaibatsu* with subsidies and other support fits in with this point of view. Heavy industry was uneconomic in the technical sense from the beginning and continued to be so even to the present. It was always dependent on government support and the great concerns which controlled Japan's heavy industry were always to be understood as a sort of political capitalism tied in with government in a dozen ways, and in the long run, more told than telling. It is interesting to note that the basic principles of this political attitude toward the economy were well worked out already in the Tokugawa Period, as was shown in Chapter V.

So far we have attempted to show that it was only the *samurai* class which could have led a movement for basic social changes in Tokugawa Japan, that its motivation for doing so was primarily political—the desire to restore the emperor and increase the national power—and that utilizing their newly created modern state apparatus they encouraged the development of the economy with, again, the primary aim of increasing national power. How, then, was the economy developed, what groups took leadership and what groups responded to the government's desires in these directions?

It is not surprising that in the leadership of the new industries above all were to be found the *samurai*. The old legal distinctions between classes had been abolished and there was no prohibition on *samurai* entering industry, rather it was encouraged, and the government was especially helpful to *samurai* who wished technical training. The *samurai* had those qualities of initiative and leadership which the merchants of Tokugawa days had relatively little opportunity to develop. Furthermore, it was felt natural in a society where status considerations were still strong that those of formerly high status should fill the important positions, and many of the most important of the new positions were in the economy. But all of this, it seems to me, would not have availed to make industrialists and business men out of former *samurai* if the *samurai* ethic had been that romantic militarism of the late European nobility.[10] That it was not so I hope is abundantly clear from the analysis of *Bushidō* in chapter four. Bernard Makihara, in a most interesting honors thesis, has shown that the "*samurai* spirit" was still a strong force activating the Meiji industrialists and finds the ethic of *Bushidō* a powerful factor in "capitalist" development. For example, he quotes the house rules of the *samurai* Iwasaki, founder of Mitsubishi, which is a most interesting adaptation of the *samurai* ethics to the situation of the modern industrialist:

Article 1. Do not be preoccupied with small matters but aim at the management of large enterprises.
Article 2. Once you start an enterprise be sure to succeed in it.
Article 3. Do not engage in speculative enterprises.
Article 4. Operate all enterprises with the national interest in mind.
Article 5. Never forget the pure spirit of public service and *makoto.*
Article 6. Be hard-working and frugal, and thoughtful to others.
Article 7. Utilize proper personnel.
Article 8. Treat your employees well.
Article 9. Be bold in starting an enterprise but meticulous in its prosecution.[11]

If the *samurai* class supplied a large number of capable and vigorous entrepreneurs, what about that other important human component which seems to be a precondition for industrialization, a disciplined labor force? I hope that it is apparent from what has been said in this study already that an obedient, hard-working and frugal labor force was to be found in abundance among both the farmers and the city classes. Actually the division between entrepreneurs and labor force, outside of the larger enterprises, is somewhat misleading when applied to Japan. The vast majority of businesses were of very small size, with five workers or less, and were basically family enterprises. It was these small businesses with the help of electrical equipment later on, which produced the bulk of Japan's light goods, always the main export and the basis of the economy. In these small businesses the "entrepreneur" was merely the family head, certainly in most cases a farmer or townsman rather than a *samurai,* and the "labor force" was the family members and perhaps a few additional workers largely assimilated to the family pattern. The rigid discipline, long hours and incredibly low overhead of these establishments were certainly one of the primary sources of Japan's economic rise, and these are impossible to understand without an idea of the peasant and *chōnin* ethic and the peculiar way the family fits into them. It is interesting to note that competition was not any more conspicuous in the realm of small industry than in the field of large industry. The small enterprises were usually under the direction of large trading firms, or were organized in trade associations under government direction. Improvements of standards or shifting of type of production was usually a result of compliance with orders from above, often directly from the government, rather than the sensitive response to a competitive market situation. Of course the large firm or government was sensitive to such market situations, especially relative to the export trade, but this has quite a different meaning than if each small business were thus sensitive. The economy continued to be penetrated by political values.

To summarize this cursory glimpse of the post-Tokugawa situation, we may say that the central value system which was found to be present in the Tokugawa Period remained determining in the modern period, in perhaps even more intense and rationalized form. The adaptations of that central value system which had been worked out as the status ethic of the various classes proved very favorable for handling the new economic responsibilities which fell to each class. In spite of the growth of a modern economy the polity remained the dominant sphere of national life and the economy was permeated with political values.

At many points in this study implicit or explicit comparisons with China have been made. This has usually been prompted by the fact that so much of the cultural and religious tradition is common to both, whereas the process of modernization took such a different course in China and Japan. We have usually attempted, wherever this subject has come up, to use the basic value systems of the two societies as a primary reference point in explaining the differences. We have said that China was characterized by the primacy of integrative values whereas Japan was characterized by primacy of political or goal-attainment values. While it is clearly beyond the scope of this study to give an adequate comparison of the two value systems, a somewhat more extended statement of what is meant by integrative values in China might assist the reader in understanding the logic behind those comparisons that have already been made.

A society characterized by the primacy of integrative values is more concerned with system maintenance than with, for example, goal attainment or adaptation; more with solidarity than with power or wealth. The pattern variables which are coordinate with the integrative subsystem are particularism and quality. This implies with respect to human relations that one is more concerned with particularistic ties, of which kinship is the type case but which may include common local origin, etc., than with universalistic attributes. It also implies that one is more concerned with qualities than performance, in Chinese terms, with "virtue" rather than deeds. Kinship relations perhaps more than any others symbolize the values of particularism and quality, and a great deal of Chinese society can be seen as the symbolic extension and generalization of kinship ties. Even the imperial government was strongly "familistic" in its structure, though at the same time a powerful locus of political values. In concrete terms the Chinese saw the problem of system maintenance in terms of a determinate set of human relations that only needed to be kept in a state of mutual adjustment for a harmonious and balanced social system to result. An adjusted equilibrium was indeed the ideal of Chinese society.[12]

Just as we have seen that system maintenance was an important if secondary value in Japan, so goal attainment with its consequent emphasis on performance was an important if secondary value in China. The main locus of these "political" values was naturally enough in the imperial government. The comparison of the place of political and integrative values, of the polity and the integrative system in China and Japan, can perhaps be revealing of both the similarities and the differences of the two countries. The relative importance of loyalty and filial piety may be taken as an important index of this contrast. As we have already seen, in Japan loyalty clearly superseded filial piety. In China:

> . . . if one chose to join the official rank, one had "to transform filial piety into loyalty to the sovereign"; but . . . when these two virtues seriously conflicted it was the duty of the son as son that should receive first consideration. This is further evidence that the family system was the foundation of traditional Chinese society and filial piety the basis of its moral principles.[13]

Not only did the value of filial piety take precedence over loyalty, but loyalty itself had a very restricted focus. We have seen in Japan that loyalty permeated the whole society and became an ideal of all classes. In China, on the other hand, it did not even apply strongly to the whole gentry class but only to those in office:

> One does not have a chance to choose one's father. That is something determined by fate. But one can choose one's sovereign, just as a girl, before her marriage, can have a choice as to who should be her

husband. It was a common saying that "the wise bird chooses the right tree to build his nest; the wise minister chooses the right sovereign to offer his service." It is true that traditionally all the people of the Chinese Empire were theoretically subjects of the emperor. But it is also true that traditionally the common people had not the same obligation of allegiance toward the emperor as those who entered the official ranks of the government. It was to the officials that the relationship between sovereign and subject was specially relevant. So even in the time of unification when there was only one sovereign, one could still choose whether to join the official ranks or not, just as the girl might choose to remain single, even though there were only one man whom she could marry. In Chinese history, if a scholar chose to remain outside the official ranks, he was a man, as a traditional saying puts it, "whom the Son of Heaven could not take as his minister, nor the princes take as their friend." He was a great free man, without any obligation to the emperor except the paying of taxes.[14]

Such an attitude toward one's political superior would be quite without support in the Japanese value system. In fact, while political power penetrated to the lowest units of society in Japan, it was much more circumscribed in China:

> The daily life of the masses was regulated by social authority, while political authority was usually confined to the activity of the *yamen*. The court, except in the case of a few tyrants, did not interfere in the going concern of society. In general a good monarch collected a definite amount of taxes and left the people alone.[15]

Not only was the generalization and extension of political power thwarted by the narrow range within which that power operated, but even in its own home ground, the imperial bureaucracy, that power was constantly being constrained by familistic and integrative considerations. Whereas the interest of the emperor may have been in the building up of national power and in taking strong, goal-oriented steps in that direction, he was constantly hampered by a bureaucracy which was not oriented to political goal-attainment values, but to the maintenance of an existing system of interests. The history of every "reform" effort in modern Chinese history (before the recent change of regime) is a tale of just such a situation, and this holds whether before or after the 1911 revolution. A perhaps overdrawn but vivid account of this situation is given by Fei:

. . . Chinese officials did not share in the political power of the emperor but served their monarch by neurtalizing and softening down his power rather than by supporting it. With his nephews in court, the uncle was protected even in secret rebellious activities. According to Chinese tradition, officials did not work seriously for the government, nor did they like to continue as officials for a long period. Their purpose in entering the government was to gain both immunity and wealth in this order. The Chinese officials when in office protected their relatives, but, when this duty to the family had been performed, they retired. Retirement and even a hermit's life were the ideal. In retirement there was no longer any authority to be served with watchful care, while the relatives who had gained protection from their kinsman official owed him a debt of gratitude. Now he need only enjoy his social prestige and grow fat and happy. As we say in China, "To come back to one's native soil, beautifully robed and loaded with honors, is the best thing in life."[16]

Of course not all officials acted in this way. There are many examples of officials who were loyal in the extreme and earnestly attempted to build up the national power. They never, however, were able to dominate the government and put through a thoroughgoing modernization program as the young *samurai* were in Japan. They were always more or less checkmated by those committed to the maintenance of the old system. Even within the framework of integrative values there is room for considerable rationalization. Weber has pointed this out in his study of the Confucian ethic. To take a concrete example, it has been written of Tseng Kuo-fan, one of the more outstandingly honest and loyal of the late Ch'ing officials:

He sought daily to improve himself by constant examination of his own mistakes and short-comings. . . . The same habits of rigid self-examination are shown in the letters which he wrote to his parents, to his brothers, and to his sons; and in the admonitions he gave to the young to live lives of frugality, diligence, and integrity.[17]

Here is indeed a rational, this-worldly ethic, the ethic of the Confucian literati. But the aim of this ethic is neither to amass wealth, nor to increase national power. Rather it is designed to maintain the adjusted equilibrium of Chinese society. Therefore it lacks the dynamism which could overcome the traditionalism of the masses or transfer the primary allegiance from the family to some larger collectivity. The rationalism inherent in the Confucian ethic seems to need to be linked with a value system in which political values have primacy if it is to have an influence in the direction of modernization. This was the case in Japan and perhaps in present-day China.

Perhaps the most interesting result of this way of comparing the value systems of China and Japan is that it maintains that they both have a strong emphasis on political and integrative values, on loyalty and filial piety, but that there is a difference with respect to primacy of stress. This comparison then is used to explain in part the dramatic differences in social development. Thus the difference in social consequences is seen not in terms of the presence or absence of certain key values, but entirely in terms of the way in which values are organized.

We are now in a position to return to some of the considerations of Chapter I and summarize the results of the present investigation for the general problems set forth there.

Our first general conclusion is that a strong polity and dominant political values in Japan were distinctly favorable to the rise of industrial society. This is not what one would necessarily have expected if one extrapolated only from the European material. The orthodox view of European economic history has generally considered the "interference" of the state in the economy as inimical to economic development, though specific policies were often viewed as favorable. A general consideration of the relation of the polity and political values to economic development in the West might significantly alter the traditional view. Nevertheless, it seems likely that the role of the polity was considerably less important in European economic development than in Japanese. The Japanese case takes on special significance when compared with other non-Western societies. All of these societies faced certain problems in common which were different from those of the West. Whereas in the West industrialism was built on centuries of slow accumulation of capital and techniques, the non-Western societies faced industrialism as an existent fact. They did not have to go through the slow process of accumulation which the West had, nor could they if they had wanted to. The capital required for modern industrialization was too great to be supplied by the existing economic mechanisms in these societies. What has happened is that in almost every case, whatever industrialization has occurred has been government-controlled or government-sponsored, because only the government has been able to marshal the requisite capital. Under these circumstances it is obvious that the strength of the polity and political values are crucial variables. Of all the major non-Western societies Japan stands out as unique in its possession of a strong polity and central political values, and it is this above all, in my opinion, which accounts for the differential acceptance of industrialization.

A consideration of the cases of Russia and China may lend further credence to this view. These societies, since they have become Communist, have certainly had strong polities and strong political values. The Soviet Union is, in fact, almost the type case of a society emphasizing goal attainment. Though Russia is a marginal case, if we include it under the category of non-Western, it is the only non-Western nation besides Japan which has been able to become a major industrial power through its own efforts. China, more clearly a non-Western society, since its shift from the traditional integrative values to the Communist political values has shown a marked spurt in industrialization and can be expected to join Japan and Russia as the third great non-Western society to industrialize. Kemalist Turkey offers a non-Communist example of the importance of a strong polity in the process of modernization. On the other hand, if we consider a society such as Indonesia, we find that although what industrialization there is is under government direction or sponsorship; a weak polity and a low emphasis on political values are important factors in the extreme hesitancy, inefficiency and weakness of the movement toward industrialization.[18] Whatever the specific form they take, and the Japanese and Communist examples are of course very different, political values and a strong polity would seem to be a great advantage and perhaps even a prerequisite for industrialization in the "backward" areas of today's world. Unfortunately any strongly goal-oriented society is perilously close to totalitarianism, if we take that term to define the situation in which political considerations tend to override all other considerations, as all of our three examples indicate.

Our second general conclusion is that religion played an important role in the process of political and economic rationalization in Japan through maintaining and intensifying commitment to the central values, supplying motivation and legitimation for certain necessary political innovations and reinforcing an ethic of innerworldly asceticism which stressed diligence and economy. That it may also have played an important part in the formation of the central values which were favorable to industrialization is at least a strong possibility.

Religion reinforced commitment to the central value system by making that value system meaningful in an ultimate sense. The family and the nation were not merely secular collectivities but were also religious entities. Parents and political superiors had something of the sacred about them, were merely the lower echelons of the divine. Fulfillment of one's obligations to these superordinates had an ultimate meaning. It ensured the continuation of future blessings and of that ultimate protection which alone could save the individual from the hardships and dangers of this transitory world.

Alternatively another set of religious conceptions was offered which also reinforced the central value system. This view accepted the structure of Japanese society and its values as in accordance with the nature of reality. Fully and wholeheartedly carrying out one's part in that society and living up to its values meant an identification with that ultimate reality. This losing the self and becoming identified with ultimate nature, a line of religious thought deriving from Mencius, also promised release from the basic frustrations of existence in a state of enlightenment. Actually the two views usually went together, they were the two lenses through which Japanese religion viewed the world; though they can be analytically separated, in practice the difference between them was usually not noticed.

Though the primary religious reinforcement of the central value system occurred in the family and national cults, a series of religious movements arose in the Tokugawa Period which developed independent institutional forms and reached large numbers of people. Some of these have been considered at length in this study. They must be seen as symptomatic of the increasing intensity of the commitment to the central values in Tokugawa times and as in turn contributing to that intensification. Doctrinally they were usually fairly simple versions of the religious conceptions we have just reviewed. They were often syncretic in origin and more concerned with piety and ethical conduct than with the fine points of doctrine. Religion in both its general and sectarian aspects, then, contributed to the integration of society in terms of a set of values which we have seen as singularly conducive to the industrialization of Japan under the special conditions in which that industrialization took place.

Furthermore, religion played a major role in political rationalization by emphasizing certain overriding religio-political commitments which could supersede all lesser obligations, thus supplying motivation and legitimation for the Restoration of the emperor, in spite of the fact that this Restoration involved breaking with many loyalties and customs of the past. This trend was clothed in nativistic and fundamentalist garb as is so often the case when religious movements are seeking to legitimize social change. Just as the Protestant Reformation proclaimed, "Back to the Bible" and Reform Islam "Back to the Koran," so the Shintō Revival movement proclaimed "Back to the *Kojiki*." Though State Shintō in modern times was in certain respects a hothouse plant, there can be no doubt that reverence for the emperor has been a major ideological force in Japan and has served to legitimize changes which would otherwise have roused the strongest sentiments of opposition. The origins of these attitudes are not restricted to a few scholars of the Kokugaku but were widely and deeply distributed in Tokugawa times. The biography of Ishida Baigan (translated as Appendix I), who was certainly no Kokugakusha, provides but one example. That powerful religious motivation is often an important factor in major political change is also indicated by the close association of Protestantism and democracy in the West and by the charismatic ideology of Communism, for most purposes to be considered as a religion, without which Communist political successes would be unthinkable.

Finally, we must consider the relation of religion to that ethic of inner-worldly asceticism which is so powerful in Japan. The obligation to hard, selfless labor and to the restraint of one's own desires for consumption is closely linked to the obligations to sacred and semisacred superiors which are so stressed in Japanese religion, as also to that state of selfless identification with ultimate nature. As we have had repeated occasion to see, Japanese religion never tires of stressing the importance of diligence and frugality and of attributing religious significance to them, both in terms of carrying out one's obligations to the sacred and in terms of purifying the self of evil impulses and desires. That such an ethic is profoundly favorable to economic rationalization was the major point of Weber's study of Protestantism and we must say that it seems similarly favorable in Japan. The importance of such an ethic is clearly relevant to the general social and cultural circumstances. An inner-worldly ascetic ethic has been described for Manus[19] and for Yurok,[20] but clearly neither of these primitive societies was in a position to industrialize. Furthermore, it is probably not uncommon among certain types of merchant class. Geertz has described the inner-worldly asceticism of the Muslim merchants of Java, which is certainly related to their economic success, but hardly sufficient to guarantee a successful industrialization in Indonesia.[21] On the other hand, such an ethic certainly seems favorable if not essential to industrialization, at least in its early stages. It is found not only in Protestantism and Japan, but in Communism. In each case the importance of religious rationalization and reinforcement is very considerable.

After all that has been said about the "functions" of Japanese religion we are finally forced to consider the meaning of those functions in terms of religion itself. If we give Japanese religion "credit" for contributing to the miraculous rise of modern Japan, we must also give it "blame" for contributing to the disaster which culminated in 1945. Such a conclusion has implications for the relation of religion and society in general. Every religion seeks to proclaim a truth which transcends the world, but is enmeshed in the very world it desires to transcend. Every religion seeks to remake the world in its own image, but is always to some extent remade in the image of the world. This is the tragedy of religion. It seeks to transcend the human but it is human, all too human. And yet tragedy is not the last word about religion, and 1945 is not the end of Japanese religion. As long as religion maintains its commitment to the source of ultimate value, which is to say as long as it remains religion, the confrontation of religion and society continues. Holding to that commitment religion turns every human defeat into victory.

Notes

1. Aston (trans.), *Nihongi,* p. 114.
2. Nippon Gakujitsu Shinkōkai, *Manyōshū,* p. 41.
3. Whitelock, *The Beginnings of English Society,* p. 31.
4. *Ibid.,* p. 37.
5. *Ibid.,* p. 29.
6. *Ibid.,* p. 38.
7. Hashimoto, "The Keystone of Medieval *Bushidō,*" p. 265.
8. For a justification of this translation see Waley, *The Analects of Confucius,* pp. 33-34.
9. Certainly many of the *samurai* who supported the Restoration were motivated by the most pressing economic needs. The ideology of the Restoration, however, was not an expression of the *economic* demands of the *samurai* class.
10. Since this chapter was written I have come across a provocative reappraisal of the role of the European aristocracy in economic development: Redlich, "European Aristocracy and Economic Development." Redlich marshals considerable evidence to show that the aristocracy had far from a negligible role in European economic development and points specifically to those aspects of their ethic favorable to initiative and daring as having economic relevance. He notes that the stereotype view of the economically hapless aristocrat is partly the result of the bias of a century of bourgeois historians. He looks forward to further research in this field before an adequate estimate of the problem can be made.
11. Makihara, "Social Values in Capitalist Development: A Case Study in Japan," p. 88.
12. Fei, *China's Gentry,* p. 74.
13. Fung, "The Philosophy at the Basis of Traditional Chinese Society," p. 31.
14. *Ibid.,* pp. 27-28.
15. Fei, *op. cit.,* p. 69.
16. *Ibid.,* p. 32.
17. Hummel (Ed.), *Eminent Chinese of the Ch'ing Period,* vol. II, p. 754.
18. This statement is based on conversation with Clifford Geertz, Jr.
19. Mead, *Growing up in New Guinea.*
20. Goldschmidt, "Ethics and the Structure of Society."
21. Geertz, "Another World to Live In: A Study of Islam in Indonesia," and "Religious Belief and Economic Behavior in a Central Javanese town."

APPENDIX

I

A Memoir of Our Teacher, Ishida

TRANSLATOR'S NOTE

THIS IS a translation of the *Ishida Sensei Jiseki,* a work composed by the pupils of Ishida Baigan in the fall of 1769, about twenty-five years after his death. It was stored in a box for more than thirty years when someone got hold of it and published an unauthorized edition. This being full of blunders, carelessness and mistakes, Uekawa Kisui (1748–1817), the adopted son of Teshima Toan, had the original manuscript recopied, and making sure that everything was correct, had it printed. This was in 1805. This history of the manuscript we are given in a note appended by Uekawa to the 1805 edition.[1] We are not told which pupils collaborated in the original writing.

This work, both in the manner of its composition and in its form and contents, is reminiscent of the *Analects* of Confucius. It is essentially a collection of the sayings and habits of the teacher, each item being more or less complete in itself, with only a minimum of arrangement by subject or chronology.

Since almost no primary material on Shingaku is available in Western languages, and since I felt it would help the reader to make an estimate of the movement if he had at hand a somewhat larger amount of primary data than could be included in quotations in the text, I decided to include a translation of one of the shorter works of Shingaku in this book. The *Jiseki* seemed a natural choice as it contains a wide range of material shedding light on both motivation and doctrine, and is of considerable intrinsic interest.

THE TRANSLATION

Our teacher's personal name was Okinaga. Another name was Baigan. The name by which he was called was Kampei. He was of the Ishida family. His father's personal name was Jōshin. His mother was a daughter of the Kado family. He was born on the fifteenth day of the ninth month of the second year of Chōkyo (1685) in the village of Higashi Agata, district of Kuwada, province of Tamba.[2]

Our teacher's character was righteous and his ability exceeded the ordinary. He received an upright rearing from his father. To cite one example, when he was about ten he went to his father's orchard, gathered five or six chestnuts, and returned. He went into his seat at lunch. When he showed them to his father, his father asked him where he got them.

Our teacher replied, "From your orchard and the boundaries of adjoining orchards."

His father said, "My chestnut trees do not extend their branches to the boundary of the orchard. The branches of the chestnut trees of the other orchards extend into the boundary of my orchard and these are really chestnuts from the other orchards." He admonished him for not discriminating in this way and, not allowing him to finish his lunch, said to him, "Take them back where you got them, quickly."

Our teacher obeyed and took them back immediately, leaving them where he had gotten them.

When he was twenty-three our teacher went up to Kyōto and took service with a certain merchant of the upper city. At first he was much attached to Shintō and his aspiration was in some way to preach Shintō. If he had no listeners he patrolled district after district ringing a bell, wishing to promote the way of man. Because of this aspiration, when going on business to the lower city he carried a book in his pocket and studied whenever he had a little leisure. In the mornings before his companions arose he faced the second story window and read a book. In the evening, after they had fallen asleep, he read books, but he did not neglect his master's business in the slightest.

Now, although he had become the chief clerk (*kashirabun*) in the house, on winter nights he left the warm sleeping places to the others and he himself slept near the door. Moreover, on summer nights when the shop boys kicked off their coverings he would get up from time to time and go around covering them.

A widely read person among his companions asked our teacher his aspiration in being fond of study (*gakumon*).

Our teacher said, "First, what is your reason?"

The other replied, "I study widely and become well versed in today's world. This is my wish."

Our teacher said, "I am not like this. I study to observe the actions of the sages of old and I hope to become an example to all men."

Then the other said admiringly, "That indeed is a better aspiration."

The mother of our teacher's master had a virtuous upbringing and was an exceptional person. One time our teacher put on a crape *haori*[3] and went to the mother of the master.

The master's mother said, "Hadn't you better wear a silk *haori?*"

Our teacher said, "I have thought about that before, but I have only this one *haori*. If I sell it and buy another it will cost money, so I have kept on wearing it."

The master's mother said, "Well then, your crape *haori* is the same as a silk *haori*," and she permitted it.

The family followed the Honganji Sect[4] and believed in the founder.[5] Although they had everyone, even the servants, go to the temple, frequently our teacher did not go. Besides, at times he expounded Shintō to his master's mother.

An old clerk in the house told the master's mother that our teacher studied Shintō and had a scanty knowledge of the [Shin] sect.

The master's mother replied, "Kampei's aspiration in studying Shintō is exceptional. Though he does not go to the temple he has faith (*shinjin*). Do not be concerned about him."

Later the master's mother became ill and daily grew worse. She said to the woman who was near her, "Now in my life there is nothing lacking. My only regret is that I will not live long enough to see Kampei's future glory."

When our teacher was about thirty-five or six, though he decided that he knew the nature (*sei*),[6] somehow or other doubts arose with respect to that nature. In order to correct this he sought a teacher hither and yon, but there was no one suitable as a teacher anywhere. Time passed and he had an interview with the old master Ryōun, and brought up the theory of the nature. Our teacher in trying to express his own knowledge was like an egg striking a great rock, and was unable to speak. Thereupon he was contented and served [Ryōun] as his master.

After that, night and day without other distraction he concentrated intensely and engaged in meditation (*kufu*). After about a year and a half had passed in this way, his mother came down sick and he went to his home village. At that time our teacher was about forty. It was in the first third of the first month, while nursing his mother, he opened a door and suddenly the doubts of former years scattered. The Way of Yao and Shun[7] is only filial piety and brotherliness (*kōtei*). Fish swim in water and birds fly in the sky. The Way is clear above and below. Knowing the nature (*sei*) to be the parent of heaven and earth and of all things, he greatly rejoiced. After that he went up to the capital and talked to his master.

After completing the greetings the master asked, "Has the meditation borne fruit?"

Our teacher said in reply, "It is indeed so."

Motioning in the air with his pipe, the master said, "What you have seen is what can be known of how things ought to be. Like the example of the blind men looking at an elephant, whether they apprehend the tail or the feet, they cannot see the whole. The eye with which you saw our nature as the parent of heaven and earth and all things remains. There must be the nature but without the eye. Now you must lose the eye."

Our teacher after that forgot to sleep or eat days and nights and practiced meditation, thus passing more than a year. Late one night, he lay down exhausted, and was unaware of the break of day. He heard the cry of a sparrow in the woods behind where he was lying. Then within his body it was like the serenity of a great sea, or a cloudless sky. He felt the cry of that sparrow like a cormorant dividing and entering the water, in the serenity of a great sea. After that he abandoned the conscious observation of his own nature.

Our teacher did not drop in on his master at all for half a year. One of the old pupils said to the master, "He ought to be a person who excels others. [Yet] he appears to have left because the master is too strict [for him]. How regrettable."

The master said, "Don't worry about him," and he showed no sign [of apprehension].

When our teacher was in the presence of his master, his master said, "In the near future you should settle down. No matter how much time you spend, months and days, just for study alone, what good will it do?"

Our teacher replied, "You need not worry," and his master rejoiced.

While our teacher was nursing his master, his master said, "I would like to smoke."

Our teacher responded, lit the tobacco, wiped the outside of the mouthpiece of the pipe with paper and offered it, but he greatly offended his master's feelings.[8] His master said, "When you do what you have just done, you show that you feel nursing me is filthy," and he at once dismissed our teacher.

Though our teacher was the only one nursing the master at the time, he did not approach him at all. He dejectedly withdrew into the next room and wept. Next morning one of his old fellow pupils came and made apology for our teacher's mistake, so that he was finally permitted to attend [his master] again.

After that for one or two days his master's illness worsened. When he was approaching the end his master said, "I would like to give you the books to which I have added my comments."

Our teacher replied, "I do not want them."

His master asked, "Why don't you want them?"

Our teacher replied, "When I face new situations, I will make a new commentary," and his master admired him greatly.

Our teacher's home village, Higashi Agata, is hemmed in by mountains before and behind. His mother loved lotus, but there was no place near in this mountainous spot where lotus could be obtained. However, there was a slight muddy place in a small stream at the edge of the mountains in front of their family garden. Though it was not a place where lotus was likely to grow, one year a stalk of lotus grew there. His mother was exceedingly happy. The next year a white lotus bravely bloomed. The time when the lotus first grew and the time when our teacher opened a lecture hall were the same.

When our teacher was forty-three he left service and after that began to lecture. When he was forty-five he took residence on the east side of Kurumayachō Street above Oike Street,[9] and for the first time opened a lecture hall. He put out a notice on a post in front, which read,

"On a certain month and a certain day there will be a lecture. There is no admission and even though uninitiated, persons who wish to may listen freely."

Whenever he lectured he put out this notice. The audience hall was divided into men's and women's sections and bamboo blinds were placed where the women were.

In the spring of the second year of Gembun (1737) he moved his residence to Sakaichō Street on the east side below Rokkaku Street.[10] When he first opened his lecture hall on Kurumayachō his audience did not exceed two or three persons, four or five persons, in the morning and evening alike. At one time there was no one but a close friend, but [our teacher] sat face to face with him and lectured.

At the lecture hall there was but one pupil one night. This pupil said, "Tonight there is no other audience, and since it would trouble you to lecture just for me, please rest tonight."

Our teacher replied, "When I began to lecture, expecting to face only the reading stand, I was satisfied if there was an audience of one," and he lectured.

Places where he went to lecture were Osaka, Kawachi and Izumi.[11] He frequently went to Ōsaka to lecture. Even in Kyōto he would lecture in different places for thirty or fifty days [at a time]. He lectured at his residence every morning and every other evening. Moreover, he held three meetings a month. As for the meetings, beforehand he had asked questions and had the pupils write replies and he also wrote replies and interpreted them.

On the first and last days of a lecture engagement he bathed to purify himself and wore a hemp ceremonial dress (*kamishimo*). Though ordinarily he lectured in his usual *hakama*[12] and *haori,* his attitude was as though he wore ceremonial dress. When he went out to lecture he wore his hemp ceremonial dress from the first day to the last.

These are the books he was always expounding: the *Four Books,* the *Classic of Filial Piety,* the *Small Learning,* the *Book of Changes,* the *Book of Poetry,* the *Diagram of the Supreme Ultimate Explained,* the *Kinshiroku,* the *Seiri Jigi,* the *Lao Tzu,* the *Chuang Tzu,* the *Warongo,* and the *Tsurezuregusa.*[13]

Ordinarily in the morning he arose before dawn, washed his hands, opened the door, swept out the house, and put on his *hakama* and *haori.* He then washed his hands, reverently lit the lamp anew, and worshipped first the shrine of the Sun Goddess, then the god of the kitchen (*kamado-no-kami*), the patron deity (*ujigami*) of his native village, the great sage Confucius, the Buddhas Amida and Sakyamuni, his teacher, his ancestors, and his father and mother. After that he sat down to his food, ate each bite thankfully, and after the meal he rinsed his mouth. After resting a little while, he began to lecture.

Also in the evening he again cleaned the house, washed his hands, lit the lamp, and worshipped as in the morning.

Once in every four or five days he always swept out the house and wiped the pillars, the threshold, and the like.

The morning lecture began at dawn and ended at 8 a.m. The evening lecture began right at sundown and ended at 8 p.m.

He had hot water before the morning lecture and tea before the evening lecture.

He kept a fire alive in the fire pan of each tobacco tray. During the day people came often, and there were persons who requested to hear a lecture not at the fixed time. Every evening until 10 p.m. the students gathered and inquired into and discussed what was doubtful in what they had heard. Thus he was busy day and night. In his spare moments he read books at his desk. Occasionally he felt sleepy due to some illness. At those times he just got up from his seat and did something, such as sweeping. When the sleepiness passed he put aside that activity and again read books at his desk. Even on short summer nights after his pupils had returned home he read books and did not go to sleep until after midnight. On winter nights he read until almost 2 a.m.

As for our teacher's clothing, in summer his everyday clothing was of *nuno*[14] and his holiday clothing was of *narazashi*.[15] In winter his everyday clothing was of cotton and his holiday clothing of *tsumugi*.[16] For his meals he often ate a sort of rice gruel made of good processed rice. Once a day he regularly prepared himself a *miso*[17] soup and a simple *sai*[18] and ate it.

He usually used fine tea. At times he would eat the boiled tea leaves with soy sauce.

In washing rice he collected the first and second rinse water in another vessel and offered it as food to the mice. As for the grains of rice left in the kettle, he put in hot water and drank them. He carefully washed what adhered to the kettle, however little, and gave it as food to the sparrows and mice. After finishing his soup, he put tea in the various soup pots and soup bowls, washed it around and drank it.

He would throw out the rotten leaves of green vegetables but he would not throw out dried up leaves, but used them.

He rarely bought fish. [When he did, he bought] *koaizaki, hakari-kujira,* or *ebizako*.[19]

In filling a pipe he did not let the tobacco come out of the pipe bowl even a little.

He split his firewood in small pieces so that it would be easy to kindle. He washed the chips which had fallen in the garden, even if but half an inch of wood, and put them in the kitchen stove. He used spills split in half widthwise. He saved the ones he had used and used them to light lanterns and other things. Even if the coals in the brazier were down to a tiny size he put them in a charcoal damper and used them.

He kept the lamp used for moxa cautery and for the light in the water closet strictly separate [from other fires]. When he had to make this sort of fire with a spill, he washed the remains of the spill and put it in the kitchen stove. If water is pure, the heart becomes pure.

He left the old well bucket rope to dry, used it as fuel, put its ashes in the fire pan or brazier and buried the coals with them because they preserve fire well.

He used the edges of old *tatami*[20] for dusting.

He always dressed his own hair. He washed his hair cord and used it repeatedly.

When he could give alms to beggars, he gave quickly, and when he was busy and could not give, he said firmly in a loud voice that he could not. This was so that he would not be stopped for a long while fruitlessly.

He did not use decorated ink sticks.[21] He scraped off what was left after grinding the ink and what adhered to the inkstone and saved it. This he saved for later use.

Generally when opening something with a seal on the paper he moistened the part of the envelope which was sealed and opened it. This was in order not to tear the paper. Although old paper which had been stretched on *shōji*[22] could not be used because there was no strength in it, this too he disjoined so as not to tear it and used it as toilet paper in the privy. Otherwise, if the paper was a little torn, he put the scraps in a basket and did not throw away any. He sold the paper scraps to someone who seemed poor and left the price up to the buyer.

Whatever the case, he did not use elegant things. He always used rough things.

Our teacher said, "Among the people there is the fear of worshipping the emperor. In worshipping the shrine of the Sun Goddess one worships both [Sun Goddess and emperor]."

When [he was to] respectfully view the imperial palace, he always bathed to purify himself before approaching, and before the south gate he passed by with the feeling of worshipping the shrine of the Sun Goddess.

When it thundered, even though late at night, he always arose and reverently sat upright.

Before having an interview with a noble he always bathed.

"It is a fearful matter for people below to use the calligraphy of exalted nobles as a model," he warned.

Before an official signboard he took off his hat and bowed at the waist as he passed. This was to show respect for the official decrees.

In doffing his hat, he took it off more than 100 yards away. This was so as not to appear presumptuous.

When inspecting an official notice he was deeply reverent.

When he was going to meet someone from the Great Shrine at Ise he bathed before he set out. He greeted the person with a heart full of reverence for the gods. When he himself went to the shrine he bathed every night at the inn.

When going to his native village our teacher always bathed at his residence before he set out. Though the road was about sixteen miles he did not relieve himself until he reached his native residence. This was so as not to dirty his body. Arriving at his native village, he worshipped at the shrine of the village deity (*ujigami*) and then visited his parents' graves and after that went to his residence.

He offered to the gods rice cake (*kagami-mochi*) supplied by his pupils and afterwards ate it. When he had bought *sake* he sprinkled some worshipfully on the kitchen stove and afterwards used it.

If he touched his foot with his hand, even through his clothes, he would arise and wash his hand.

When a letter came from someone he would accept it thankfully and later open and read it. It was as if he were actually facing the other person.

If even an old pupil was lax in his aspiration to study (*gakumon*) he would firmly refuse to accept congratulatory gifts [from him].

If when he asked someone to buy something for him, the person would not take the price of it, he would not use it but would return it even if it were a small thing.

After receiving a gift he used fine writing paper for his return [token] present. This could be used for the final draft of handwriting or some other use. This he did so that his return present could be put to use and would not be a waste.

To silver coins (*gin*) wrapped in paper which he was sending to someone, he attached *noshi,*[23] and to pennies (*sen*) wrapped in paper he tied *mizuhiki*[24] and attached *noshi.*

Every time he went to urinate he took off his *hakama* and *haori* beforehand. When going to defecate he first urinated in the urinal and then went to the water closet. He was careful in this way because farm families dislike it if urine and excrement are mixed as it is inconvenient to transport.

When he took a bath he first cleaned himself carefully, and then entered [the bath tub].

When our teacher [was dressing] to go to the funeral of an old friend, a pupil offered him his *katabira*[25] with crests[26] on a white ground, but saying it to be troublesome he wore an [ordinary] dyed *katabira.*

On a day when our teacher was to lecture in the evening and he was talking at length with people, even when it reached the close of the day he did not show any sign [of anxiety] at all.

The pupils regretted the fact that our teacher cooked for himself. When they suggested that he employ a male servant, he replied that on the contrary since it would be too much trouble for him there was no need. But when the pupils pressed him he did not resist but hired someone.

Though this man, always gadding about, was incapable of even watching the door our teacher never said one word about it, and continued to employ him. The pupils knew this and got rid of the man. Again according to the pupils' plan he hired a man, and though this man was gentle, he was stupid. He did not even know how to tie his own *obi*[27] so our teacher tied it for him. Moreover, in cold weather both his feet ached with cracks and sores. Our teacher felt sorry for him and said, "I will bundle them up for you." And he just spread his legs and let our teacher tie them up. Since this man too was a trouble to our teacher the pupils also got rid of him. After that they resigned themselves to our teacher's will and he lived for the rest of his life cooking for himself.

When our teacher was reading, children of the neighborhood came and called to him in sport. Our teacher went to answer and the children ran away laughing. Coming again they did as before and our teacher also went to answer as before.

Our teacher when coming and going on the road in summer left the shade to others and himself walked in the sunshine. In winter he left the sunshine to others and himself walked in the shade.

Our teacher said, "The attainment of benevolence (*jin,* Chinese *jen*), since it is a virtue of the heart, is important. Although it cannot be quickly attained, there will be one or two matters in which benevolence can be practiced without having any anxiety, suffering hardships in one's body or spending money. If you do something in which it is practiced even one-thousandth part, it is still benevolence, and I believe it must be good. Because of this I note down the matter.

"When coming and going on the road if you have your mind on it, there will be matters in which you can help the world, such as by fixing the road. If you ask for an example, damming a small stream at the side of the road which had been running in the middle of the road is benevolence.

"When you are going out, if you leave definite word as to where you are going, either with your parents, brothers and sisters or wife, it will put others' minds at rest and it will be benevolence. When you leave word as to your route in coming and going, one who looks for you will not miss you and it is benevolence.

"Write your characters in *oieryū,*[28] for this is easy to read, and it will set others' minds at rest, and this is benevolence.

"If you draw a symbol on various sorts of umbrellas and straw hats it will distinguish them from those without the symbol, but compared with just writing one's name it is bad. If you write your name, out of a hundred people all one hundred will know it. If you make a symbol, out of a hundred people ninety will not know it. It will trouble the minds of many people and is not benevolence. I don't do it.

"Whatever you use, use it properly according to the circumstances, as for instance one uses water on top of Atago Mountain or Hieno Mountain [differently than] one uses water at Ōi River or Kamo River.[29] Acting so as not to trouble others' minds, this is benevolence.

"Even if there is something that to some extent displeases others, there is probably not anything that will become the basis of benevolence as much as being unselfish. Even though we try bit by bit, we do not succeed in this. Even though we would like to succeed in this, we lament that in our whole life our desires will probably not be fulfilled."

Our teacher said, "Because I have observed that many people labor to nourish their fields, for thirty years when I have been on a journey of even a day or half a day, I have used a privy when I needed to relieve myself. Where there was no privy, I have always been careful to relieve myself in a field. While this is a humble, small thing, I believe that it is a frugality appropriate to me."

Wherever our teacher was when he stopped at a tea shop, he stopped at a poor and humble looking place and gave a large price for the tea.

Our teacher said, "When I was twenty years old, I had an illness in the stomach and in order to preserve my health, morning and evening I ate *zōsui*.[30] Because of this I recovered from my illness in only a month. Reasoning from this I thought it was sufficient to nourish my body with two meals a day. After that till I was about forty I lived on two meals a day. Instead of eating four *gō*[31] per day as is usual, I was satisfied with three *gō*. The remaining *gō* I gave to charity. Not only that, but if you eat often, the expense of everything is great, so I gave the rice for the remaining meal to beggars and lived on two meals a day. But one evening at the beginning of my lecture someone said, 'If one uses one's voice and one's food is too meager, it will endanger life.' Thinking [my former practice] was not in accordance with my aspiration to impart to others the Way handed down to me in this brief life, after that I ate three meals a day."

One autumn when there were floods in neighboring provinces, there was a moon-viewing party. Our teacher was invited by his pupils and went. Later a certain person came to our teacher's place and said, "There are floods in neighboring provinces and many people are in distress. Doesn't going on a moon-viewing party show one is not troubled by the distress of others?"

Our teacher replied, "It is not that I am not distressed about the floods. Nevertheless, they are not my responsibility. Besides it would be rare if every year in all the various provinces nothing went wrong. However much we lament this, what good does it do? In the habitual gathering of pupils, there are those who do not come. When they do not gather it is easy to desert learning. Worrying about this is my responsibility. Because I fulfill my responsibility I hold meetings in order to gather, though infrequently, those who are close to me. We must know the responsibility of the upper classes and of the lower and not confuse them."

Our teacher said, "I regret the taking of life for no purpose. Since I was a boy, I have added cool water to hot bath water, or to foot bath water or water in which things had been boiled before pouring it out. This was so as not to kill insects in the earth.[32] I have been able to do this about seven times out of ten. However, this is a small matter. Because I sought to extinguish a craving mind I cooked for myself. I continuously concentrated on trying to eliminate a desirous mind. If a weak person like myself comes to be without desire like this, may he not be of some small assistance in helping the minds of other men?"

Our teacher said, "Although loyalty and filial piety are not in my person, I always wish to reform the lack of loyalty and filial piety in others, and the desire to teach and guide even one person is my passion."

A certain person inquired of our teacher, saying, "Do you criticize present-day scholars for not basing themselves on the principle of nature (*seiri*) because your own position is correct? [If you do] if there is anything in you even slightly incorrect, you cannot [criticize them]."

Our teacher replied, "I do not criticize others. I lament the fact [that there are those who] do not know the basic meaning of learning (*gakumon*). Let us say, for example, that there are here today many retainers whose lords have been murdered. The present-day scholars, however, are like men who have the strength but are without the aspiration to avenge the injury. Though I have the aspiration to revenge the injury, I am like a person whose loins are unslung. This is because I am a late starter in learning and untalented. I am weak and without virtue and my actions are not valiant. It is only furtively that I know the goodness of nature. Alas, though I have the aspiration to cause others to know this, since I am called a low person there are few people who will really listen [to me]. This is as if a coward wills to avenge the injury to his lord, but he cannot do it. The present-day scholars, however, study from youth and become of broad learning and much knowledge, or they enter government service and are notable men because of being known in the world. But absorbed in literature (*bungaku*) they do not know that Yao and Shun, with the principle of nature (*seiri*) as the basis of their learning, governed the empire and only followed nature. Their not knowing this is like having the strength but not willing to avenge the injury. Knowing that these men, if they knew the nature, could revive the Way, I lament."

Though our teacher always said to the pupils that they should know their own nature, there were only two or three who believed this. Among these Saitō Zemmon deeply believed it, and day and night concentrated on meditation (*kufu*) as much as possible. One night, unexpectedly hearing the sound of a drum, he knew the nature. Hereupon, more and more, conviction arose, was daily nourished and finally became complete. Thereupon, Zemmon from the depth of his conviction helped his friends, but still their aspiration was weak. Kimura Shigemitsu from the beginning strongly believed and after a lapse of time his meditation bore fruit. One winter while covering *shōji,* he suddenly knew his own nature. Greatly rejoicing he came to our teacher's home to show what he had attained, "Wonderful! Marvelous! This, well, this, ah . . ."

Our teacher on this occasion granted that Shigemitsu knew the nature.

From this the pupils really believed that the nature could be directly known. When they concentrated their minds in meditation, and faith penetrated to the marrow, they each forgot to eat and sleep and either engaged in quiet sitting (*seiza*) or earnestly enquired. Those who shortly came to know their natures were many.

Our teacher, speaking to a pupil who had come to know his nature, said, "What learning creates is that one reflects on righteousness and unrighteousness so that one will only follow righteousness. To cultivate the nature without accumulating righteousness is not the Way of the sages." He often made this point.

Our teacher said, "My natural disposition was argumentative, and I was from an early age disliked by friends. I was often unkind but at about 14 or 15 I suddenly came to my senses and regretted this, and though I thought that by about 30 I had in general corrected this, still it showed in the edges of words, and at 40 I felt there was still a little sourness like burnt plum pickle, but by about 50 I felt my bad disposition was quite gone."

Till about 50 when our teacher was in someone's presence and there was something on which their minds differed, it seemed that he showed a sour face, but at about 50 he did not show the slightest sign whether there was something on which they differed or not, and at about 60 he said, "Now I have become [completely] at ease (*raku*)."

Our teacher's mother now and then came up from her native village. When it was spring he accompanied her to such places as Gion[33] and Kiyomizu,[34] or he accompanied her to a theater to amuse her. He said to his mother, "Though I live in Kyōto I seldom see things such as plays. This is so as to become a model for others who come in contact with me. Only because my mother comes to Kyōto, I go sight-seeing in a leisurely way." [Hearing this,] his mother was happy.

When our teacher was thirty-two his father died and when he was fifty-two his mother died. He felt his grief to the full in the mourning period.

There was a Zen nun who came to our teacher's lecture hall, but one year she visited around in Yamato and went to places where women probably ought not to go. When she came and brought her travel diary and showed it to our teacher he sent her away saying, "Do not come again."

In the summer of the third year of Gembun (1738) our teacher, accompanied by five or six pupils, went for the hot baths to Tajima,[35] but even there our teacher night and day corrected the proofs of *Toi-mondō*. One day, taking a small boat together with his pupils, he [went to] view the Seto.[36] They put out to sea, and in the north there was [open] sea of unknown extent. Suddenly the wind began to blow fiercely. The pupils were greatly frightened. Our teacher remained unmoved. Then they landed the boat on an islet of piled up rocks, called Nochigashima and ascending it he looked around. Gradually the wind subsided and the waves became calm and the surface of the sea extended far and wide. Then our teacher pointed to the boundlessness of the sea and showed what a small thing is the human body. The pupils profited from this.

In the great drouth of the third year of Gembun (1738) when those above and below together were praying for rain, our teacher also daily bathed and privately prayed for rain. From the night of the 21st of the seventh month it rained heavily and the joy of noble and humble had no limit. On that day at the home of a nearby disciple our teacher and his pupils gathered and were rejoicing in the rain when a small wind began to blow. Our teacher with a troubled expression as though something were the matter said, "For a brief while I am returning home. I will come back," and leaving his seat he went out.

After a little while he returned and his disciples inquired as to the reason for his going home. Our teacher said, "When I looked up into heaven with the wind blowing as it was, the clouds appeared to be going toward the northwest. This is the sign of a wind arising. If there should also be a fierce wind when there is a great rain like this, it is very likely to injure the crops. Returning home, I bathed and secretly prayed." The words of the prayer were,

> *Ame o koi kaze shizuka ni to inoru nari*
> *Mamorase tamae futabashira no kami.*
> I pray for rain and calm wind,
> Protect us, O two-pillar god.[37]

When there was a fire anywhere it troubled our teacher's heart. This was because he lamented the affliction to men and the destruction of property. On a winter's night of a certain year there was a great fire in Shimo Okazaki Village. Feeling that if food were lacking it would be hard to bear since it was the dead of winter and the middle of the night, our teacher gathered together his pupils in the middle of the night, cooked rice, made it into rice balls, and, accompanied by his pupils, brought it to Okazaki and gave it out to all persons in distress.

On an occasion when four or five pupils were gathered at our teacher's house a fellow pupil brought an otter. Though the idea was to kill it and divide it among them, since none of them was accustomed to doing it they asked what they should do. Though our teacher also was unaccustomed to doing it, he sharpened a small knife well and killed the otter. He easily killed it and divided it.

From the winter of the fifth year of Gembun (1740) to the following spring there were many suffering people in all parts of upper and lower Kyōto. That winter, there were only stories of distress, but there were no people distributing alms. Our teacher deeply lamented this, and sent his pupils in groups to various places and had them seek out those in distress. Because there were many pitiful things worse than they had heard [our teacher] divided his pupils into groups of three or four, went to those places from the 28th of the last month and distributed small coins as alms. From the second day of the first month of the next year, those distributing alms from place to place became very numerous.

One time when our teacher was lecturing in Ōsaka a certain Shintoist started saying, "This lecture which forces Japanese people into a Chinese spirit is indeed wrong. We must drive out such an enemy of the gods. Let us meet and put the matter to rights."

Repeatedly he said that he would come up and settle the matter. Our teacher, pretending to be occupied, did not take it up and tried to avoid an incident. But he continued interrupting our teacher, saying, "If you don't meet me you must stop lecturing here at once."

Because he was forcibly hindered our teacher had no choice, but said, "All right, I give in to your wish. We will meet."

When the Shintoist accompanied by five or six pupils came to our teacher's place, our teacher said, "Well, I feel great joy in your faith in Shintō. I hear that you call me an enemy of the gods. I do not understand it at all. Since I do not at all feel that way, I honestly teach others our country's Shintō without the slightest duplicity, using the counsels of Confucianism and Buddism. I will make an oath that I am thoroughly loyal to the gods and do not lie when I say this. Not only do I lack duplicity, but I will have two or three pupils who are now in this hall likewise make an oath. If you ask me to add the other pupils not present, I will comply with your request. You also must make an oath without a wicked intent and have all your pupils likewise make an oath. I will give you anything to prove this oath. With this oath we will dispel doubts between us as to whether or not we are thoroughly loyal to the gods, and after that we can converse at leisure."

The Shintoist said, "As for the matter of an oath I really think it reasonable, but nevertheless it is a fearful thing. Having heard that your intention is without duplicity I will not go on to the oath," and he declined the offer.

A certain Mr. Yukifuji and a certain Mr. Mori read *Toimondō*. Mr.

Mori enquired of our teacher about certain doubtful places in the book. Mr. Yukifuji twice spent the whole day in discussion. Since the matters [discussed] were many, only one or two are presented here.

Mr. Yukifuji asked, "Are mind (*kokoro*) and nature (*sei*) different?"

Our teacher replied, "When you say mind, it contains both nature and feelings (*jō,* Chinese *ch'ing*), there is motion and rest (*dōzei*), essence and function (*taiyō*).[38] When you say nature, since it is essence, it is at rest. Mind being in motion is function. If we talk about the essence of the mind, it is what resembles nature. The essence of the mind is that, with respect to changing, it is no mind (*mushin*). The nature is also no mind. The mind belongs to substance (*ki,* Chinese *ch'i*), nature belongs to principle (*ri,* Chinese *li*). Principle is included in everything and is not something manifest. The mind, however, is manifest, and changes as it contacts things. When we are speaking from the point of view of man, substance is before and nature is after. When we are speaking from the point of view of the principle of heaven and earth, there is principle and afterwards substance arises. When we speak of the whole (*zentai*), principle is one thing. To illustrate the fact that principle is in everything but is not manifest, there is an *uta*[39] of the monk Dōgen:[40]

Yo no naka wa nani ni tatoen mizutori no
hashifuru tsuyu ni yadoru tsukikage.
To what shall we compare the world?
Moonlight reflected in the drops shed by a waterfowl.

"It is like the fact that all the moonlight is reflected in even the smallest fragment of the falling drops. Though we say that principle does not appear, we must know that it exists within. When we perceive our own nature with enlightenment, there is not anything like the *kami,* the Supreme Limit, or the Buddha.[41] Therefore if we comprehend this nature, we can say that even Confucians, Taoists, Buddhists, the hundred schools[42] and the myriad talents, are branch shrines of this, our land of the gods. A certain book says, 'If we say that Japan alone is a land of the gods, being broad, it is [actually] narrow [that is, limited]. But if we say that there is a land of the gods in even the smallest particle, being narrow [limited in space] it is actually limitless."

Mr. Yukifuji, saying, "It is so," noted down this *uta.*

Mr. Yukifuji asked, "In instructing your pupils do you teach making the mind (*kokoro*) the whole of it?"

Our teacher replied, "It is not thus. I teach by means of conduct."

Mr. Yukifuji inquired, "If it is thus, then do you teach making the five relations the whole of it?"

Our teacher replied, "It is so."

Mr. Yukifuji asked, "The teacher has no wife. How is that?"

Our teacher replied, "My aspiration is to propagate the Way. But if I were encumbered with a wife I fear I would lose the Way so I live alone."

Mr. Yukifuji said, "I have doubts here. Is it not the Way to take a wife, however difficult [that may be]? Your teaching makes the five relations the whole of it, but to me this destroys the five relations. How about this?"

Our teacher replied, "Yes, but nevertheless what you propose is a position like that of Yen Tzu.[43] Though Tzu Lu and Jan Ch'iu were very virtuous, putting service first, Jan Ch'iu was unprofitably led into the wrong path of the Chi family, and Tzu Lu mistook righteousness and, participating in unrighteousness, died in battle. It is because they did not come up to Yen Tzu. How much less can a person such as I at all come up to the behaviour of Yen Tzu! For this reason I live alone. Since I have brothers and nephews, the worship of the ancestors will not be abandoned. I have no strong desire for flourishing descendants who will worship me. My humble wish is that, though I throw away myself, I will see the Way practiced. This is my desire."

One summer when our teacher went to lecture at the home of Kurosugi Masatane in Shiraki Village, Ishikawa District, Kawachi Province, he saw that a running stream had been channeled near a fence. He inquired, "Has this running stream always been here?"

Masatane replied, "As you say, this running stream has always been here."

Our teacher said, "I inquire because it is the season when farmers need water."

He wondered if they had contrived this stream so that he would escape the heat and if so he was afraid of interfering with farming.

On the way from the inn to the lecture hall he looked at the grass in the fields. Though wearing his ceremonial garment he put his hand into the muddy earth and took some grass. He said, "This is bad grass which steals the manure," and showed it to his pupils. People of that region came to exert themselves in their family occupation after they heard our teacher lecture.

At the end of the lectures when Masatane offered a package of silver as a present, our teacher would not accept it. Though he repeatedly pressed it on him, he would not accept and said, "On top of my receiving from you the expenses of my stay and of the journey, there is no reason for me to accept a gift," and in the end he did not accept it.

The Kyōto pupils went to meet our teacher, and arrived the day the lectures were to end. Masatane said to our teacher, "Since this is the first visit of those who have come to meet you, they should stay a day or two and allow me to show them the sights and historic places of the neighborhood."

When our teacher told the pupils Masatane's thought, the pupils replied. "Although we are grateful, we do not desire pleasure excursions, but only wish your return to the capital." Thus they set out early the next morning.

After they returned to Kyōto he recounted to his pupils the events of his stay in Kawachi and said, "In Kawachi this time I did not accept Masatane's gift because it exceeded propriety. What would have been suitable?"

Each pupil replied and our teacher said, "One *ryō*[44] of silver and one cotton handkerchief. This would have been suitable to the occasion."

When on another day the pupils who had come to meet him were at his side he said, "I do not like staying over for pleasure excursions after my business is completed, no matter where it is," and he rejoiced at their not staying.

There are two books which our teacher wrote on the request of his pupils. The first was based on rough drafts of the words with which he replied to the inquiries of people every day. He collected these, made them into a book and called it *Toimondō*. It was printed in the fall of the fourth year of Gembun (1739), the seventh month. The other book [originated as follows]: in the fall of the third year of Kampō (1743) the pupils, having asked about ordinary matters of economy in order to put this into practice, made a book out of the gist of what they had heard and showed it to our teacher. Our teacher approved of this. After that when the pupils were all practicing economy a certain man argued with our teacher, saying it was bad for the pupils suddenly to practice economy. Writing up this argument and making a book, our teacher called it *Seikaron*. It was printed in the summer of the first year of Eikyō (1744), the fifth month.

Our teacher became ill on the night of the 23rd of the ninth month, the fall of the first year of Eikyō (1744), and died on the 24th at noon in his dwelling. He was sixty years of age. He was buried at Toribe Mountain, southeast of Kyōto. After his death the things which remained in his house were only three boxes of books, the drafts of his replies to the daily questions of people, his reading stand, his desk, his inkstone, his clothes and the utensils of his daily use.

Notes

1. *Jiseki*, SGSS, vol. 6, p. 319.
2. Characters for personal names may be found in Appendix III, List of Chinese and Japanese Names. Characters for other names may be found in Appendix II, List of Chinese and Japanese Words.
3. A kind of coat. From what follows we must assume that a silk *haori* would have been more in keeping with his status.
4. Another name of Jōdo Shinshū.
5. Shinran Shōnin.
6. Nature is used in the broadest

philosophical sense, meaning one's own nature and at the same time the nature of the universe.

7. Legendary Chinese rulers often cited by Confucians for their ideal government.

8. Apparently by wiping the mouthpiece.

9. Kurumayachō is a street in Kyōto which runs north and south. "Above" means north toward the imperial palace.

10. Sakaichō is a street in Kyōto which runs north and south. "Below" means south away from the imperial palace.

11. Kawachi and Izumi are nearby provinces.

12. A kind of trousers.

13. For explanation of these books see Chapter VI, notes 12 and 13.

14. Linen, cotton or hemp cloth.

15. "A hempen stuff woven and bleached at Nara in the province of Yamato." (Brinkley)

16. Pongee.

17. Bean paste.

18. A side dish eaten with rice.

19. Varieties of fish.

20. Straw matting.

21. Japanese ink comes in dry sticks and is rubbed on an inkstone and mixed with water before being used. Decorated ink sticks are more expensive than plain ones.

22. A sliding screen or door.

23. "The long thin strip of dried sea-ear always attached to a present." (Brinkley)

24. "A fine paper cord usually red or white for tying presents." (Brinkley)

25. Summer garment made of hemp.

26. Crests are distinguishing symbols belonging to families.

27. A kind of belt or sash.

28. "A style of handwriting originated by Son'en Hōshinnō, the son of the Emperor Fushimi." (Brinkley)

29. The Ōi River (another name for the Katsura River) drains Atago Mountain and the Kano drains Hieno (Hiezan). All are in the vicinity of Kyōto. The idea is that one uses water differently on top of a mountain where all water must be hauled up than one does near a river. Thus one should always act in accordance with the situation.

30. "A kind of gruel containing *miso* and chopped vegetables [and rice], a medley soup." (Brinkley)

31. A *gō* is 0.318 pint.

32. This custom appears to be of Buddhist origin.

33. "Gion is a ward of Kyōto formerly celebrated for its cherry trees, which when in blossom attracted thousands of visitors." (Papinot)

34. Kiyomizu was a famous temple east of Kyōto built in 780.

35. A province.

36. The Inland Sea. The open sea of unknown extent in the next sentence is the Pacific Ocean.

37. The two pillars refer to the inner and outer shrines at Ise.

38. The paragraph following is a very condensed statement of some of the central problems of neo-Confucian philosophy. The essential idea is that though the mind has within it the *li* or principle (almost a Platonic idea), it is composed of *ch'i* or ether which is subject to change. Thus when it is said that there is no mind it means either that there is no *ch'i* and only *li* remains, or more likely that the *ch'i* is now opaque to *li*. The thought is that of Chu Hsi. On this problem as handled by Chu Hsi see Fung, *History of Chinese Philosophy*, vol. II, pp. 534-546.

39. A 31-syllable Japanese poem.

40. Dōgen (1200-1253) was the founder of the Sōtō sect of Zen.

41. Nature transcends the specific conceptions of the three religions. *Kami* is the Shintō word for god. The Supreme Ultimate is the Confucian conception of the absolute.

42. A loose term covering the various schools of Chinese philosophy.

43. Yen Tzu, Tzu Lu, and Jan Ch'iu were all disciples of Confucius.

44. A unit of coinage.

APPENDIX

II

List of Chinese and Japanese Words

(The following list supplies characters for all Chinese and Japanese words used in the text, including place names and other names with the exception of personal names which are included in Appendix III. A brief identification follows each term but it is not possible to give a complete definition. In those cases where a rather detailed explanation of a term has appeared in the text a reference is given to the page or note where such explanation may be found.)

CHINESE

ch'eng	誠	Sincerity.
ch'i	氣	Ether, substance.
chih	知	Wisdom, knowledge.
Chin Ssu Lu	近思錄	See Chapter VI, note 12.
ching	敬	Earnestness.
ch'ing	情	Feelings, emotions.
Hsiao Hsüeh	小學	The *Small Learning*, a compilation by Chu Hsi.
hsiao t'i	孝悌	Filial piety and brotherliness.
hsin	心	Heart, mind.
hsin	信	Good faith.

hsing	行	Action.
hsing	形	Form.
hsing	性	Nature in the philosophical sense.
hsing li	性理	The principle of nature.
Hsing-li Tzu-i	性理字義	See Chapter VI, note 12.
i, yi	義	Righteousness.
jen	仁	Benevolence.
li	理	Principle, reason.
li	利	Profit.
ming	命	Fate, destiny, decree.
shih	士	Knight.
T'ai-ch'i T'u-shuo	太極圖說	*Diagram of the Supreme Ultimate Explained,* see Chapter VI, note 12.
tao	道	The Way.
yamen	衙門	Civil or military court, the seat of the local magistrate.
Yin	殷	Another name for the Shang Dynasty, 1766-1137 B.C.

JAPANESE

Ama no Oshihi no Mikoto	天忍日命	A Shintō deity.
Amaterasu O-Mikami	天照大神	The Sun Goddess.
Amida	阿彌陀	The Buddha Amitabha.
ashigaru	足輕	Common foot soldier.
Atago	愛宕	A mountain near Kyōto.
bakufu	幕府	The shogunate, literally "tent government."
bantō	番頭	Chief clerk.
Bukyō Shōgaku	武教小學	A work by Yamaga Sokō.
bundo	分度	See p. 130.
bungaku	文學	Literature.
bushi	武士	A *samurai.*
Bushi no Michi	武士の道	Same as *Bushidō.*
Bushidō	武士道	The Way of the Warrior.
chō	町	A city ward.
Chōkyō	貞享	Year period, 1684-1688. Also read Teikyō.
chū	忠	Loyalty.
chūgen	中間	*Samurai's* attendant.
chūnen	中年	See p. 51.
Daijingū	大神宮	A shrine dedicated to the Sun Goddess.
daikan	代官	See p. 43.
daimyō	大名	The lord of a *han.*
Dainihonshi	大日本史	*History of Japan.*
dansho	斷書	See p. 169.
detchi	丁稚	An apprentice.
dōwa	道話	A moral discourse, another name for *kōshaku.*

dōzei	動静	Motion and rest.
ebiza	海老ざこ	A kind of seafood.
Edo	江戸	Old name for Tōkyō. The Tokugawa Period is sometimes called the Edo Period.
Edokko	江戸っ子	An inhabitant of Edo.
Eikyō	延享	Year period, 1744-1748.
Engishiki	延喜式	A collection of regulations for ceremonies, etc., compiled in 927 A.D.
gaku	學	Learning, study.
gakumon	學問	Learning, study.
gakusha	學者	A scholar, a learned man.
Gekū	外宮	The Outer Shrine of Ise. Sometimes read Gegū.
gembuku	元服	Ceremony of coming of age.
Gembun	元文	Year period, 1736-1741.
Genroku	元祿	Year period, 1688-1704.
gi	義	Righteousness.
Gion	祇園	A ward of Kyōto.
gin	銀	Silver (coin).
giri	義理	Right.
gō	合	0.318 pint.
Gokōsatsu Dōwa	御高札道話	*Lectures on Government Notices,* a work of Nakazawa Doni.
gonin-gumi	五人組	Five-family group.
Gorakusha	五樂舍	A *kōsha.*
gōshi	鄉士	See p. 41.
Hagakure	葉隱	A 17th century work on *Bushidō.*
hakama	袴	A kind of trousers.
hakari-kujira	はかり鯨	A kind of fish.

han	藩	A fief.
hannin-mae	半人前	See p. 49.
haori	羽織	A sort of coat.
hatamoto	旗本	Direct retainer to the *shōgun*.
Hieno	日枝	A mountain near Kyōto.
Higashi Agata	東縣	Home village of Ishida Baigan.
Hizen	肥前	A province.
Hōei	寶永	Year period, 1704-1711.
hojinshi	輔仁司	See p. 168.
Hokekyō	法華經	The *Lotus Sutra*.
hōkō	奉公	Service.
Honganji	本願寺	The Shin sect.
honshin	本心	One's true (basic) heart or mind.
hōon	報恩	Repayment of blessings.
hotoke	佛	The Buddha.
Hōtoku	報德	Movement founded by Ninomiya Sontoku. The term means repayment of blessings.
ichiri	一理	One principle.
Inari	稻荷	A folk deity, the god of harvests.
inkan	印鑑	A seal.
Ise	伊勢	A province.
Ishikawa	石川	A district in Kawachi province.
Izanagi no Mikoto	伊弉諾命	Male creator deity of Shintō mythology.
Izanami no Mikoto	伊弉冊命	Female creator deity of Shintō mythology.
Izumi	和泉	A province.
Izumo	出雲	A province.

jiai	慈愛	Affection, love.
jin	仁	Benevolence.
jinsha	仁者	A benevolent person, a good man.
jiri-rita	自利利他	The harmony of profiting self and others.
Jishūsha	時習舎	A *kōsha.*
Jizō	地藏	A folk deity, protector of children.
jō	情	Feelings, emotions.
Jōdo	淨土	Pure Land, a Buddhist sect.
Jōdo Shinshū	淨土眞宗	True Sect of Pure Land, the Shin sect.
jokun	女訓	Shingaku lectures for women.
kagami	鏡	A mirror.
kagami-mochi	鏡餅	A round mirror-shaped rice cake offered to a deity.
kagura	神樂	A sacred dance.
kaidoku	會讀	Reading in turn.
kaiho	會輔	Shingaku discussion meeting.
Kaimokushō	開目鈔	*The Awakening to the Truth,* a work by Nichiren.
kaiyūshi	會友司	See p. 168.
kakun	家訓	House rules, family precepts.
Kamado no kami	竈の神	The god of the kitchen.
Kamakura	鎌倉	Place name.
kami	神	Native Japanese word for god. A Shintō deity.
Kami no Michi	神の道	Same as Shintō.
kamidana	神棚	Household Shintō shrine.
kamishimo	裃	Ceremonial dress.
Kamo,	賀茂	A river near Kyōto.

Kampō	寛保	Year period, 1741-1744.
Kansai	關西	Ōsaka-Kyōto area.
Kantō	關東	Tōkyō area.
kashirabun	頭	Chief.
katabira	帷子	A hemp gown for summer.
Katsura	桂	Another name for the Ōi River.
Kawachi	河内	A province.
Kegon	華嚴	A Buddhist sect.
kei	形	Form.
keizai	經濟	The economy.
kenshō	見性	Enlightenment, knowing the nature.
kenyaku	儉約	Economy, thrift.
ki	氣	Ether, substance.
Kinshiroku	近思錄	See Chapter VI, note 12.
Kishū	紀州	A province.
Kiyomizu	清水	A temple near Kyōto.
kō	孝	Filial piety.
kō	講	Confraternity.
koaizako	こあいざこ	A kind of fish.
Kogaku	小學	The *Small Learning,* a compilation by Chu Hsi.
Kojiki	古事記	*Record of Ancient Things,* compiled in 712 A.D.
kokoro	心	Heart, mind.
Kokugaku	國學	National studies, particularly the school of which Motoori and Hirata are the outstanding members.
Kokugakusha	國學者	A member of the Kokugaku school.

kokuon	國恩	The blessings of the nation.
kokusan	國產	Domestic (as opposed to foreign) production.
kokutai	國體	National polity.
kōsha	黌舍	Shingaku lecture hall.
kōshaku	講釋	A lecture.
kōshi	講師	See p. 168.
koshōgumi	小姓組	See p. 44.
kōtei	孝悌	Filial piety and brotherliness.
kufu	工夫	Meditation.
kun	君	Lord.
Kunshikun	君子訓	A work by Kaibara Ekiken.
kunshin ittai	君臣一體	Unity of lord and subject (retainer).
Kuwada	桑田	A district in Tamba province.
Kyūshū	九州	The southernmost of the four large islands of Japan.
Kyūhanjō	舊藩情	An essay by Fukuzawa Yukichi on conditions in the old *han*.
Manyōshū	萬葉集	Ancient anthology of poems compiled in the eighth century.
mappō	末法	"The latter end of the Law," designating a period of religious degeneracy.
matsurigoto	政	Literally "religious observances," used to designate affairs of state.
Meiji	明治	Year period, 1868-1911.
Meirinsha	明倫舍	*A kōsha.*
mi o tsutsumi	身を敬み	Behave prudently.
mikado	帝	The emperor of Japan.
miso	味噌	Bean paste.
Mitogaku	水戸學	The Mito Learning, a school centered in the Mito fief.

Mitsubishi	三菱	One of the *zaibatsu* corporations. Owned by the Iwasaki family.
Mitsui	三井	One of the *zaibatsu* corporations. Owned by the Mitsui family.
mizuhiki	水引	See Appendix I, note 24.
moto	本	The foundation, the essentials.
mukashi banashi	昔話	Old tales.
mura	村	A village.
mushin	無心	No mind.
Nabeshima	鍋島	A *han*.
Nagasaki	長崎	Place name.
nakakoshō	中小姓	See p. 44.
Nakatsu	中津	Place name.
nanushi	名主	Head of a village.
naraza-ra-shi	奈良晒布	See Appendix I, note 15.
Nihongi	日本紀	*Chronicles of Japan,* compiled in 720 A.D.
Ninōkyō	仁王經	*Sutra of the Benevolent Kings.*
noshi	熨斗	See Appendix I, note 23.
nuno	布	See Appendix I, note 14.
obi	帯	A sort of belt or sash.
Ōi	大井	A river near Kyōto also known as the Katsura.
oieryū	御家流	See Appendix I, note 28.
Oike	御池	A street in Kyōto.
Okina Mondō	翁問答	A work by Nakae Tōju.
okonai	行い	Action.
Ōmi	近江	A province.
on	恩	Blessings.

Onna Daigaku	女大學	*The Great Learning for Women,* a work by Kaibara Ekiken.
raku	樂	Ease, pleasure.
rinkō	輪講	Construing a book in turn.
Rokkaku	六角	A street in Kyōto.
roku	祿	Stipend.
Rinzai	臨濟	A branch of the Zen sect.
rōyū	老友	See p. 168.
ryō	兩	Unit of coinage.
ryōshin	良心	The good heart, the true heart.
sai	菜	A side dish eaten with rice.
Sakaichō	堺町	A street in Kyōto.
sake	酒	Rice wine.
samisen	三味線	A three-stringed musical instrument.
samurai	侍, 士	A warrior.
samurai no michi	侍の道	Same as *Bushidō.*
sangū	參宮	A pilgrimage to the shrine of Ise.
sankyō itchi	三教一致	The harmony of the three teachings, Shintō, Confucianism and Buddhism.
sansha	三舍	The three *kōsha* which formed the Kyōto nucleus of Shingaku.
sansha inkan	三舍印鑑	The seal of the *sansha.*
Sanzensha	參前舍	A *kōsha.*
sei	性	Nature in the philosophical sense.
seigaku	性學	See Chapter VI, note 79.
seiri	性理	Principle of nature.
Seiri Jigi	性理字義	See Chapter VI, note 12.

seiza 靜坐 Contemplation, quiet sitting.

Sekigahara 關ヶ原 The battle in which Ieyasu won his decisive victory, 1600.

sen 錢 Penny.

seppuku 切腹 Suicide by disembowelment.

Seto 瀨戸 The Inland Sea.

shashu 舎主 Head of a *kōsha*.

shi 士 A *samurai*.

shihainin 支配人 A manager.

Shimo Okazaki 下岡崎 Place name.

shin 臣 Retainer.

Shingaku 心學 A movement founded by Ishida Baigan. The term means heart or mind learning.

Shindai Kuketsu 神代口訣 A work by Imbe no Masamichi, 1367.

shinjin 信心 Faith, a believing heart.

shinkō 信仰 Faith, belief.

Shinshū 眞宗 The True Sect of Pure Land. The Shin sect.

Shintō 神道 The Shintō religion. The Way of the gods.

Shintō Gobusho 神道五部書 A Shintō work compiled probably in the 13th century.

Shiraki 白木 Place name.

shiyō 枝葉 Details, inessentials.

shōgun 將軍 The military ruler of Japan.

shōji 障子 Paper sliding door or screen.

shōjiki 正直 Honesty.

shokubun 職分 Status, occupation.

shokugyō 職業 Occupation, calling.

shōnin 商人 Merchant.

shonyū 初入 Student.

Shōwa 昭和 Year period, 1926-

shōya 庄屋 Village headman.

Shūseisha 修正舎 A *kōsha.*

shūshi 宗旨 A religion, a faith.

sonnō 尊王 Revere the emperor.

sonnō jōi 尊王攘夷 Revere the emperor; expel the barbarians.

Sōtō 曹洞 A branch of the Zen sect.

tai 體 Essence, literally "body."

Taikyoku Zusetsu 大極圖說 See Chapter VI, note 12.

Tajima 但馬 A province.

Tamba 丹波 A province.

tatami 疊 A mat, matting.

tedai 手代 A clerk.

Tempō 天保 Year period, 1830-1844.

Tendai 天臺 A Buddhist sect.

tendō 天道 The Way of heaven.

tenshoku 天職 A vocation, a calling.

tensoku 店則 Shop rules.

Tōdaiji 東大寺 Buddhist temple at Nara erected in 728.

tokō 都講 See p. 167.

tokonoma 床の間 An alcove.

Tokugawa 德川 Shogunal house 1600-1868.

tomokoshō 供小姓 See p. 44.

Toribe 鳥邊 Mountain southeast of Kyōto where Ishida was buried.

toshiyori 年寄 An elder.

tozama 外樣 The outside lords.

tsumugi 紬 Pongee.

Tsurezuregusa 徒然草 See Chapter VI, note 13.

ujigami 氏神 Tutelary or patron deity.

uru 得る Attain.

uta 歌 A 31-syllable Japanese poem.

Warongo 和論語 *Japanese Analects.*

Yamaga Gorui 山鹿語類 A work by Yamaga Sokō.

Yamato 大和 A province, more broadly Japan.

yō 用 Function, use.

Yonezawa 米澤 *Han* of the Uesugi family.

zaibatsu 財閥 The supercorporations of modern Japan.

Zen 禪 A Buddhist sect.

zendō 禪堂 Zen meditation hall.

zenkun 前訓 Shingaku instruction for children.

zentai 全體 The whole.

zōsui 雜炊 See Appendix I, note 30.

APPENDIX
III

List of Chinese and Japanese Names

CHINESE

Ch'eng Hao 程顥
Chou Tun-yi 周敦頤
Chu Hsi 朱熹
Chuang Tzu 莊子
Fei Hsiao-tung 費孝通
Fung Yu-lan 馮友蘭
Hsün Tzu 荀子
Jan Ch'iu 冉求
Lao Tzu 老子
Shun 舜
Tzu Lu 子路
Wang Yang-ming 王陽明
Yao 堯
Yen Tzu 顏子

JAPANESE

Dōgen	道元
Eisai	榮西
Fukuzawa Yukichi	福澤諭吉
Fushimi Tennō	伏見天皇
Gamō Kumpei	蒲生君平
Hayashi Shihei	林子平
Hirata Atsutane	平田篤胤
Hōnen Shōnin	法然上人
Hosoi Heishū	細井平洲
Ichida	市田
Imbe no Masamichi	忌部正通
Ise Teijo	伊勢貞丈
Ishida Baigan (Okinaga, Kampei)	石田梅巖，興長，勘平
Ishida Jōshin	石田淨心
Ishikawa Ken	石川謙
Iwasaki	岩崎
Jimmu Tennō	神武天皇
Kada Azumamaro	荷田春滿
Kado	角
Kaibara Ekiken	貝原益軒
Kaihō Seiryō	海保青陵
Kamo Mabuchi	加茂眞淵
Kawabe no Omi	河邊臣

Kawakami Tasuke 川上多助
Keichū 契沖
Kimura Shigemitsu 木村重光
Kitabatake Chikafusa 北畠親房
Kumazawa Banzan 熊澤蕃山
Kurosugi Masatane 黒杉政胤
Kuroyanagi 黒柳

Meiji Tennō 明治天皇
Minamoto Yoritomo 源頼朝
Mitsui Takafusa 三井高房
Miura Baien 三浦梅園
Miyamoto Mataji 宮本又次
Mori 森
Motoori Norinaga 本居宣長
Muro Kyūsō 室鳩巣
Musō Kokushi 夢窓國師
Naitō Kanji 内藤莞爾
Nakae Tōju 中江藤樹
Nakai 中井
Nakamura 中村
Nakatomi 中臣
Nakazawa Dōni 中澤道二
Negi 禰宜
Nichiren 日蓮

Ninomiya Sontoku 二宮尊徳
Oguri Ryōun 小栗了雲
Okudaira 奥平
Rennyo Shōnin 蓮如上人
Saitō Zemmon 齋藤全門
Shinran Shōnin 親鸞上人
Shōmu Tennō 聖武天皇
Son'en Hōshinnō 尊圓法親王
Suiko Tennō 推古天皇
Suzuki Daisetsu 鈴木大拙
Tachibana no Moribe 橘守部
Takata Zenemon 高田善衛門
Takayama Masayuki 高山正之
Takechi 高市
Takeda Shingen 武田信玄
Takekoshi Yosaburo 竹越與三郎
Teshima Toan 手島堵庵
Tokugawa Ieyasu 徳川家康
Tokugawa Mitsukuni 徳川光圀
Tokugawa Nariaki 徳川齊昭
Tokugawa Yoshimune 徳川吉宗
Tomita Kōkei 富田高慶
Takano Shōseki 高野昌碩
Uekawa Kisui 上河淇水

Uesugi Harunori	上杉治憲
Wakizaka Gidō	脇阪義堂
Watsuji Tetsurō	和辻哲郎
Yamaga Sokō	山鹿素行
Yamagata Hantō	山片蟠桃
Yodoya	淀屋
Yoshida no Kaneyoshi	吉田兼好
Yoshida Shōin	吉田松陰
Yukifuji	行藤

Bibliography

WORKS IN JAPANESE

Azuma Shintaro: *Kinsei Nihon Keizai Rinri Shisō Shi* (The History of Modern Japanese Economic Ethical Thought, A Study of the Economic Ethical Thought of Japanese Confucians in the Early Edo Period). 461 pp. Tōkyō, 1944.

Hasegawa Kōhei: "Chōnin Seikatsu to Shingaku Shisō" (*Chōnin* Life and Shingaku Thought). *Shingaku,* Vol. 1. 70 pp. Tōkyō, 1941.

_______________: "Shingaku Kenkyū no Genjō" (The Present State of Shingaku Studies). *Shingaku,* Vol. 7. 98 pp. Tōkyō, 1942.

Hirano Gitarō: "Keizai Rinri to Shokubun Shisō" (The Economic Ethic and the Idea of *Shokubun*). *Shakai Seisaku Jihō,* No. 223 (4), pp. 1-17. Tōkyō, 1939.

Ishida Baigan: *Seikaron* (Essay on Household Management). *Shingaku Sōsho* (The Shingaku Library), Vol. 1, pp. 135-165. Tōkyō, 1904.

_______________: *Toimondō* (City and Country Dialogue). *Shingaku Sōsho,* Vol. 3, pp. 87-231. Tōkyō, 1904.

Ishida Baigan Jiseki (A Memoir of Our Teacher, Ishida. Written by his pupils). *Shingaku Sōsho,* Vol. 6, pp. 289-319. Tōkyō, 1904.

Ishikawa Ken: *Sekimon Shingaku Shi no Kenkyū* (A Study of the History of Sekimon Shingaku). 1367 pp. Tōkyō, 1938.

_______________: "Shingaku Gaisetsu" (An Outline of Shingaku). *Shingaku,* Vol. 1. 87 pp. Tōkyō, 1941.

Kachibe Sanenaga: "Sekimon Shingaku Shiron" (A Historical Essay on Sekimon Shingaku). *Shingaku,* Vol. 7. 123 pp. Tōkyō, 1942.

Kawashima Takeyoshi: "Kō ni tsuite" (Concerning Filial Piety). In *Nihon Shakai no Kazoku teki Kōsei* (The Familistic Structure of Japanese Society). Tōkyō, 1948.

Kōno Shōzō: *Kokumin Dōtoku Yōron* (A Survey of the National Morality). 274 pp. Tōkyō, 1935.

Miyamoto Mataji: "Sekimon Shingaku to Shōnin Ishiki" (Sekimon Shingaku and the Merchant Consciousness). *Shingaku,* Vol. 2. 64 pp. Tōkyō, 1942.

Naitō Kanji: "Shūkyō to Keizai Rinri" (Religion and the Economic Ethic, Jōdo Shinshū and the Ōmi Merchants). *Shakaigaku* (Sociology), Vol. 8, pp. 243-286. Tōkyō, 1941.

Nishi Shinichirō: *Tōyō Rinri* (Oriental Ethics). 331 pp. Tōkyō, 1935.

Shiraishi Masakuni: "Shingaku Kyōka no Hōhō" (Shingaku Teaching Methods). *Shingaku,* Vol. 4, 82 pp. Tōkyō, 1942.

Takenaka Seiichi: "Shingaku no Keizai Shisō" (Shingaku Economic Thought). *Shingaku,* Vol. 5. 77 pp. Tōkyō, 1942.

Watsuji Tetsurō: "Gendai Nihon to Chōnin Konjō" (Modern Japan and the *Chōnin* Spirit). In *Zoku Nihon Seishin Shi Kenkyū* (Further Studies in the Japanese Spirit), pp. 247-383. Tōkyō, 1935.

WORKS IN WESTERN LANGUAGES

ABBREVIATIONS

HJAS	Harvard Journal of Asiatic Studies (Cambridge, Mass.)
KUER	Kyōto University Economic Review (Kyōto)
MN	Monumenta Nipponica (Tōkyō)
TASJ	Transactions of the Asiatic Society of Japan (Tōkyō)
TPJSL	Transactions and Proceedings of the Japan Society, London

Anesaki, Masaharu: *History of Japanese Religion,* London, Kegan Paul, 1930. 409 pp.

______________: *Nichiren, The Buddhist Prophet,* Cambridge, Mass., Harvard University Press, 1916. 160 pp.

______________: Review of Robert Cornell Armstrong, *Light From the East; Studies in Japanese Confucianism, Harvard Theological Review,* 8 (1915), Cambridge, Mass., pp. 563-571.

Anon.: *Principle Teachings of the True Sect of Pure Land,* Kyōto, Otaniha Hongwanji, 1915. 89 pp.

Armstrong, Robert Cornell: *Just Before the Dawn, The Life and Works of Ninomiya Sontoku,* New York, Macmillan, 1912. 272 pp.

______________: *Light from the East; Studies in Japanese Confucianism,* Toronto, University of Toronto, 1914. 326 pp.

______________: "Ninomiya Sontoku, The Peasant Sage," *TASJ,* 38 (1910).

Asakawa, K.: "Notes on Village Government in Japan After 1600," *Journal of the American Oriental Society,* 30-31 (1910-1911), pp. 259-300, 151-216.

Aston, William G.: *Nihongi, chronicles of Japan from the earliest times to a.d. 607, TPJSL,* Supplement I, 2 Vols., London, The Japan Society, 1896. 407; 443 pp.

______________: *Shintō, The Way of the Gods,* London, Longmans, Green, 1905. 337 pp.

Benedict, Ruth: *The Chrysanthemum and the Sword,* Boston, Houghton Mifflin, 1946. 324 pp.

Blacker, Carmen, tr.: "*Kyūhanjō by Fukuzawa Yukichi*," *MN*, 9 (1953), pp. 304-329.

Bodde, Derk: "Harmony and Conflict in Chinese Philosophy," in Arthur F. Wright, ed., *Studies in Chinese Thought, American Anthropologist,* Memoir 75, Vol. 55 (1953).

Boxer, C. R.: *The Christian Century in Japan, 1549-1650,* Berkeley, University of California Press, 1951. 535 pp.

Buchanan, Daniel Crump: "Inari, Its Origin, Development, and Nature," *TASJ,* Second Series, 12 (1935), pp. 1-191.

Caudill, William: *Japanese American Personality and Acculturation,* Genetic Psychology Monographs 45, Provincetown Journal Press, 1952. 102 pp.

Chamberlain, B. H.: *Kojiki or Records of Ancient Matters,* London, Kegan Paul, 1932. 495 pp.

Chen Huan Chang: *The Economic Principles of Confucius and His School,* New York, Columbia University, 1911. 730 pp.

Clement, Ernest W.: "Instructions of a Mito Prince to His Retainers," *TASJ,* 26 (1898).

Coates, Harper Havelock and Ryugaku Ishizuka: *Hōnen, The Buddhist Saint,* translated from the original by Shunjō, the authorized biography, Kyōto, Chionin, 1925. 955 pp.

Coleman, Horace: "Life of Yoshida Shōin," *TASJ,* 45 (1917), pp. 117-188.

De Benneville, James S.: *The Yotsuya Kwaidan,* Philadelphia, Lippincott, 1917. 286 pp.

Dening, Walter: "Confucian Philosophy in Japan. Reviews of Dr. Tetjirō Inoue's Three Volumes on the Philosophy," *TASJ,* 36 (1908), pp. 101-152.

Department of Education: *History of Japanese Education,* Tōkyō, 1910.

Devereux, Edward C., Jr.: Elements of Gemeinschaft and Gesellschaft in Tokugawa Japan, Honors Thesis, Harvard, 1934.

De Visser, M. W.: *Ancient Buddhism in Japan,* 2 Vols., Paris, Librairie Orientaliste Paul Geuthner, 1928. 763 pp.

Droppers, Garret: "A Japanese Credit Association and its Founder," *TASJ,* 21 (1893).

Dubs, Homer H.: *Hsüntze, The Moulder of Ancient Confucianism,* London, Probsthain, 1927. 293 pp.

______________: *The Works of Hsüntze,* London, Probsthain, 1928.

Ehara, N. R. M.: *The Awakening to the Truth or Kaimokushō,* by Nichiren, Tōkyō, International Buddhist Society, 1941. 102 pp.

Eliot, Sir Charles: *Japanese Buddhism,* London, Arnold, 1935. 431 pp.

Fanfani, Amintore: *Catholicism, Protestantism, and Capitalism,* New York, Sheed and Ward, 1935.

Fei, Hsiao-tung: *China's Gentry,* Chicago, University of Chicago Press, 1953. 287 pp.

Fisher, Galen M.: "Daigaku Wakumon. A Discussion of Public Questions in the Light of the Great Learning, by Kumazawa Banzan," *TASJ*, Second Series, 16 (1938), pp. 259-356.

______: "Kumazawa Banzan, His Life and Ideas," *TASJ*, Second Series, 16 (1938), pp. 223-258.

______: "The Life and Teaching of Nakae Tōju, The Sage of Ōmi," *TASJ*, 36 (1908).

Florenz, Karl: "Ancient Japanese Rituals," *TASJ*, 27 (1900), pp. 1-112.

Fujimoto, Ryukyo, tr.: *The Tannishō*, Kyōto, Hompa Hongwanji, 1932.

Fukuzawa, Yukichi: *Autobiography*. See Kiyooka, Eiichi.

______: *Kyūhanjō*. See Blacker, Carmen.

Fung, Yu-lan: *A History of Chinese Philosophy*, 2 Vols., Princeton, Princeton University Press, 1952. 407; 721 pp.

______: "The Philosophy at the Basis of Traditional Chinese Society," in F. S. C. Northrop, ed., *Ideological Differences and World Order*, New Haven, Yale University Press, 1949.

Geertz, Clifford, Jr.: "Another World to Live in: A Study of Islam in Indonesia," Cambridge, ms., 1952. 73 pp.

______: "Religious Belief and Economic Behaviour in a Central Javanese Town: Some Preliminary Considerations," Cambridge, mimeo., 1955. 33 pp.

Goldschmidt, Walter: "Ethics and the Structure of Society: An Ethnological Contribution to the Sociology of Knowledge," *American Anthropologist*, 53 (1951), pp. 506-524.

Greene, D. C.: "The Remmon Kyokwai," *TASJ*, 29 (1901), pp. 17-36.

Grinnan, R. B.: "Feudal Land Tenure in Tosa," *TASJ*, 20 (1892), pp. 228-248.

Gubbins, J. H.: "A Samurai Manual," *TPJSL*, 9 (1910), pp. 140-156.

Hall, J. Carey: "Teijo's Family Instruction: A Samurai's Ethical Bequest to His Posterity (1763)," *TPJSL*, 14 (1915), pp. 128-156.

Hall, Robert King: *Kokutai no hongi*, Cambridge, Harvard University Press, 1949. 200 pp.

______: *Shūshin: The Ethics of a Defeated Nation*, New York, Bureau of Publications, Teachers College, Columbia University, 1949. 244 pp.

Hammitzsch, Horst: "Kangaku und Kokugaku," MN, 2 (1939), pp. 1-23.

______: *Die Mito-Schule*, Tōkyō, Deutsche Gesellschaft fur Natur- und Volkerkunde Ostasiens, 1939. 95 pp.

______: "Shingaku," *MN*, 4 (1941), pp. 1-31.

Hashimoto, Minoru: "The Keystone of Medieval Bushidō," *Cultural Nippon*, 4 (1936), pp. 263-272, 345-354.

Henderson, Dan F.: "Some Aspects of Tokugawa Law," *Washington Law Review*, 27 (1952), pp. 85-109.

Hepner, Charles W.: *The Kurozumi Sect of Shintō,* Tōkyō, Meiji-Japan Society, 1935. 263 pp.

Hibbett, Howard S., Jr.: Ejima Kiseki and the Hachmonjiya: A Study in 18th Century Japanese Fiction, Ph.D. Thesis, Harvard, 1950.

Holtom, Daniel Clarence: "The Meaning of Kami," *MN,* 3, 1 (1940), pp. 1-27.

______________: *The National Faith of Japan,* London, Kegan Paul, 1938. 316 pp.

Honjō, Eijirō: "Economic Ideas in Tokugawa Days," *KUER,* 13, 1 (1938), pp. 1-22.

______________: "Economic Thought in the Early Period of the Tokugawa Era," *KUER,* 14 (1939), pp. 1-17.

______________: "Economic Thought in the Latter Period of the Tokugawa Era," *KUER,* 15, 4 (1940), pp. 1-24.

______________: "Economic Thought in the Middle Period of the Tokugawa Era," *KUER,* 15, 2 (1940), pp. 1-33.

______________: "The Formation of 'Japanese Political Economy,'" *KUER,* 17, 2 (1942), pp. 1-19.

______________: "The Original Current of 'Japanese Political Economy,'" *KUER,* 17, 3 (1942), pp. 1-19.

______________: "A Survey of Economic Thought in the Closing Days of the Tokugawa Period," *KUER,* 13, 2 (1938), pp. 21-39.

______________: "Views in the Taxation on Commerce in the Closing Days of the Tokugawa Shogunate," *KUER,* 16, 3 (1941), pp. 1-15.

Horie, Yasuzō: "Clan Monopoly Policy in the Tokugawa Period," *KUER,* 17, 1 (1942), pp. 31-52.

______________: "The Encouragement of *Kokusan* or Native Products in the Tokugawa Period," *KUER,* 16, 2 (1941), pp. 43-63.

______________: "Development of Economic Policy During the Latter Tokugawa Period," *KUER,* 17, 4 (1942), pp. 48-63.

______________: "An Outline of Economic Policy in the Tokugawa Period," *KUER,* 15, 4 (1940), pp. 44-65.

______________: "An Outline of the Rise of Modern Capitalism in Japan," *KUER,* 11, 1 (1936), pp. 99-115.

Hoshino, Ken: *The Way of Contentment,* translations of selections from Kaibara Ekiken, London, Murray, 1930.

Hummel, Arthur W., ed.: *Eminent Chinese of the Ch'ing Period,* 2 Vols., Washington, U. S. Government Printing Office, 1944.

Ishikawa, Ken: "On Kaibara Ekiken's Thought and Reasoning as expressed in his *Yamatozokukun,*" *Cultural Nippon,* 7, 1 (1939), pp. 23-35.

Ito, Lucy S.: "*Kō,* Japanese Confraternities," *MN,* 8 (1952), pp. 412-415.

Iwado, Tamotsu: "'Hagakure Bushidō' or the Book of the Warrior," *Cultural Nippon,* 7, 3 (1939), pp. 33-55; 7, 4, pp. 57-78.

Jacobs, Norman: The Societal System: A Method for the Comparative Analysis of Social Institutions, with Special Reference to China and Japan, Ph.D. Thesis, Harvard, 1951.

Katō, Genchi: "A Study of the Development of Religious Ideas among the Japanese People as Illustrated by Japanese Phallicism," *TASJ,* Second Series, 1 (1924), Supplement. 70 pp.

______________: *A Study of Shintō, The Religion of the Japanese Nation,* Tōkyō, Meiji Japan Society, 1926. 214 pp.

______________: "The Theological System of Urabe no Kanetomo," *TPJSL,* 28 (1930-31), pp. 143-150.

______________: "The *Warongo* or Japanese Analects," *TASJ,* 45 (1918).

Kawakami, Tasuke: "Bushidō in its Formative Period," *Annals of the Hitotsubashi Academy,* 3, 2 (1952), pp. 65-83.

Keene, Donald: *The Japanese Discovery of Europe: Honda Toshiaki and Other Discoverers 1720-1798,* London, Routledge and Kegan Paul, 1952. 233 pp.

Kirby, R. J.: "Ancestral Worship in Japan," *TASJ,* 38 (1910), pp. 233-267.

Kiyooka, Eiichi, tr.: *The Autobiography of Fukuzawa Yukichi,* Tōkyō, Hokuseido Press, 1934. 360 pp.

Knox, George Wm.: "A Japanese Philosopher," *TASJ,* 20 (1893), pp. 1-133.

______________: "A System of Ethics: An Abridged Translation of 'Okina Mondo,'" *The Chrysanthemum,* 2 (1882), pp. 100-104, 160-171, 245-256, 344-350.

Kobayashi, Abbot: *The Doctrines of Nichiren,* Tōkyō, Kelly and Walsh, 1893. 29 pp.

Kōno, Shōzō: "Kannagara no Michi," *MN,* 3, 2 (1940), pp. 9-31.

Koyama, Matsukichi: "Yamaga Sokō and his Bukyō Shōgaku," *Cultural Nippon,* 8, 4 (1940), pp. 67-87.

Legge, James: *The Chinese Classics* (second edition, revised), 7 Vols., Oxford, 1893.

Levy, Marion and Kuo-heng Shih: *Rise of the Modern Chinese Business Class,* New York, Institute of Pacific Relations, 1949. 64 pp.

Lloyd, Arthur: *The Creed of Half Japan,* London, Smith, Elder and Co., 1911. 385 pp.

______________: "Developments of Japanese Buddhism," *TASJ,* 22 (1894).

______________: "Historical Development of the Shushi (Chu Hsi) Philosophy in Japan," *TASJ,* 34 (1906), pp. 5-80.

______________: "The Remmonkyō," *TASJ,* 29 (1901), pp. 1-16.

______________: Shinran and his Work, Studies in Shinshu Theology, Tōkyō, Kyōbunkwan, 1910. 182 pp.

Lockwood, William Wirt: The Economic Development of Japan: Growth and Structural Change, 1869-1938, Ph.D. Thesis, Harvard, 1950.

Longford, Joseph H.: "Note on Ninomiya Sontoku," *TASJ,* 21 (1893).

Lowell, Percival: "Esoteric Shinto," Parts I, II, and III, *TASJ,* 21 (1893); Part IV, *TASJ,* 22 (1894).

______________: *Occult Japan,* Boston, Houghton, Mifflin, 1895. 377 pp.

Makihara, Bernard Minoru: Social Values in Capitalist Development: A Case Study of Japan, Honors Thesis, Harvard, 1954. 105 pp.

Minami, Hiroshi: "Human Relations in the Japanese Society," *The Annals of the Hitotsubashi Academy,* 4, 2 (1954).

Mitsui, Takaharu: "Chōnin's Life under Feudalism," *Cultural Nippon,* 8, 2 (1940), pp. 65-96.

______________: "Travel in the Tokugawa Era," *Cultural Nippon,* 7, 3 (1939), pp. 69-80.

Murdoch, James: *A History of Japan,* Vol. 3, *The Tokugawa Epoch 1652-1868,* London, Kegan Paul, 1926. 823 pp.

Nakai Gendo: *Shinran and his Religion of Pure Faith,* Kyōto, Shinshu Research Institute, 1937. 250 pp.

Nichiren: *Kaimokushō.* See Ehara, N. R. M.

Nippon Gakujitsu Shinkōkai: *Man'yoshu,* Tōkyō, Iwanami, 1940. 502 pp.

Norman, E. Herbert: "Ando Shoeki and the Anatomy of Japanese Feudalism," *TASJ,* Third Series, 2 (1949). 340 pp.

______________: Japan's Emergence as a Modern State, New York, Institute of Pacific Relations, 1946.

Nukariya, Kaiten: *The Religion of the Samurai,* London, Luzac, 1913. 253 pp.

Onishi, Goichi: "Ninomiya Sontoku, An Agrarian Economist of Feudal Japan," *Cultural Nippon,* 8, 1 (1940), pp. 75-99.

Papinot, E.: *Historical and Geographical Dictionary of Japan,* Ann Arbor, Overbeck Co., 1948. 842 pp.

Parsons, Talcott: " 'Capitalism' in Recent German Literature: Sombart and Weber," *Journal of Political Economy,* 37 (1928, 1929), pp. 31-51.

______________: *Essays in Sociological Theory,* (revised edition), Glencoe, Free Press, 1954. 459 pp.

______________: "H. M. Robertson on Max Weber and his School," *Journal of Political Economy,* 43 (1935), pp. 688-696.

______________: The Integration of Economic and Sociological Theory, The Marshall Lectures, University of Cambridge, mimeo., 1953. 69 pp.

______________: *The Social System,* Glencoe, Free Press, 1951. 575 pp.

______________: *The Structure of Social Action,* New York, McGraw Hill, 1937. 817 pp.

Parsons, Talcott, R. Freed Bales and Edward A. Shils: *Working Papers in the Theory of Action,* Glencoe, Free Press, 1953. 269 pp.

Parsons, Talcott and Niel Smelser: *Economy and Society,* 1956.

Pelzel, John: "The Small Industrialist in Japan," *Explorations in Entrepreneurial History,* 7, 2 (1954), pp. 179-193.

______________: Social Stratification in Japanese Urban Economic Life, Ph.D. Thesis, Harvard, 1950.

Petzold, Bruno: "Characteristics of Japanese Buddhism," *Studies on Buddhism in Japan,* Tōkyō, International Buddhist Society, 3 (1941), pp. 33-70.

______________: "On Buddhist Meditation," *TASJ,* Third Series, 1 (1948), pp. 64-100.

Ponsonby-Fane, R. A. B.: *Studies in Shintō and Shrines,* Kyōto, Ponsonby Kinenkai, 1943. 504 pp.

Redlich, Fritz: "European Aristocracy and Economic Development," *Explorations in Entrepreneurial History,* 6, 2 (1953), pp. 78-91.

Reischauer, August Karl: "A Catechism of the Shin Sect (Buddhism)," *TASJ,* 38 (1911), pp. 331-395.

______________: "Genshin's Ojo Yoshu: Collected Essays on Birth into Paradise," *TASJ,* Second Series, 7 (1930), pp. 16-97.

______________: *Studies in Japanese Buddhism,* New York, Macmillan, 1925. 361 pp.

Reischauer, Edwin O.: *Japan Past and Present* (revised edition), New York, Knopf, 1953. 292 pp.

______________: *The United States and Japan,* Cambridge, Harvard University Press, 1950. 357 pp.

Richards, I. A.: *Mencius on the Mind,* London, Kegan Paul, Trench Trubner, 1932.

Robertson, H. M.: *Aspects of the Rise of Economic Individualism: A Criticism of Max Weber and his School,* Cambridge, Cambridge University Press, 1933. 223 pp.

Sadler, A. L.: *The Beginner's Book of Bushidō by Daidoji Yuzan (Budo Shoshinshu),* Tōkyō, Kokusai Bunka Shinkokai, 1941. 82 pp.

______________: *Diary of a Pilgrim to Ise by Saka,* Tōkyō, Meiji Japan Society, 1940. 84 pp.

Sakai, Atsuharu: "Kaibara Ekiken and 'Onna Daigaku,'" *Cultural Nippon,* 7, 4 (1939), pp. 43-56.

______________: "The Memoirs of Takeda Shingen and the Kai no Gunritsu," *Cultural Nippon,* 8, 3 (1940), pp. 83-108.

Sansom, G. B.: *Japan, A Short Cultural History,* New York, D. Appleton-Century, 1931. 525 pp.

______________: "The Tsuredzure Gusa of Yoshida no Kaneyoshi," *TASJ,* 39 (1911), pp. 1-146.

______________: *The Western World and Japan,* New York, Knopf, 1950. 504 pp.

Sasaki, Gessho: *A Study of Shin Buddhism,* Kyōto, The Eastern Buddhist Society, 1925. 139 pp.

Satomi, Kishio: *Japanese Civilization: Nichirenism and the Japanese National Principles,* New York, Dutton, 1924. 231 pp.

Satow, Ernest: "Ancient Japanese Rituals," Parts I, II, and III, *TASJ,* 7 (1879), pp. 95-126, 393-434; 9 (1881), pp. 183-211.

______________: "The Mythology and Religious Worship of the Ancient Japanese," *Westminster Review,* London, July, 1878, pp. 27-57.

______________: "The Revival of Pure Shin-tau," *TASJ,* 3, Appendix (1874). 98 pp.

______________: "The Shin-tau Temples of Ise," *TASJ,* 2 (1874), pp. 101-124.

Schwartz, W. L.: "The Great Shrine of Izumo," *TASJ,* 41 (1913), pp. 493-681.

Shively, Donald H.: A Japanese Domestic Tragedy of the 18th century. An Annotated Translation of the Love Suicide at Amajima, by Chikamatsu, Ph.D. Thesis, Harvard, 1951.

Simmons, D. B. and John Wigmore: "Notes on Land Tenure and Local Institutions in Old Japan," *TASJ,* 19 (1891), pp. 37-370.

Smith, Neil Skene: "Materials on Japanese Social and Economic History: Tokugawa Japan," *TASJ,* Second Series, 14 (1937), pp. 1-176.

Smith, T. C.: "The Introduction of Western Industry to Japan during the Last Years of the Tokugawa Period," *HJAS,* 11 (1948), pp. 130-152.

Spae, Joseph John: *Itō Jinsai,* Monumenta Serica, 12, 1948. 250 pp.

Suzuki, Daisetz Teitaro: *The Training of the Zen Buddhist Monk,* Kyōto, The Eastern Buddhist Society, 1934. 111 pp.

______________: *Zen Buddhism and its Influence on Japanese Culture,* Kyōto, The Eastern Buddhist Society, 1938. 278 pp.

Tachibana, S.: *The Ethics of Buddhism,* London, Oxford University Press, 1926.

______________: "Indebtedness, as Buddhism Teaches it," *The Young East,* 4, 11 (1934), pp. 34-37.

Takaishi, Shingoro: *Women and Wisdom of Japan,* London, Murray, 1905.

Takekoshi, Yosaburo: *The Economic Aspects of the History of the Civilization of Japan,* 3 Vols., London, Allen and Unwin, 1930.

Teng, Ssu-yü and John K. Fairbank: *China's Response to the West,*

A Documentary Survey, 1893-1923, Cambridge, Harvard University Press, 1954. 296 pp.

Tillich, Paul: *The Courage to Be,* New Haven, Yale University Press, 1952. 197 pp.

______________: *Systematic Theoology,* Vol. I, Chicago, University of Chicago Press, 1951.

Troup, James: "The Gobunsho or Ofumi of Rennyo Shōnin," *TASJ,* 17 (1889), pp. 101-143.

______________: "On the Tenets of the Shinshu or 'True Sect' of Buddhists," *TASJ,* 14 (1885), pp. 1-17.

Tsuchiya, Takao: "An Economic History of Japan," *TASJ,* Second Series, 15 (1937).

Utsuki, Nishu: *The Shin Sect, A School of Mahayana Buddhism,* Kyōto, Publication Bureau of Buddhist Books, Hompa Honganji, 1937. 45 pp.

Van Straelen, Henri: *Yoshida Shōin, Forerunner of the Meiji Restoration, A Bibliographical Study,* T'oung Pao Monograph, Vol. 2, Leiden, Brill, 1952. 149 pp.

Waley, Arthur: *The Analects of Confucius,* London, Allen and Unwin, 1938. 268 pp.

______________: *Three Ways of Thought in Ancient China,* London, Allen and Unwin, 1939. 275 pp.

______________: *The Way and its Power,* London, Alle and Unwin, 1934. 262 pp.

Weber, Max: *Ancient Judaism,* translated and edited by H. H. Gerth and D. Martindale, Glencoe, Free Press, 1952. 484 pp.

______________: *From Max Weber: Essays in Sociology,* translated, edited, and with an introduction by H. H. Gerth and C. Wright Mills, New York, Oxford University Press, 1946. 490 pp.

______________: *Max Weber on Law in Economy and Society,* edited by M. Rheinstein, translated by E. Shils and M. Rheinstein, Cambridge, Harvard University Press, 1954. 363 pp.

______________: *The Protestant Ethic and the Spirit of Capitalism,* translated by Talcott Parsons, London, Allen and Unwin, 1930. 292 pp.

______________: *The Religion of China,* translated and edited by H. H. Gerth, Glencoe, Free Press, 1951. 308 pp.

______________: *The Theory of Social and Economic Organization,* translated by A. M. Henderson and Talcott Parsons, edited with an introduction by Talcott Parsons, New York, Oxford University Press, 1947. 436 pp.

Wheeler, Post: *The Sacred Scriptures of the Japanese,* New York, Schuman, 1952.

Whitelock, Dorothy: *The Beginnings of English Society,* Harmondsworth, Middlesex, Penguin, 1952. 256 pp.

Yoshimoto, Tadasu: *A Peasant Sage of Japan,* London, Longmans, Green, 1912. 254 pp.

Index